Best Sermons 4

Best Sermons 4

James W. Cox, Editor

Kenneth M. Cox, Associate Editor

HarperSanFrancisco
A Division of HarperCollins*Publishers*

FIRST EDITION

Library of Congress Catalog Card Number 88–656297
ISSN 1041–6382

91 92 93 94 95 HAD 10 9 8 7 6 5 4 3 2 1

This edition is printed on acid-free paper that meets the American National Standards Institute Z39.48 Standard.

Contents

Preface   ix

I. EVANGELISTIC

1. The Word Comes among Us
   George Beasley-Murray   3

2. Have You Ever Heard John Preach?
   Fred B. Craddock   10

3. Joseph's Story   *John E. Kelso*   18

4. Spread, O Spread, Thou Mighty Word
   J. Donald Waring   24

5. How to Become a Christian   *David E. Leininger*   29

II. EXPOSITORY

6. Infant Arms: Epiphany   *Leo Sands*   39

7. When All Is Said and Done   *Mark Trotter*   41

8. Mary, Mother of God   *Steven P. Vitrano*   48

9. Remember Rahab   *David R. Wilkinson*   55

10. He's Back   *William H. Willimon*   64

11. The Tragicomedy of the Gospel
    C. Michael Fuhrman   69

12. Dirty Work   *Jeffrey L. Ruff*   77

13. Joseph   *Neta Pringle*   83

III. DOCTRINAL/THEOLOGICAL

14. He Is Going before You *Chevis F. Horne*   89

15. The Bible: Its Diversity and Its Unity
     Bruce M. Metzger   95

16. The Big One and the Not-So-Big One
     Ronald D. Sisk   101

17. God Remembers *Krister Stendahl*   107

18. Jesus, the Liberator *Bill J. Leonard*   111

19. The Saints: Dogged Blunderers toward Heaven
     Carroll E. Simcox   118

20. An Hour's Work and a Day's Pay
     L. Alan Sasser   124

IV. ETHICAL

21. The Things That Make for Peace
     Elizabeth Achtemeier   133

22. A Kind of Loving, for Me *Walter J. Burghardt*   140

23. The Distorted and the Natural
     Allan M. Parrent   147

24. Caught in the Act *James Ayers*   154

25. Is Sex Ever Safe? *Richard Groves*   160

26. God and the "L-Word" *Howard W. Roberts*   167

V. PASTORAL

27. Your Religion: Method or Motive—Which?
     Donald Macleod   177

28. Not All Saints, But Surely Some Saints
     W. Sibley Towner   184

29. When Life Crashes In *William Powell Tuck*   189

30. The Servant of the Lord *Pavel Filipi*   197

31. Through Flood and Fire   *Paul W. Nisly*   201
32. It Is Something to Us   *Vernon Murray*   210
33. Doing and Being   *Byron C. Bangert*   215

VI. DEVOTIONAL

34. What to Do about God   *Welton Gaddy*   223
35. What Easter Means to Christians
    A. Leonard Griffith   229
36. Intimacy with God   *John Killinger*   237
37. The Gracious Guest   *Albert J. D. Walsh*   243
38. Going to Hell for the Right Reason
    Tom W. Boyd   248
39. Consider the Monkeys   *Robert John Versteeg*   253
40. Pretending, Self-Justification, and Grace
    Clifford Williams   258

Index of Contributors   265
Index of Sermon Titles   267
Index of Scriptural Texts   269

Preface

As we watched and heard Bill Moyers's recent television documentary "Amazing Grace," we were struck by the remarkable variety of styles, places, and people depicted as the hymn was rendered again and again. Yet the same theme, the same words, and essentially the same melody came to expression in a kaleidoscope of captivating music. Something like that happens in the preaching of the church: Week after week, in churches large and small, ministers tell the same old story of God's love, with fascinating variations. An earthquake in San Francisco and demonstrations for freedom in Prague give the message individually different sounds; the preachers speak different languages; the listeners hear a message of special relevance for them. And so it must be—always—if the sermon meets the real needs of real people.

The most important criteria in the selection of sermons for *Best Sermons 4* were originality, scriptural and/or Christian basis, relevance, clarity, and interest. These criteria applied to the commissioned sermons as well as to the sermons from the international competition.

Judges for the competition were as follows:

James W. Cox, Lester Professor of Christian Preaching, Southern Baptist Theological Seminary

Donald Macleod, Francis Landey Patton Professor of Preaching and Worship, Emeritus, Princeton Theological Seminary

Henry H. Mitchell, author of *Black Preaching: The Recovery of a Powerful Art*

Ralph V. Norman, Professor of Religious Studies and Vice Provost, University of Tennessee, and editor of *Soundings*

Katherine Paterson, author of *Bridge to Terabithia* and *Jacob Have I Loved*

Ferrol Sams, M.D., author of *Run with the Horsemen* and *The Widow's Mite*

Joseph Webb, Professor of Communication and Preaching, Milligan College

Once again, we thank all those who submitted sermons for the competition, and we encourage those and others to send us more of your best sermons.

JAMES W. COX
KENNETH M. COX

Best Sermons
P.O. Box 6029
Louisville, Kentucky 40207

I. EVANGELISTIC

1. The Word Comes among Us

George Beasley-Murray

In the beginning was the Word,
and the Word was with God,
and the Word was God.
He was in the beginning with God
All things came into being through him,
and apart from him not a thing came into being.
What has come into being had its life in him,
and the life was the light of men;
and the light shines on in the darkness,
and the darkness did not grasp it. . . .

—John 1:1–18

I vividly recall reading these words as a new Christian, as a teenager. I was fifteen years of age when I became a Christian, won by the love of Christ when somebody made it very clear that that love included me. I got hold of a copy of the New Testament, and I opened it, glancing at the Gospels of Matthew, Mark, Luke. When I saw the one that was according to John, I thought I would start just there. I read, "In the beginning was the Word, and the Word was with God, and the Word was God." I was absolutely foxed! I hadn't any idea what it meant. I knew it must have something to do with Jesus. But how can God be a word? I just didn't understand it. It was a long while before I heard anybody talk about it. I now realize that if I had been of that age in the first century, anywhere in the old world that was ruled by the Roman Empire (it wouldn't have mattered if it was east

---

George Beasley-Murray is former principal of Spurgeon's College, London, and until his retirement was professor of New Testament at the Southern Baptist Theological Seminary, Louisville, Kentucky. Dr. Beasley-Murray is the author of *Baptism in the New Testament* and *Jesus and the Kingdom of God.*

or west), I would have understood those words. All the world knew about the Word. In this connection, I may say that I opened the *Living Bible* to see what the translator had done with these words. He put it in this way: "Before anything else existed, *there was Christ.*" Now in the first century nobody outside Palestine other than Jews and Christians would have had the faintest idea what that meant. What is a Christ? Who is the Christ? People had never heard of him. But they all knew about *the Word!*

We read in the Book of Acts of a lengthy and impassioned sermon by the first man to lay down his life for Christ—Stephen, the deacon, as we call him. He gave a review of Israel's history, in the course of which he said, "Moses was learned in all the wisdom of Egypt." Naturally, that was quite right. Moses was brought up as a prince. Do you know that as a young man, when Moses pursued his studies, he would have read poems about the Word of God, who was the Wisdom of God? In Egypt, they spoke of the great God from whom the Word came. It was like an effluence coming out of his mouth, and he created all things and maintains all things. They knew about him in ancient Iran and Iraq, that is, in Assyria and Babylonia. They spoke of the terrible power of the Word of God that was like the bursting of a dam, like a net that was spread all over the sea that nothing can escape.

> The Word of God heaven cannot contain him.
> The Word of God earth cannot contain him.

The ancient Greeks learned about the Word from the ancient folk in the east. They were not the inventors of this concept. They simply thought about it and developed it in very instructive ways. The old Stoics, the great teachers of ethics in those days, thought of the universe as a great body and the Word of God as the soul of the universe. A Jew named Philo, who was a contemporary of Jesus, lived in Egypt. He wrote books for the educated folk in the ancient world to let them know about the teaching of the Bible. He stated that nobody can really know God as he is, but the Word of God is the God we can know. "The Word is the God of us imperfect men." And so the Word is the high priest through whom we come to God. He is the advocate for the forgiveness of sins, the firstborn Son of God, the pilot of the universe.

In the early centuries of the Church, a man named Augustine came on the scene. He was a towering figure in that time. As a young man, he became a great orator but was a real yuppie and lived a wild life. When he became a Christian and read the Gospel of John, he said, "I have read all this before, about the Word that was in the world at the beginning, and that he was with God and was God, and that all things were created through him." "But," he said, when he came to verse 14, "I've never read in any of those books the Word became flesh and lived among us."

I can well imagine people picking up this book in the world of that time and reading about all these things: "The Word was in the beginning with God. All things came into existence through him and apart from him not a single thing came into being. In him was the life, and the life was the light of men. And the light shines on in the darkness, and the darkness hasn't grasped it." Yes, they would. That's excellent. What a neat way of putting it! But when they read the statement, "The Word became flesh and pitched his tent among us," they became excited. "Whenever did that happen?" they asked. " 'We gazed on his glory'—When was this?" " 'Nobody has ever seen God. The only Son, who lives with him, has made him fully known'— How can we learn about this?" "Read on," said John, "and you'll find out!" This is the most superb piece of communication of the good news of God that has ever been penned. So then, let's look a little more carefully at the way John put it.

I have entitled this address, "The Word Comes among Us." When did he do that? The answer is "From the very beginning." The Word, we are told, was the life and the light of men, and the light is shining in the darkness still. Some people wondered if John the Baptist was that Word. No, said the evangelist. John came to tell people about him. The Word was the *true* light, and as he comes into the world, he gives light to every man. Notice, he gives light to *everybody!* The Word of God has always been teaching the world. He "illuminates," as we say, the minds of people everywhere. All the truth we have ever gained about the world and God has come from him. Have you ever wondered how it is that in the fifth chapter of the Book of Genesis it could be written of a man (his name was Enoch) that "he walked with God"? Long before Moses, long before Exodus, long before the revelation of God at Sinai, he came to be known as "the man who walked with God." Have you ever wondered how it was that the man named Abraham, through whom the Jewish race began, was called by God to go and leave the land where he lived and become a pilgrim in Israel's land? Paul actually understood this perfectly. He must have nearly startled the Jews out of their skin when he pointed out that the statement in the Bible—"Abraham was justified by faith"—was written about Abraham before he became a Jew and received the sign of the covenant of God. Abraham the heathen, justified by faith! The Book of Genesis tells us of an occasion when Abraham had to go out and do battle with some petty kings who had captured his nephew Lot. After rescuing Lot, Abraham met a strange individual, Melchizedek, who is described as "priest of the most high God." Abraham acknowledged that he was a genuine priest of God, and he gave him a tenth of all that had been taken of the spoils of war. Yes, Paul understood this perfectly. He told some country pagans, "God has never left himself without witness at any time in this world." And so when he stood on Mars Hill in Athens and addressed the rulers and learned men of the city, he quoted from the poets and prophets whom they knew and approved what they said. "We are offspring of God," said one man. "In him, we live and move and have our being," said another. Remember, Paul wasn't talking to a Christian church or Sunday school class. He was talking to people who had never heard the name of Jesus until Paul preached to them, and what Paul had been saying to them had sounded strange. That's why they had asked him to explain it to them. So Paul told them that the philosopher who said that all of us live and move and have our being in God was quite right. We all live by the mercy of God, and he speaks to us through his Word. But alas, so many don't comprehend! You know, we should thank God that we know who the Word is. We know what he has taught in the flesh and what he has done for the world's salvation, and so we ought to be very thankful for this.

I was very glad that even before I started my theological course in Spurgeon's College, looking to the ministry, I got hold of a little book by a man who in those days all the preachers used to talk about. He was an Indian named Sadhu Sundar Singh, a mystical kind of man, but a most powerful evangelistic preacher in India. When he was persuaded to come to England and to this country, too, he found that people thought he had come from a heathen home simply because he and his family were Sikhs (a special branch of Hinduism). "No, no, no," said he. "I had godly parents. Day-by-day they prayed to God, and they walked with God, and it was easy for me to open my heart to Jesus when I learned of him." So our task when we meet with people who are obviously seeking to walk with God is to do what

Paul did when he preached in Athens and said, "Whom you ignorantly worship, I make known to you." For he is the God revealed in Jesus.

But, of course, there came that wonderful time when it all came out in the open, as it were. "The Word became flesh." That sounds rather strange language. But it was quite deliberate. Instead of saying, "The Word appeared among us," the evangelist used the strongest language possible to make sure that men and women understood. It wasn't a case of God giving us little visions of himself, God coming among us, as it were, a man. No, he *became* flesh and blood; he really *became* one of us.

We are then told, "He pitched his tent among us." The translations don't put it quite like that, but that is the literal meaning of the statement, and there was a reason for John writing this. You see, John was a Jew, and he knew his Old Testament. The Book of Exodus tells how God showed his presence among the people he had rescued out of Egypt. He brought them through the desert to Mount Sinai and then to the Promised Land. You will remember that in those days there was a tent where they used to gather to worship God. We call it the Tabernacle. That is simply an old-fashioned word for a tent. Above that tent there constantly stood the pillar of cloud and fire. It was a symbol of the presence of God, guiding his people through the dangerous wilderness that they might at last reach the Promised Land. As God was with his people in those days, so he came among us in Jesus, the man who revealed God in his glory.

We gazed on his glory, said John, with a glory such as the only Son of the Father could show. What sort of glory was that? Dazzling light? Gorgeous clothing? Gold and diamonds? No, of course not. "We gazed on his glory, *full of grace and truth.*" *Grace* is a wonderful Christian word that isn't always understood. It really is love, but a special sort of love. It is love for the needy; love for the undeserving; love that comes to the rescue. Jesus, the Word made flesh, was full of that sort of love. I think many of you know that Ruth and I no longer live in London, but we have gone now to live by the ocean. We don't call it the ocean in Britain; it's simply the English Channel. But the English Channel can get pretty rough, let me tell you. Now, our house is merely a block or so away from the sea. There is a main road there, running from east to west, and our road runs at right angles to it. Now, when it is sunny, which isn't every day, as you know, in England, sometimes between noon and one o'clock, the reflection of the sun on the sea is so bright, I cannot keep my eyes on it. The sea is just a dazzling sight of golden glory. It could almost make you think that God in his glory is at the end of our road! So he is, of course! Indeed, not merely at the *end* of the road, he's all along it! They who understand that the glory of God is revealed in the love of Christ are able to recognize that he comes to any home where he's welcome.

Now the wonderful thing about the Word who has come to mankind in Jesus is that he comes to us still. He comes to us in all kinds of ways, and we especially know about his coming who come to church and listen to his speech. The great thing to know is that, as the Bible puts it, "He is the same yesterday, today, and forever," which means that he is the same as when he was among people in the days of his flesh. You remember what they called him? "The friend of publicans and sinners." "And," said the shocked Pharisees, "he evens eats with them!" He does today, of course. You will recall those beautiful words, spoken to a church that had not only lost its first love but had lost almost all its love: "I stand at the door and knock; if anyone will hear my voice and open the door, I will come in." But don't stop there! The risen Lord adds, "I will come in to him, *and eat with him and he with me.*" That is, the Lord wishes that we and he share life together, just as he did with the ordinary folk whom the religious elite despised. He does that now, as he has ever been doing.

Let me tell you about a very famous picture. It is inspired by those words I have just quoted: "I stand at the door and knock." Jesus stands outside a door, which is all overgrown with ivy and weeds, and there is no knocker or handle on the outside. He is waiting, having knocked, to enter. That picture is in St. Paul's Cathedral in London, and it is called "The Light of the World." No reproduction of it can ever do it justice. Now because it has been for many years in St. Paul's, right in the heart of London, at a juncture of many busy roads, it began to lose its color through the accumulation of dust. So the cathedral authorities decided to have it cleaned. It was sent to an art specialist who does that sort of thing. When the men who were assigned to do the job took the picture out of its frame, they saw words in writing that no man was ever intended to read. They were written by the artist and this is what he wrote: "Forgive me, Lord Jesus, that I kept you waiting so long." He had known about Jesus and his readiness to share life with him, but it was evidently a long, long time before he responded to the invitation of the Lord. But in the end he did, and by his picture he sent the message to unknown thousands who have gazed upon it.

Maybe we need to pray that prayer. Let's be humble enough to do it and receive that indescribable blessing of the friendship of God.

2. Have You Ever Heard John Preach?

Fred B. Craddock

Mark 1:1–8

If Jesus were here tonight, and I had asked for names of preachers most influential for whom we're grateful, his voice would have listed the name John the Baptist. There is no question about that. There is no human being more influential upon the life and career of Jesus than John. We don't know how their association began. We know that a day came, an hour came when Jesus untied the apron strings, lifted the carpenter's apron over his head, put it on the bench, and left the shop. We don't know why that day, that hour, just then. We do know the eighteen solid years, we understand that. They had to be. They had to be silent years—you don't hear roots growing. They had to be silent years. Jesus had a wise mother—she didn't push him out into the show windows of the world like a child star. She let him grow.

But why this day, why this hour? I don't know. He may have heard the groaning and crying from south of town. When Jesus was a teenager, the Romans rounded up in Nazareth and environs a lot of people they considered to be troublemakers or suspected to be such and hanged them on poles, like power poles running along the road south of town, and the screaming of the women and sisters and daughters and wives and the moaning of the victims could not have

Fred B. Craddock, an ordained minister in the Christian Church (Disciples of Christ), currently holds the Bandy Distinguished Chair in New Testament and Preaching at the Candler School of Theology at Emory University in Atlanta, Georgia. His seven books include the text *Preaching.* This sermon was presented at a seminar on preaching at Kirkridge, Bangor, Pennsylvania.

gone unnoticed by young Jesus. Maybe he still remembers, and he can't stay a carpenter anymore. I don't know.

It might have been the lessons droned away in the synagogue that nobody heard but everybody heard. It might have been a mother's prayer over the kitchen stove. It might have been the stirrings of God in his heart in ways mysterious still to us and probably to him. It might have been that the word came into town about John in the desert. Have you heard John? Have you heard John? Maybe that was it, because Jesus left. He went through the dark gap of the Valley of Jezreel into the heated Jordan valley to the desert country in the south of Palestine where this man, this extraordinary man, was preaching.

They became close. They were already close, Luke said. Luke says they were about the same age—within six months of each other, Jesus being at that time thirty years old. Luke says they were cousins, their mothers being kin—Elizabeth the old woman and Mary the young girl. Maybe they already were close. We don't understand. We don't know. We don't have the information. But Jesus came to John. Heard John. Was with John. Was influenced by John.

The whole New Testament announces that this is one of the most extraordinary figures in the history of God's work in the world. Mark calls John the beginning of the gospel of Jesus Christ. John, in his Gospel, starts with that marvelous poem, this hymn to Christ, and twice he interrupts it, by saying, "Now there was a man sent from God whose name was John; he was not the light." Why does he interrupt his own song with a little prose footnote that says, "I'm not singing about John"? Because that man was so great, some would think, "Ah, that's John." Like Herod Antipas after John was dead, when he heard about Jesus, he said, "That's John again."

Luke says in the Book of Acts that there was a very eloquent preacher who came from North Africa to Corinth, Greece, and wanted to preach in the church, and his first sermon was John, the Christ of God. He had to be straightened out on one minor detail, and then he was all right. Luke says that when Paul went to Asia and stopped in the great city of Ephesus he found a little gathering of disciples, and he met with them, and he talked with them, and they said, "We're followers of John." Did you know that by the year 50 on three continents there were groups following John?

And the power of that man over Jesus. He baptized Jesus. The first sermon that Jesus ever preached was the sermon of his model, his leader, John. Repent, the kingdom of heaven is at hand. Same sermon. But what did you expect? It was his first sermon. All of the synoptics say that he did not even begin his preaching until John's ministry was shut up in prison. And the silencing of that great man said to Jesus, You continue. And so he came into Galilee, preaching like John.

They were so much alike. Herod said of Jesus, "That's John again." According to Acts, the resurrected Christ, the postglorious Christ just before ascending, quoted John the Baptist. When Jesus got word that John had been killed, he said to his disciples, "Let's go somewhere else." And they got in a boat and crossed the sea. But he owed the man a funeral, and so he said to the crowd, "What did you go out to see? A man dressed up in fine clothes? They belong in king's houses. What did you go out to see? A reed shaken by the wind? Oh, no, no. A prophet? Greater than a prophet. In fact," said Jesus, "there has never been anybody born of woman greater than John the Baptist." You cannot study the life of Jesus unless you study John.

What an extraordinary man. Did you ever hear him preach? A lot of people did. If you take all the Gospels together, all the Gospels together, they came from what today we would call Lebanon, Syrophoenicia, Syria, Jordan, Israel, Arabia. Think about it. In the desert. Standing under the burning sun, sand swirling in your face, people standing together who had sworn on their mother's grave, "I wouldn't be caught dead with those people!" Jews and Arabs standing together because, when the Word of God is preached, you tend to forget why it is you hate this person next to you.

Oh, a lot of people came, I'm sure, some of them came out of curiosity. I can imagine the teenagers in that country, sitting around on the hoods of the camels, nothing to do. "Have you heard of John?" "No." "Well, let's go out there." "What are you doing?" And they go out; I'm sure there was a lot of that. And you can't blame them. He was an oddity. He had long hair, and when I say he had long hair, I don't mean he just had long hair. It wasn't like the young businessmen in Atlanta with a little ponytail. He never cut his hair. I mean, he never cut his hair. He had a long beard, not a neat beard like some of you have. I mean, he had never trimmed his beard. He was a Nazarite. And he was strange. He dressed in an unusual way—camel's hair and a leather band around the waist. And his food—he never went home with anybody for lunch, and I'm sure nobody accepted his invitation. "I'll take a rain check on that, John." He lived in the desert.

But they came. All the Gospels say, the crowds came. Left the plow in the furrow, left the bread in the oven, turned school out early. Have you ever heard John preach? Absolutely riveting, I'm sure. Fred Robertson used to say that here was no chef offering up fancy dishes. He broke the break of God with his bare hands and said, "Eat it and live." He was no politician trying to make *yes* sound like *no* and *no* sound like *yes*. He said, "The judge is coming, and I'm here to serve subpoenas." He was no candle in the sanctuary; he was a prairie fire with a stump or a rock as his pulpit. The sun and moon and stars as chandeliers. And the Jordan River, his baptistry. And they came. And I imagine listening to his sermons was like the kind of meal you have after holidays. After all that sweet stuff and fruitcake and turkey and again turkey—and how many ways can you fix turkey? And you finally give up and just have some cornbread and milk and vegetables. That's what it was like. It must have been. And the persuasive form of his character. We used to talk a lot about the character of the preacher being important for preaching. But I'm listening to it now from the rhetoricians. The old Greek rhetoric professors used to say, "For all of your oratory, the most persuasive part of your argument is your character." And there's John, the rough grain of his character shining through. What he said and what he was cut out of the same cloth. And it must have been persuasive, because all the multitudes came out there. And when the sermon was over, they came over and said, "John, what are we to do?" And he said, "If you have any food, share it. If you have any clothes, share it." The tax collectors came and said, "What are we to do?" He said, "Don't take any more than is your due." And the soldiers were standing on the rim of the crowd, and when everybody else was gone, they shuffled awkwardly up to the pulpit and said, "Any word for us?" And he said, "No violence and don't intimidate the people and don't forage around here trying to supplement your income. Be content with your wages."

Persuasive. Did you ever hear him preach? It's kind of frightening. Oh, not just the images he used. He did use some strong images. Ax at the root of the tree. God can raise up children of Abraham from these stones. The winnowing fork is in his hand. Wheat and chaff. Chaff is burned, save the wheat. Are you ready? Repent! (Pause.) It's kind of, you know . . . But that's not what was frightening about it. What's frightening about listening to John preach is that he puts you in the presence of God. And that's what everybody wants, and that's what everybody doesn't want. Because the light at the altar is different from every other light in the world.

In the dim lamps of this world, we can compare ourselves with each other, and all of us come off looking good. We convince ourselves that God grades on the curve, and what's the difference? We're all okay. And then you come in the presence of God, and you're at the altar, and it's all different. For if our hearts condemn us, think of this—God is greater than our hearts and knows everything. It's called, in literature, a moment of truth. The whining is over. There's no way to modulate the human voice to make a whine acceptable. The whining is over. The excusing is over. It's the school, it's the church, it's the board, it's the government. It isn't! All that's over. It just stops. Like a skipping rock across the water, when it slows down—boom. Like waking from a dream of palaces and patios to find the roof leaks and the rent's due. Like shutting off the stereo, and you still hear the rat gnawing in the wall. That's just the fact of it.

In my mind, I serve God. But there's another force in my life, and I say, "I'm going to do that." I don't do it. I say, "I'll never do that." I do it. Crucified between the sky of what I intend and the earth of what I perform. That's the truth. You know what the moment of truth is. We all want it; we don't want it. We don't talk about it a lot. I don't like to talk religion carelessly and carefreely, like some people do. They're just full of Jesus talk and Spirit talk everywhere and all. I just can't do that. But that doesn't mean it isn't there. You can bury it as deep as a bone—it's there. If you live in the fast lane or the slow, it doesn't matter—it's there. You don't have to be down and out— that's a mistake many of the churches make. They think you can minister to people only when they're down and out, got a crisis, family falling apart, got fired, on drugs, this and that, and in swoops the church. "Can I help you?"

Look, the people who are up walking around and doing great, they have the same need. That's not the difference. We don't wait until somebody's down and out, circling overhead like a vulture. "One of these days you'll go down, and then we can help you." And finally there you are up over a little general store, in one room, 15-watt bulb swinging overhead, and you're on a bare mattress, cigarette butts floating in urine and stale beer, and then we come and say, "You need the Lord." That's what the person needed before.

You see, it doesn't matter whether you're on the centr[?] at the Olympics crying through the national anthem with medal around your neck or you're wheeled into the servic[?] because you have muscular dystrophy. Your need is the same. doesn't matter if you're at the peak of your income power or lean your face into the post office window and say, "Are the checks late again?" It's all the same. It doesn't matter if you have bowed your neck at the university to receive the doctoral hood or you're a fifty-three-year-old enrolled in a literacy class—it's all the same.

Now those moments come to us, sometimes in an afternoon that you spend in the monastery of your mind, sometimes in some violent exchange. But they come. Glen Adsett, a schoolmate of years ago, ministered mostly in China. He was under house arrest in China when the soldiers came one day and said, "You can return to America." They were celebrating, and the soldiers said, "You can take two hundred pounds with you." Well, they'd been there for years. Two hundred pounds. They got the scales and started the family argument—two children, wife, husband. Must have this vase. Well, this is a new typewriter. What about my books? What about this? And they weighed everything and took it off and weighed this and took it off and weighed this and, finally, right on the dot—two hundred pounds. The soldier asked, "Ready to go?" "Yes." "Did you weigh everything?" "Yes." "You weighed the kids?" "No, we didn't." "Weigh the kids." And in a moment, typewriter and vase and all became trash. Trash. It happens.

When I was pastoring in Tennessee, there was a girl about seven years old who came to our church regularly, to Sunday school, and sometimes her parents let her stay for the worship service. They didn't come. We had a circular drive at that church. It was built for people who let their children off and drove on. We didn't want to inconvenience them, so we had a circular drive. But they were very faithful—Mom and Dad. They had moved in there from New Jersey with the new chemical plant. He was upwardly mobile, they were both very ambitious, and they didn't come to church. There wasn't really any need for that, I guess. But on Saturday nights, the whole town knew of their parties. They gave parties, not for entertainment, but as part of the upwardly mobile thing. That determined who was invited—the right people, the one just above, finally on up to the boss. And those parties were full of drinking and wild and vulgar things. Everybody knew. But there was a beautiful girl every Sunday.

One Sunday morning I looked out, and she was there, and I thought, "Well, she's with her friends." But there were Mom and Dad. And after the sermon, at the close of the service, as is the custom at my church, came an invitation to discipleship. And Mr. and Mrs. Mom and Dad came to the front. They confessed faith in Christ. Afterward, I said, "What prompted this?" They said, "Well, do you know about our parties?" And I said, "Yeah, I heard about your parties." They said, "Well, we had one last night again, and it got a little loud, and it got a little rough. And there was too much drinking. And we waked our daughter, and she came downstairs, and she was on about the third step. And she saw that we were eating and drinking, and she said, 'Oh, can I have the blessing? God is great, God is good, let us thank him for our food. Goodnight, everybody.' She went back upstairs. Oh, my land, it's time to go, we gotta be going. We've stayed. . . . Within two minutes the room was empty." Mr. and Mrs. Mom and Dad are picking up crumpled napkins and wasted and spilled peanuts and half-sandwiches and taking empty glasses on trays to the kitchen. And with two trays, he and she meet beside the sink on either side, and they look at each other, and he expresses what both are thinking: "Where do we think we're going?" The moment of truth.

Did you ever hear John preach? Most refreshing thing in the world. Most refreshing thing in the world. He said, "God's Messiah is coming. The kingdom is at the door. God's Messiah is right next door." What a thrilling thing! Oh, of course, everybody jumped at that, like it was going to be the cure for everything. They were going to be turned around, of course, because their old motto, "Where the Messiah is, there is no misery," was going to be reversed: "Where there is misery, there is the Messiah." But they didn't know it now. How exciting it was, and hope-filling it was. Oh, not everything was going to be fixed. That's not the point of the Kingdom of God, to fix everything. Some things cannot be fixed. Some things happen in our lives, in our relationships, that all the king's horses and all the king's men can't put together again. That's just the way it is.

Do you remember that couple in Thomas Hardy's novel? They had a daughter named Elizabeth, and Elizabeth died. And they agreed that if they had another child and it was a girl, they would name her Elizabeth, and maybe it would help. And they had another child, and it was a girl, and they named her Elizabeth. And it didn't help. And they realized they could have had fifty daughters and named them all Elizabeth—they would still miss Elizabeth. Some things you don't fix. But this is what John said: "The Messiah is coming; get ready by repenting and confessing your sins." And they confessed their sins and were washed in the Jordan, and they were forgiven. They were forgiven. They were forgiven. What's that like? The Bible has so many images for that—new creation (don't let that slip past you). New creation? Morning has broken like the first morning? Yeah. Blackbird like the first bird? Yeah. New creation, that's what the Bible calls it. The Bible calls it a new beginning. Picture a child, third grade, trying to do arithmetic, in a hurry, bell's about to ring, teacher's fussing, "Hurry up, children," try to erase a mistake, tear the paper, make a black smear, start to cry, teacher comes by, "Oh, my goodness," and teacher slides a new sheet of paper there and says, "Why don't you just start over?"

The Bible calls it a new birth. You've been to that window, haven't you? The maternity ward, the nursery, and all that stuff up there in that big window? And all the men outside trying to figure out which one it is? You know, Julie is in there somewhere, and I know she's the prettiest one, and you can't read those little old bands where the arm comes down and the hand joins and there's a deep wrinkle and there's that band, and it's so small, and you say, "Well, I think that's . . ." And the Bible says, That's what it is, that is it. And John offered that.

The Bible says it's like a snowfall. You get up in the morning early, and you look out: about four inches and there's not a print in it yet. And you look across the alley, and what yesterday afternoon was the ugly garbage dumpster is now a mound to the glory of God. That's what the Bible calls it. And John is offering it. Did you ever hear John preach? If you haven't, you will. Because the only way to Nazareth is through the desert. Well, that's not really true. You can get to Nazareth without going through the desert. But you won't find Jesus.

3. Joseph's Story
John E. Kelso

Matt. 1:18–25

Christianity begins with a story. From the many ways by which we approach our faith—with some giving emphasis to doctrine and theology and others to practice and ethics—during the Advent and Christmas seasons, all Christians come together around a story. We are captivated by the drama of the story that we tell to each other over and again in Scripture readings, in carols, in pageants and processions and portray in countless nativity scenes that we create on the church lawn or set up in miniature on our mantle at home.

The Christmas story is powerful because its central event, the unique and unfathomable miracle of God's Incarnation, occurs in the telling of a familiar miracle: the miracle of human birth. Who among us, when we have seen a newborn child cradled in its mother's arms, has not experienced some of the wonder of God's presence and love breaking into the world? Or more, when we have done the cradling ourselves? So at Christmas time, the holy baby and mother rightly and naturally get most of our attention. But surrounding the main characters and the central event are costars and subplots that remind us that this story is not of an ordinary birth. Shepherds in the fields have a powerful vision while they watch their flocks by night. Seers from faraway lands in the East make an incredible journey to Bethlehem, following a star. We meet the terrible Herod, the wonderful seniors Elizabeth and Zacharias, and the enig-

John E. Kelso is associate pastor at the Stone Church of Willow Glen in San Jose, California. Ordained to the Presbyterian Church (USA), Kelso received his master of divinity at Princeton Theological Seminary and his B.A. at Cleveland State University. Pastoral ministry is a second career for Kelso; previously he was employed in business management.

matic Simeon and Anna. These characters and their stories fascinate us, and with excitement fitting to the occasion, we proclaim and portray their parts in the birth of the Savior. But all do not get equal attention.

Among the principles who crowd the stage for the Christmas pageant—angels and kings, mothers and fathers, prophets and prophetesses, shepherds, perhaps even a donkey and a lamb or two—there is one we hardly notice. Although Matthew tells his story, he is not even given a speaking part. Near the manger, but not too near, just off to one side, quietly kneeling, is Joseph. But this quiet man, Joseph, has much to tell us about the child in the manger. For as little attention as we pay to him, it may be true that, among all the assembled cast, Joseph knows most intimately the identity of the one who is born. Joseph has a story to tell, and Joseph's story is of the power of Jesus to bring justice, righteousness, and salvation.

One reason we shunt Joseph off to the side of the crèche is, I think, because of the indelicate nature of the problem he faced when he was confronted with Mary's pregnancy. It's so much nicer to think about Joseph sitting in the stable, being quietly supportive of the mother and child, than it is to think about what Joseph may have been thinking about when he first got the news.

One thing that he was surely thinking about was taking the steps that would lead to Mary being stoned to death. Regardless of his inclinations or good nature, that was the law. More to the point, even if it offends our present standards of mercy, it was a useful law. Marriage and family were of utmost importance to all the people. Palestine was a harsh land ruled by a harsh government. To be a woman cut off from family or an orphaned child of unknown lineage in a time and place of subsistence living was to be lost. In a society that could not afford, even if it could have imagined, government welfare services, the network of relationship and responsibility found only in families offered some hope for the elderly and the infirm. Marriage began with the bethrothal, and the period that followed before the man took his bride into his home was a time when trust was built between two families coming together. The betrothal period was also often a time for the couple themselves to build a relationship of trust, respect, and even love. To violate that respect and trust—in the way it was obvious to Joseph that Mary had done—was not only a deep personal wound; it also threatened the stability and security of the family. Such a thing was a great evil, and the law justly demanded that both the woman and the man involved in this evil be put to death.

Joseph's mind had to be full of terrible thoughts, and perhaps it is well that he remains silent in Matthew's account, because to put words to those thoughts would surely damage for all time our image of gentle Joseph. Matthew says that Joseph was a just man, and justice demanded that all the facts be known and the guilty be punished. Yet somehow, faced with the most indelicate of personal crises, a violence to trust and security that cried out for traditional justice, Joseph, precisely because he was a just man, decided to forego public vindication of himself and to, instead, quietly break off his relationship with Mary. Understand that this was no mere kindness: for in doing this he would not only free Mary's family to close around her protectively, but he would also certainly then have to suffer the consequences of inevitable speculation and rumor that would arise about his own responsibility for the baby. He would lose the respect of the people. His reputation would suffer, probably also his livelihood, and possibly even his chances for marriage and family.

If Joseph was a just man, then Joseph's justice is a new kind of justice: justice in which someone would freely choose to suffer in order to save the life of another; to suffer with love so that she might have new life; to suffer the consequences for what he understands to be another's sin. What could have motivated this man? What kind of justice is this? It is the child who is coming. It is the justice of Christ.

Another reason we don't often pay attention to Joseph is that, while we approve of what he does, I'm afraid that it's very difficult for us to take him seriously—to believe in him. I first encountered my own difficulty with Joseph's story during seminary when my class was asked to name the most unbelievable character in the Bible. Our professor, who spoke with a German accent and brandished the wooden pointer he carried like a riding crop, was known to inspire within his students fear and trembling along with the disciplined analytic thinking he sought. Fear and trembling was certainly the first order of business with this question. Seminarians like to think they are where they are because of what they believe—or at least to find out what they believe. Being asked to speak publicly of the stumbling blocks to belief is a frightening call to strip off the protective garb of vocation and face the challenge of faith without pretense. So we began to respond slowly, but eventually, with growing enthusiasm, we built quite a list of biblical characters we thought were unbelievable. We included Samson and his magical hair; Jonah, who was swallowed by the big fish; and even Baalam's ass, the talking donkey. Finally, the good professor threw up his hands in disgust and announced that none of us knew what we were talking about. We were confusing, he said, what we doubted to be factual with what was unbelievable. The power of a story, he said, is to be measured by its ability to inspire reflection, response, and imitation in life and art. The truly unbelievable, he said, has no power to capture human imagination. Yet, for every character we had named, no matter how fantastic, he could find any number of parallels in art and literature that have inspired imagination, reflection, and response. "You have not yet named," he roared, "the most unbelievable character in the Bible. Find for me one other story, anywhere, in which a man is told a story like the one Mary told Joseph, in which that man believes what he is told."

The lesson had its effect on me. I began to understand that stories that have the power of truth are not limited to what is easily believable as fact. I even thought I knew why I had paid so little attention to Joseph's story. But on reflection, years later, it seems to me that there is more to learn. Do we really ignore Joseph's story just because it is not powerful enough to be believable? Is there perhaps too much, rather than too little, power here—power that we avoid confronting when we require more of this particular story than of others?

The mechanism we use to dismiss Joseph's story is peculiar in its irony. We do not easily believe in Joseph simply because Joseph so easily does believe. As if it is not enough for him to undertake a courageous act of justice—a kind of justice as new to the world as the child in Mary's womb—Joseph then chooses to believe in the reality of Mary's virtue, and that belief is almost too much for us to abide. Where is the evidence? In a dream? Why, reality is far too delicate to be confirmed on the evidence of a dream. Sometimes it takes little to make us doubt even what we have experienced with our senses while wide awake, and we must look for hard evidence.

A few weeks ago, it was my turn to be liturgist and make the parish announcements during Sunday service. Our head of staff, Bob, was preaching that day, and he wrote a note on my bulletin so that I would be sure to announce the Christmas concert and Advent party scheduled for the evening. Dutifully, I made that announcement first of all, but as I sat down—just as the choir was rising for the anthem—Bob jumped up, came to the pulpit, and to everyone's surprise, began to repeat the concert announcement. At first I thought I had done something wrong: perhaps giving you the wrong time or place. But as he pressed on with his usual competent authority, I actually began to doubt that I had made the announcement at all. Then, suddenly, he hesitated, and for a moment, each unsure of his own reality, we waited for the congregation to tell us the truth.

It was easy to forgive Bob's daydream, and I expect you will also understand my momentary lack of confidence. Reality is a slippery thing. Just so, it is very difficult to understand how Joseph could take such confidence from his own dream. When it is so easy to doubt what our experience and reason tell us must be true, how could Joseph possibly believe what his experience and reason surely told him was a lie? Against all evidence, save the evidence of a dream, Joseph chose to believe—to have faith in the faithfulness of Mary. And by this unbelievable act of believing, a miracle was wrought. Mary was vindicated. A terrible situation crying out for justice was transformed. The power of Joseph's believing was so great that the righteousness of the Lord was brought forth: righteousness that is the sign of God's relationship with us—a relationship so powerful that, unbelievably and against all evidence, we, too, are vindicated before the Lord. This is the righteousness of Christ.

The final stumbling block for us may be that Joseph's story does not end with his choice to believe. There is more to the story, and it asks much of those who would believe in it. Once believing, Joseph did more: He chose also to make something concrete from his faith. He made a commitment. He committed himself to be the father of the child in every way that he could. He committed himself to the risk and joy of what all stepparents know to be the ambiguous and full, frustrating and fulfilling, the scary and wonderful task of loving and caring for children who fill your life, yet will always, rightly, call another "Father."

In faith, Joseph made his commitment, and his commitment turned his faith into the transformation of his life. And just so, the Christ, yet unborn, claimed his fist soul: gentle Joseph, who believed and then responded with life-changing commitment to Jesus. Who, with the power to inspire faith and commitment that could transform life, can this child be but the Son of God?

Kneeling by the manger, close, but not so close as to keep the child from our sight, is Joseph. And we know the story of how this child grew to be one who will suffer for the sins of others and will have such faith and commitment to God's work that millions will respond. Who among us cannot say, who cannot believe, that the Son of God is not also truly the son of Joseph? Amen.

4. Spread, O Spread, Thou Mighty Word

J. Donald Waring

Matt. 28:16–20

In the name of the Father and of the Son and of the Holy Spirit. Amen.

"Now the eleven disciples went to Galilee, to the mountain to which Jesus had directed them. And when they saw him, they worshiped him. . . . "

If anyone else here today is a preacher's kid, then you know what it's like to be the thinly disguised subject of one sermon illustration after another. I always knew that someday I would have justice. And today, I'm up here, and Dad is out there. So this would seem to be my supreme opportunity.

When I was a very small boy, I saw in an old family photo album a picture of my father wearing the clothing of a prison inmate. Apparently, he'd been in a play back in college, and his part was the character of a convict. But I didn't know that. All I knew was that here was this picture of my father dressed in a striped outfit with a ball and chain attached to his ankle. And as far as I was concerned, this could only mean that he, at one point in his life, had been in prison.

J. Donald Waring is assistant rector of Christ Church Cranbrook in Bloomfield Hills, Michigan. An Episcopalian, Waring received his master of divinity at General Theological Seminary in New York City. Before his appointment at Christ Church, Waring served as a seminarian intern at Grace Episcopal Church and St. Thomas Episcopal Church, both located in New York City. This sermon was preached at the commencement Eucharist for General Theological Seminary, New York City, May 1989.

Now, at my young age, this was the coolest thing I could possibly imagine. I had no idea what prison was all about; all I knew was that tough guys went there, cowboys went there, and apparently my dad had been there. I told all of my little kindergarten buddies, and they told their buddies, and they told their buddies. Very quickly, this rumor—this rumor that my father had been to jail—was all over the class. And this rumor had power: I became an instant hero; all the kids wanted to come and meet my father. It lasted, of course, until they met him—wearing his clerical collar.

Rumors are powerful. They are persistent, and they take on a life of their own. First we hear them, and then we spread them like wildfire. It's often impossible to prove them either true or false. But we spread them anyway. The rumor about my father was false—I think. But rumors always have their basis in something. And every once in a while, one turns out to be true.

The gospel for today consists of the last five lines of the Book of Matthew. We know it as the Great Commission. This is Matthew's version, Matthew's record, of what happened to the disciples on Easter Day: He reports that they've all rushed to Galilee because they've heard strange, unbelievable *rumors* about Jesus—Jesus who had been dead now since Friday. Suddenly, Jesus appears to them; this rumor that he was alive turns out to be true. Jesus appears and charges them—commissions them—to "make disciples of all nations, baptizing them in the name of the Father and of the Son and of the Holy Spirit."

That's the Great Commission. It is a calling for all Christians to take the truth of Christ into the world and incorporate people into the Church. It is a calling to bring people into the very specific faith of Christianity. Often that requires very up-front sharing about who we think Jesus is. But that's never an easy thing to do, and I'm sure many of us here feel that this business of witnessing publicly to our faith, this work of calling people to Christ, is probably the least enjoyable, most uncomfortable aspect about being a disciple. But in light of this Great Commission, we feel that the burden is somehow upon us to go out there and transform, not only the world, but everybody in it as well.

When I was working as a hospital chaplain, one of the patients I was to see was an altogether healthy ninety-five-year-old man, in for only a minor problem. He was affiliated with no church, and never in his life had he been religious. But he was truly one of the happiest people I've ever met—completely at peace with his agnosticism and all of its implications. And, of course, he was immune to any of my attempts to interest him in Christ. It was enough to drive me crazy. He was open; he listened; but it was as if he had no need for any of it. I couldn't prove anything to him. And so what do we do with the Great Commission?

Well, we are to go out anyway into a world of science, a world of religious pluralism, and a world that no longer shelters the Church. We go out as the baptized who have promised to proclaim Jesus Christ; we go out as the Episcopal church entering a decade of evangelism, and our task is to do more than just fill pews. Our task is to persuade people that the health of the world depends upon Jesus Christ and that they, too, need to be baptized. Baptism is a very specific thing. It involves professing that Jesus Christ is the ultimate answer. Now, nobody can prove that we're wrong about this, but neither can we prove that we're right. And so what do we do with the Great Commission? It seems like an impossible task.

Let's go back to our reading from the end of Matthew. Now, the most striking thing to me about this account is that the disciples are worshiping Jesus. They are already at the point where we profess to be ourselves and where we hope to bring the world. They are worshiping Jesus, even though only hours before they had completely abandoned him. Then they fled in terror; now they worship. They worship him, and eventually all will go to their deaths proclaiming the name of Jesus Christ—building the Church and fulfilling that Great Commission, which they understood as their calling.

So the central question for all of us has to be this: What happened to the disciples after Jesus died and before they saw him again? Something happened. What is it that would take the disciples from abandonment to martyrdom; from denial to death; from total betrayal to total commitment? What is the key ingredient to such a complete conversion? We all know the events that occurred: The cock crowed for Peter, and the last disciple fled. Jesus was delivered to Pilate. He was subjected to a corrupt trial, beaten by soldiers, whipped, and finally crucified. And when he was dead, Joseph of Arimethea buried him in a family tomb. Then on the third day, Jesus rose from the dead. These are the things that we've all heard many times. This is our story.

But what is less apparent about the events that week is the gathering effect of a *rumor*. For centuries, this rumor had echoed among the people of Israel. It told them that God accepted them and was with them. It told them that God was loving and very near, no matter what the outward circumstances would suggest. This was all rumor. Nobody could prove it. And this rumor—this rumor that made the people of Israel who they were—told them that someday in the future someone was going to come and set things right. Rumor had it that the Messiah would come.

Jesus himself throughout his life gave voice to this rumor. It attached itself to him; it followed him; it lived within him. It was him (John 1:1). He spread the rumor, and he redefined it. He claimed to be one with God (John 10:30). He claimed to be the Christ and said, "The Son of Man will be raised on the third day" (Mark 8:31). "Destroy this temple, and in three days I will raise it." (John 2:19). This rumor had power: It would not go away; it had a life of its own. And it was the driving force of that crucial week.

The people knew something of this rumor, and they hurled it back at Jesus when he hung on the cross: "You who would destroy the temple and build it again in three days, save yourself!" (Matt. 27:40). Pilate and his cohorts knew of it. They knew this rumor that Jesus would rise. And they tried to silence it by sealing the tomb, posting guards around it (Matt. 27:64), and afterwards inventing the tale that the disciples stole Jesus' body (Matt. 28:-13). But this rumor—this Word—would not be silenced. It was a light shining in the darkness, and the darkness could not overcome it (John 1:5).

And finally, this rumor exploded on Easter morning. It erupted first among the women at the tomb, and there something convinced them beyond a doubt that Christ was alive. They saw him. For them, this rumor was no longer a rumor but the truth. *Jesus lives.* They could do nothing but rush to the disciples and tell them: *Christ is alive!* And then this rumor that had been at work erupted in the disciples. It hit them. They saw Jesus. They knew he lived. They knew that the hand of God was behind it all. And they worshiped him. They went out among the nations, baptizing them in the name of the Father and of the Son and of the Holy Spirit.

But what about us? What do we do with the Great Commission? What do we do about an individual and a world that seem immune to even our mightiest efforts to change them? We can't prove the truth of Christ to them, as much as we'd like to do that. We can't do this, because it is our faith that God does it. But what we can do, and what God asks us to do, is to keep the rumor going—keep the word alive that Jesus lives.

Jesus lives. That's a loaded statement. But it's precisely this loaded statement that we are to bring to the world. This is our task before anything else. *Jesus lives.* This is the Great Commission: *Christ is alive!* That is not a platitude; it is our very foundation as a people. It's the beginning and the ending of who we are. *Jesus lives!* And when we proclaim this truth, we give voice to the rumor—we give voice to the word God has unleashed upon this world. We give voice to God's Word, which works to bring all people and nations back into his loving arms. He has promised that this Word will stand forever and will not come back to him empty (Isa. 40:8).

Here, I can't help but think of the words to a familiar hymn:

> Spread, O spread, thou mighty word, spread the
>   Kingdom of our Lord,
> that to earth's remotest bound all may heed the
>   joyful sound;
>
> Word of life, most pure and strong, word for which
>   the nations long,
> spread abroad, until from night all the world
>   awakes to light.[1]

Jesus lives. That means we live. By the power of the Spirit, he is with us until the end of time. Spread this word. Spread it while we still have time. Because rumor has it that he's coming again. Amen.

NOTE

1. Jonathan Friedrich Bahnmaier (1774–1841), "The Church's Mission," in *The Hymnal 1982* (New York: Church Hymnal Corporation, 1982), 530.

5. How to Become a Christian
David E. Leininger

John 3:1–8

In a recent summer while spending a week of retreat and study at Columbia Seminary, I attended chapel one morning and heard Ben Johnson preach. (Ben is a professor there.) I do not remember the sermon (a malady that I understand I share with many others), but I recall a story he told. A young man came to the door of a monastery with a large duck in his arms. His uncle, who happened to be one of the monks, answered the knock. "Here, Uncle, this is a gift for you and the others. Eat it in good health." The uncle was very grateful, and that night, with the duck dressed and stuffed, he and the others enjoyed a generous repast.

A few days later, another knock came on the monastery door. "I am a friend of the nephew who brought you the duck. I have been a bit down on my luck lately, and I wonder if I might impose on you for a bite to eat and a place to sleep for the night?" "Of course, my son, you are most welcome." And that night, he joined the monks for some warm duck soup.

A few days later, another knock on the door. "Hi, I am a friend of the friend of the nephew who brought the duck. Could I impose on you for a bit of hospitality?" He too was welcomed . . . more duck soup. A few days more went by. Another knock. "Hello, I am a friend of the friend of the friend of the nephew who brought the duck." That night at dinner he was presented with a steaming hot bowl of

David E. Leininger is senior minister of First Presbyterian Church in Fort Myers, Florida. Leininger attended Lutheran Theological Southern Seminary where he received his master of divinity. His doctorate of ministry is from Erskine Theological Seminary. Previously, Leininger served as minister at two Presbyterian churches in South Carolina.

water. He tasted it, looked up, and asked, "What's this?" "Well, this is the soup of the soup of the soup of the duck that my nephew brought."

As I heard the story I was struck by the similarity of that experience with the way so many come to Christianity. It is often second-, third-, or fourthhand and ends up exceedingly watered down. Sad.

Over the past several weeks, the sermons from this pulpit (in case you have forgotten) have been focusing on some of the problems that have resulted in the decline of the mainline church in this nation along with some ideas concerning how the trend might be reversed—in particular, through a much greater commitment to evangelism: sharing the faith. But in reflecting further, I wonder whether or not we might be getting ahead of ourselves. After all, it does no good to encourage people to share their faith if they are not quite sure what faith it is they are being asked to share. Perhaps we can do something about that this morning.

Our Scripture lesson is as basic in that regard as any you can find. Those of you who grew up in the church in generations past probably heard over and over, "Ye must be born again." George Whitefield, the great evangelist of the eighteenth century, preached over three hundred sermons on that text. When asked why he did that so often, his reply was simply, "Because ye must be born again!" A century later, another great evangelist, Dwight L. Moody, said, "This doctrine of the new birth is the foundation of all our hopes for the world to come. It is really the ABC of the Christian religion. My own experience has been that if a person is unsound on this doctrine, he will be unsound on almost every other fundamental doctrine in the Bible."[1]

In recent years, however, the phrase *born again* has gone out of favor in the mainline vocabulary. It has become associated with a far-right religious/political viewpoint that many consider intolerant, if not intolerable. Among us cerebral Presbyterians, being born again seems long on feeling but short on doing and thus slightly disreputable and not worthy of our attention.

I wonder if that might not have been Nicodemus's problem. For a good Jew, he seems very Presbyterian to me. He was financially secure (as are most Presbyterians). He was a leader in his community (as are many of you). He understood matters of religion as doing, not just feeling; that what we believe determines how we behave (the same as Presbyterians). He was intellectually curious, not content to blindly accept things without investigation—a thinker (just like most Presbyterians). Nicodemus was an admirable fellow, but there was something lacking in his life, so one night he came to talk to Jesus.

In a way, that by itself was remarkable. Of course, word had spread everywhere of the incredible impact of this Nazarene. But some of Nicodemus's good friends and fellow "Presbyterians" had been terribly disturbed at some of the goings-on: the crowds that were attracted to Jesus, this preacher's obvious dislike of what was then the mainstream religious practice, and all this talk about miraculous signs and wonders. One part of Nicodemus told him to avoid this Jesus like a bad shekel, but another part could not be content with that—the stories of crippled legs made strong, of withered arms made straight, of blind eyes restored to sight came too frequently to ignore. So Nicodemus came and, as the two sat quietly together, he shared his sense of unease with Jesus. "Rabbi, we know that you are a teacher come from God; for no one can do these signs that you do, unless God is with him."

Reading between the lines of the Gospel account, there must have been further conversation between Nicodemus and Jesus, words or gestures from this Jewish "Presbyterian" that fairly shouted out his sense of the inadequacy of his own religious experience. Clever teacher that he was, Jesus made a statement that would be certain to provoke further thought. He said, "Truly, truly, I say to you, unless one is born anew (or, depending on the translation, "born from above," or the one with which we grew up, "born again"—all are legitimate), he cannot see the Kingdom of God."

"Now wait a minute, Teacher. You have done a lot of miracles, but this is one even *you* cannot manage. People cannot be born again when they are old!" Jesus replied, "Oh, yes they can. Just as they once began life physically, they can begin spiritually . . . and if they do not, they will never really experience the presence of God in their lives."

The look on Nicodemus's face must have been quizzical. It was obvious that he was still trying to sort out what he had just heard. The example of birth was plain enough—every life has to start somewhere, even the spiritual life. But good analytical, "Presbyterian" Nicodemus wanted to know more. "How does it happen?"

Jesus explained. "There are some things that we know but we do not know *about*. The wind, for example. It blows whenever and wherever it wants. It came from somewhere; it goes somewhere. We see and feel what it does. It defies explanation. It is the same with the new birth. It simply happens."

Now, take a giant mental leap ahead nineteen centuries, out of the Judean courtyard and onto a patio in southwest Florida. Imagine a conversation with a modern Nicodemus. Imagine you are him. You have come to church for years. You went through the confirmation class just like the other twelve-year-olds. You stood up before the congregation and answered, "I do," when the pastor asked if you acknowledged yourself to be a sinner and if you accepted Jesus Christ as your Lord and Savior. You had to say, "I do," or you would have looked like a fool, and your parents would have grounded you for months. But the words were just that—words. That was many years ago. Now you have grown up, and even though you have always thought of yourself as a Christian, a feeling inside says that you have been missing something. You have been living on the faith of the faith of the faith that someone once told you you ought to have. So one evening you come to a respected friend, a Christian, for some answers. "Friend, you are a Presbyterian just like me. But your religion is different from mine. You seem to have a sense of peace and joy that I have never experienced. I don't understand. Help me. How do I become a Christian like you?"

Your friend replies. "Nick, the place to begin is at the beginning, and the best way to explain is with an analogy. Once upon a time you were going on your merry way, muddling through without help from anyone. But then you met a lady. She treated you well—kind, gentle, caring, and so on. You continued to spend time with her. You got to know her. Then one day you realized that, to you, life without her would not really be living. This woman was different from any you had ever known, and something was born in you that made you feel that from that moment you wanted to spend your life with her.

"Can you explain all that? Could anyone explain love? Of course not. It just happened. And frankly, if you had waited for an explanation, you would never have taken the next step. One day you took a leap of faith—you declared your love for her and asked her to become your wife. She accepted, and since then it has been happily ever after. Oh, ups and downs, of course. But the love you felt in your salad days has grown and matured into something that is very real but equally inexplicable.

"Now, Nick, move that thought up a notch. You have met Jesus and, like most everyone else, agree that this is a remarkable man, regarded by all with respect and admiration. After all, the Bible says he was God in the flesh. But something about him is vaguely disquieting. His perfect example, his way of gracefully meeting even the worst that life has to offer, sets a standard for humanity that you do not meet. But you would like to. Something is born in you that makes you realize you want to know him more.

"You spend more time with him, get to know him even better. Finally, you take another leap of faith. You make a commitment to begin. That is what Jesus meant so long ago when he told another Nicodemus, 'Ye must be born again.' You say, 'Lord, I know I am not all I should be, but I believe you can help me. Starting now, I want you to come into my life.' It is that simple."

You still look quizzical. "I am still not sure I understand it all," you say. "Don't worry," your friend says. "This is something better experienced than understood—just like falling in love and getting married."

"But this seems *too* simple. Really being a Christian means upholding certain standards, acting in an ethical way, being a decent citizen, trying to correct the abuses and injustices of society—doesn't it?"

"Well, yes and no," your friend answers. "Think again about your relationship with your wife. You have been married a long time now. The love the two of you have for one another is as strong, if not stronger, than ever, but it is different from those early days. As you have grown together, you have both matured. You probably treat each other differently now than back then. You think more alike now, so the questions you might have asked in the beginning are no longer necessary. You have more common interests and concerns now (your children, for example), so you are more inclined to want to do the same things. You know what makes each other angry or uncomfortable, so you automatically avoid those things. All that is *now*. But to get to *now*, you had to have a then. You had to *begin* somewhere . . . [Bridal Chorus] . . . and then came the growing and learning together. Had you skipped the beginning, there would have been no growing and learning. Sure, certain behavior is appropriate for a Christian, just as it is for a husband. But to try get to that point without first going to the altar leads to all sorts of trouble."

Your friend continues. "Perhaps that is why Jesus used the words *born again*. There had to be a beginning of the relationship between you and your wife, just as there has to be a beginning to your relationship with the Lord. It does not just happen, and nothing symbolizes beginning like birth."

"I don't know," you say. "I am still kind of stuck on all this born-again talk. So-called born-again Christians have always turned me off."

"No problem," responds your friend. "If all that is keeping you from making this leap of faith is words, let's *change* the words. Instead of calling yourself a born-again Christian, substitute something like a *begun* Christian. It says the same thing. In fact, in this day and age it might even be more helpful. What bothers you about born-againers is the same thing that sometimes bothers me about them—they seem to give the impression that the new birth means they have finally reached the ultimate in spiritual development. But birth is not an end; it is a beginning, the first halting movements on the road to maturity. If you and I simply call ourselves *begun* Christians, then we might take more seriously the fact that we have a long way to go.

"Nick, would you like to become a *begun* Christian? Pray this simple prayer. 'Lord Jesus, I know I am not what I ought to be, and I hardly imagine what I *can* be. But I want to begin.' That is how you become a Christian."

Now, take one more mental leap, off the patio and back to the pew. Hear the preacher ask a question. Have you ever made a prayer like that? If you have never made that decisive beginning for yourself, you are living on the faith of the faith of the faith that someone once had. But by now it is so watered down that the sense of joy and peace that comes from a personal relationship with Jesus Christ is not there.

Or perhaps you *did* make such a prayer once long ago, but in all the hurry and scurry of modern life, you let the once joyous relationship you had with your Lord slip to the side. Just like husbands and wives who grow apart through the years through lack of communication. Perhaps you need a new beginning.

Now it is decision time. If you are satisfied with a watered-down faith, you can tune this invitation out. But if you are not, if you would like to become a *begun* Christian or even a begun-*again* Christian, I invite you to pray silently where you are and ask Jesus Christ to become Lord of your life.

Let us pray.

Oh, Lord, thou hast heard the prayers of thy people. Give us the strength to take our commitment seriously, never again content with a watered-down faith. Give us enough faith so that we always have plenty to share. We pray in Christ's name. Amen.

NOTE

1. Quoted by Harry M. Lintz, *Birth Marks of the Born Again* (Wheaton, IL: Van Kampen Press, 1953), 50.

II. EXPOSITORY

6. Infant Arms: Epiphany
Leo Sands

Isa. 60:1–6; Psalm 71; Eph. 3:2–3, 5–6; Matt. 2:1–12

I'll never forget that night. It was cold over Persia as my fellow stars and I journeyed together across the December sky. It was the winter solstice—the longest night of the year. But the sky was clear—not a cloud—and I knew that we could be clearly seen from planet earth.

Suddenly, I was jolted from my course. It was the hand of God. He called to me and told me to change my way. I was to forget about myself and my own brightness. He wanted me to be humble. "I have a special mission for you," he said, "to lead others to me. Head west toward the hill country of Judaea. Three men will follow you. Take them to the little town called Bethlehem." Sure enough, I looked down, and there they were, on camels: three men, wise and good, royally dressed as if they were kings. God must have spoken to them, too, because they were looking up, waiting for me to lead them.

So I began to direct them that night and was renewed in the process. I forgot about myself and devoted my attention instead to helping my three companions. When the moon would be covered and the night dark, I would shine extra bright so that they wouldn't stumble and fall. When they would get tired and discouraged, I'd twinkle and twinkle till they would feel better again.

We stopped off in Jerusalem for a while. The wise men went into the palace of the king. Soon we arrived in Bethlehem. God had me stop over a stable on the hillside, and I could see inside a young

Leo Sands is professor of preaching and communications at the University of St. Michael's College, Toronto School of Theology, Canada. He is a member of the Academy of Homiletics and served as a judge for the sermon competition in *Best Sermons 2*.

mother and father with their newborn baby boy. He was so tiny that he couldn't have been more than a few days old. He was sleeping, then crying, and then being fed by his mom, the way all babies that size are. At the door were shepherd boys gazing in.

Then my friends got down from their camels and took precious objects from their packs. They confidently walked toward the stable like men who had finally found what they had long been searching for. Inside they introduced themselves, knelt down in front of the child, and began to pray. They prayed for a long time. Then one of them turned to the father to ask him the child's name. He told them that his name was Jesus. The men presented their gifts, handing them to the father but clearly intending them for the child. One offered a vessel containing incense. That was strange, because incense is usually used in praise of God. The second man presented a jar filled with myrrh, a costly ointment often used to anoint the bodies of the dead. That I found odd, too. I wondered if the baby were sick, whether perhaps he would not live long. The third man's gift was gold, which is ordinarily presented to kings.

I did a lot of wondering that night. Who was this child? Why had God brought us halfway around the world to see him? I asked God for more light. I knew that even though I was a star, I was still much in the dark. God answered my prayer, and I began to understand.

I was aware that somehow on the day the child below me would die, my sister sun, who always shone so brightly, would be eclipsed. On that day, even at noon the earth would be in darkness. I realized, too, that the child was a king, not just for Bethlehem but for the whole world. I wanted to go to every city and village on planet earth, east and west, north and south, all nations, all races, all religions, and lead them all to Bethlehem, to the child, because I knew that he was holding out his infant arms to them all, loved them all, could take away the sins of the world, could bring it peace, and wanted to do just that.

Last of all, I wondered what I would do now that I was his messenger. I wanted like everything to bring him a present as my comrades had done. But since I had to stay in my star track, I couldn't. But if I were able, what would I give him? What would my gift be? I thought of bread and wine, just plain bread and wine. And with that I would tell him that he could have me, too, that I wanted to give him myself. I knew I wasn't much but that he would want me anyway.

7. When All Is Said and Done
Mark Trotter

Text: Ezek. 34:11–24; Matt. 25:31–46

I want you to imagine a testimonial banquet honoring a beloved teacher. All his colleagues are there. Former students have returned to pay honor to this great man. There are speeches of praise and gifts given in gratitude. Then the teacher is asked to say a few words in response.

This will be his last opportunity to speak to all those who have been his students, his disciples, through the years—the ones who sat at his feet and listened to everything he said. What will he say to them on an occasion such as this? This is his last address to them.

He will undoubtedly summarize what he has said to them over a whole career of teaching. He will put in capsule form the essence of his message. And since he is a skilled teacher, he will state it as simply as possible. It will be simple in structure but dramatic in impact because he will want them always to remember this.

In fact, if something is really profound, it can be stated simply. That's the nature of truth: simplicity. All great teachers are able to state simply what we know deep down to be true, even though we may not be able to articulate it ourselves.

I want you to imagine that scene as we look at the New Testament lesson for this morning, the twenty-fifth chapter of the Gospel of Matthew, the vision of the last judgment. Sometimes it is known as the parable of the sheep and the goats, although it is technically not a parable.

This is Jesus' last word to his disciples as he retires from the vocation of teacher. The twenty-fifth chapter of Matthew is the end

Mark Trotter has served since 1976 as senior minister of the First United Methodist Church in San Diego, California, and is the author of *Grace All the Way Home.*

of a long teaching section. With the twenty-sixth chapter begins what is called the "passion narrative," the story of his suffering and dying. So this is the end of his teaching. This is kind of a farewell speech. It is delivered on the Mount of Olives outside of Jerusalem. It is a long speech, taking up several chapters and concluding with the story of the last judgment.

The disciples sit expectantly, waiting for the teacher's final words. They will always remember this. When he says, "In conclusion...," they strain forward with expectation. He begins, "When the Son of man comes in his glory and all of the angels are with him, then he will sit on his glorious throne." And with that ominous beginning, he sets his last words to us in the context of last things in order to give them more weight.

"When the Son of man comes...." The Son of man was a code word for Messiah, the one who will come to make things right in a world gone wrong. The Son of man was the one who will bring in the Kingdom of God. Almost everyone expected the Son of man to come in those days. There were those who hoped that Jesus was the Son of man, that is, the Messiah-king, or a Messiah-warrior. So when the words "When the Son of man comes" are spoken, they pierce deeply and directly to the longings of the people gathered there.

They knew exactly what he was talking about. He was talking about ultimate things now. He was talking about the way it will be "when the curtain falls," when "the scales of history are balanced," "when all is said and done." Then, "the Son of man will come with all of the angels, and he will sit on his glorious throne."

"And before him will be gathered all of the nations of the world." So this is the last judgment, the final one, when everybody is there, the time when our lives are to be judged for what they really were. This is the judgment from which there is no appeal.

I have been asked many times who will be saved and how can we know. Sometimes the question comes when someone we care about dies, and we wonder what will happen to them. Sometimes it comes when somebody, spouting Scripture, seems to know definitively who is going to be saved and who is going to be damned. Or maybe we've seen one of those billboards out on the highway in the desert that shouts at us, "Where will you spend eternity?"

One way the Bible answers these ultimate questions is to paint the scene of the last judgment. That's what Jesus is doing in this passage. There are other judgment scenes in the Bible; some don't agree with this one. But this is Jesus' vision, so I would take it seriously. "All the nations will be there," which means everyone. Different religions will be there. Those of no religion will be there. The whole world will be there before the Son of man sitting on his throne.

Then he describes the judgment by means of an analogy. He says it will be like a shepherd who at the end of the day separates the sheep from the goats, a common practice in that pastoral country where several flocks would use the same pasture. But at the end of the day they would be separated. This shepherd will send the sheep to his right hand and the goats to his left. The sheep will go into the Kingdom of God, and the goats into eternal punishment.

Now that's a harsh description of the last judgment. It is indeed an analogy, so you do not need to take the details literally. The details are there so that you will take it seriously, much the same way Flannery O'Connor described her use of the "grotesque" in writing her stories: "For people whose eyesight has grown dim, you have to write in large figures. And for those who are deaf, you have to shout." She does that, and so does the Bible, especially in scenes like the last judgment, where the attempt is to penetrate dulled and insensitive souls and minds. Judgment scenes are painted in the Bible on large, bold canvases. They virtually shout at you to get your attention so that you will take them seriously and, in turn, take the life that you are living seriously. So when the Son of man comes, he will judge everyone, as a shepherd separates the sheep from the goats at the end of the day.

He's got our attention now. Jesus is talking not only about ultimate things but about our ultimate destiny. This is serious business. The question that is on everybody's mind is, Who are the sheep? Who are those who are shepherded into the kingdom? Will I be in that number?

Then comes the revelation. And it is indeed an amazing revelation. It breaks down conventional expectations. It shatters the standards that the world uses to determine who is going to be saved and who is not.

He begins by describing those who are going to be saved. "I was hungry, and you gave me food. I was thirsty, and you gave me drink. I was a stranger, and you welcomed me. I was naked, and you clothed me. I was sick, and you visited me. I was in prison, and you came to me."

That shattered the expectation of the world. The world expects that judgment will be on the basis of our personal behavior. Jesus says judgment will be on the basis of our relation to other people. The world expects that we will be judged on whether or not we were righteous. Jesus says we will be judged on whether or not we were compassionate.

It's revolutionary but not a surprise to those gathered to hear these final words. They had heard them from him before, many times. From the beginning, he had shocked the conventionally righteous by treating those labeled "unrighteous" as if they were human beings. The righteous said, "Those people are sinners, and therefore they deserve whatever fate they get." Jesus replied, "None of us get what we deserve in this life. Most of us get better than we deserve."

They said to him, "If you love foreigners, if you love your enemies, they will not return the favor. We will guarantee you that." Jesus says, "You have not loved if you do it for reciprocation. That's not love; that's bartering. Love gives without any expectation of return."

They said, "Well, we want to visit those who are sick, and we want to give food to those who are hungry, but the rules won't let us. And we should always obey the Law." Jesus said, "That's using the Law of God to run away from what God is really calling you to do. If someone is hungry, feed him. Don't evaluate their worthiness. If somebody is in need, help them. If somebody is hurt, heal their wounds."

What he is saying is no surprise. But here, in the context of the last judgment, it has more weight. You will be judged, he says, not by your righteousness but by your compassion.

Those on the right hand are dumbfounded at this. They ask, "Lord, when did we see thee hungry and feed thee, or when did we see thee thirsty and give thee drink, and when did we see thee a stranger and welcome thee or naked and clothed thee or sick or in prison and visit thee?" And the king will answer them, "Truly I say to you, as you did it to one of the least of these, you did it to me."

They can't believe it. They are totally surprised. They don't remember doing those things. They can't recall any of those deeds. When did we do them? Which means they did them humbly. They did them not to get recognition, not to earn their salvation. They couldn't even remember doing them because they didn't do them for themselves. They didn't do them for reward or attention. They did them out of compassion for somebody else.

I would guess that another reason they couldn't remember them was because they were such simple, little things. No big deal really. The kind of things that after you do them you can't remember them, but the person you did them for will never forget them.

Things that don't solve any of the world's great problems like hunger or disease—they just give somebody who is hungry a meal, and they treat a stranger or a foreigner hospitably or an enemy decently. They just visit somebody who is sick and hold their hand. That's all.

And what Jesus is saying is that those simple deeds have ultimate consequences. Not that saving the world isn't important, but it means that even those who are busy saving the world will be asked the same question: Did you help the person at your doorstep or that person in your own family or the neighbor down the street that nobody has heard from for about a month?

That's the meaning of the conclusion, when those who were rejected ask, "When did we see you in such dire straits?" And he will say to them, "If you did not do it to one of the least of these, you did not do it to me."

Well, the goats are just as surprised as the sheep. They thought that they were doing great things, and they probably were. It's just that we can be so absorbed in doing great things that we miss the important things. And Jesus came to make it clear that the most important thing in this world is your neighbor in need. If you ignore him or her, then all of your other good deeds simply don't matter— probably because, if we ever stopped to look at it, we could see that we often use noble causes and even religious activities to shield us from the harder and more demanding task of helping those who are closest to us.

Jesus was particularly hard on religious people with that criticism. The parable of the good samaritan can be read as a condemnation of those who are so busy doing important things, even religious things, that they don't have time to help the person in real pain on the side of the road. Jesus taught that lesson consistently. But in case you didn't get it, he spells it out in the scene of the judgment. Some old goat asks, "When did we see thee?" And he answers, "Every person that you refused to help was me."

Ray Balcomb talked about an editorial that he read in the newspaper about those "New Age" seminars that are so popular now all around the country, preaching a "new spiritual consciousness," they say. But it really isn't new at all. It's the same old business about looking after yourself and feeling good about yourself. The editorial pointed out that spirituality is really much deeper than that, genuine spirituality is. It suggested that one of the important criteria is the test, "By their fruits ye shall know them." Which reminded Balcomb of the story that Bishop Roy Nichols liked to tell. Nichols said he grew up in a kind of charismatic black church where there was a lot of enthusiasm, a lot of shouting and jumping. Nichols said that his mother told him once, "It isn't so much how high you jump but what you do when you come down."

Jesus said the same thing. It was Jesus who said, "By their fruits ye shall know them." He also said, "Not those who say, 'Lord, Lord,' but those who do the will of my heavenly Father will be in the kingdom." And he told the parable about two sons who were sent into the field to work. One son said, "I will go," but he did not go. And the other said, "I will not go," but he went. Now which one, Jesus asks, did the will of the father?

It is the same message consistently, repeated here in his closing remarks, that what you say religiously in church is not as important as what you do compassionately in the world.

And if you come to the end, and you say, "But I was a good person," but you did not feed the hungry, and you did not do the simple deeds of love to those in need, then everything else that you did will count for nothing. To paraphrase Bishop Nichols, it won't matter how high you have climbed in this world, it won't matter how much virtue and piety you have accumulated in this world, if you haven't the compassion that leads you to stoop to help somebody in need.

Carroll Simcox tells of the time he was in Damascus in Syria. He was in the hospital there for a very painful attack of kidney stones. I understand from those who have suffered it that it is an incredible pain. It occurred when he was alone in a hotel room in the middle of the night. He called the desk of the hotel and asked for a doctor. The desk called. The doctor said he couldn't be there until the morning.

In the early morning he was writhing on his bed when the chambermaid walked in to clean the room. She saw him there on the bed.

Her expression was of horror and terror. As she came closer to the bed her expression changed to compassion. She stretched her hands upward and said, "Allah!" as a kind of prayer. Then she said to Simcox, "Good soon." Then she left the room. She returned with a cup of tea. No words were spoken. She lifted his head, put the cup to his lips, and he drank.

He said, "The Lord stretched his hand to me through a stranger of another faith. It was like communion. I recalled what Christ said, 'If you have done it unto the least of these, you have done it to me.' " In that situation, in that country, five thousand miles from home, all alone, he said, "I was the least of these."

"When the Son of man comes with all of the angels, he will sit on his glorious throne. And before him will be gathered all of the nations." They will all be there. Everyone will be there—Jew, Christian, Muslim, Hindu, believer, nonbeliever. And he will ask only one question: "Did you help the least of these?"

8. Mary, Mother of God
Steven P. Vitrano

As Protestants, we do not venerate or canonize Mary; we ignore her. True, we do not believe she was immaculately conceived or that she in any sense serves as a mediator or dispenser of divine grace. But if we believe in the virgin birth of Jesus and that he was divine—the second person of the Godhead—then surely she occupies a unique place in salvation history. She is the mother of "God manifest in the flesh," and that makes her special as a woman and as a mother.

But what do we know about Mary? Not a great deal, to be sure. But what we do know is told in a series of sketches that should give us cause for serious reflection.

Consternation

See this girl, possibly sixteen or seventeen years of age, going about her daily chores—sweeping the floor, washing the dishes, making the bed, or whatever—when suddenly she is confronted with an angel who says, "Hail, O favored one, the Lord is with you!" (Luke 1:28, RSV). Surprised? Thunder-struck? Luke's account is an understatement: "she was greatly troubled at the saying" (v. 29). Greatly troubled, indeed! Put yourself in her place. How troubled would you be? But the angel continues: "Do not be afraid, Mary, for you have found favor with God. And behold, you will conceive in your womb and bear a son, and you shall call his name Jesus" (vv. 30, 31).

Hold everything! This is too much. "How can this be, since I have no husband?" (v. 34). She is engaged to be married, but there has not been nor will there be premarital sex. She's not that kind of girl. How is she to have a baby?

Steven P. Vitrano, until his recent retirement, was professor of preaching, liturgics, and evangelism at the Seventh-Day Adventist Seminary in Berrien Springs, Michigan. Dr. Vitrano is the author of three books and numerous articles.

The Holy Spirit will come upon you,
and the power of the Most High will overshadow
   you;
therefore the child to be born will be called Holy,
the Son of God. (v. 35)

It is too easy to take this story for granted. Mary is a girl who lived many years ago in an obscure Palestinian village called Nazareth. She was of good lineage but not "high born." She was not perfect but apparently of a pious, spiritual nature. She was secure in the fact that she would be married, not having to suffer the reproach (in her day) of living her life as a spinster. Her circumstances were normal and ordinary, far from sensational. Put it all together and you know she was more than shocked at what she heard; she was filled with consternation! This can't be true; it must be a dream—forget it!

Acceptance

Mary could have done just that, forgotten it. But to her credit she didn't. Her religious experience was genuine. She recognized the call of God when she heard it—unbelievable as it may seem—and she accepted it. "Behold I am the handmaid of the Lord; let it be to me according to your word" (v. 38). Her faith was a simple but complete trust. Such faith is and always has been redemptive.

It is not by accident that Mary's expression of that faith has been etched in the tradition of the Church. Through centuries of time, the Magnificat has been a part of its liturgical heritage.

My soul magnifies the Lord,
and my spirit rejoices in God my Savior,
for he has regarded the low estate of his
   handmaiden.
For behold, henceforth all generations will call me
   blessed;
for he who is mighty has done great things for me,
and holy is his name. (vv. 46–49)

Fulfillment

The Christmas story is well known. It tells of shepherds and angel songs, of stars and stables, of wise men with their gifts, and the birth of a baby. But this is the story of Mary. She is holding her newborn in her arms. She has become a mother! What joy! What wonder! What fulfillment!

In the days that follow his birth, routines are changed, adjustments are made. It is a time of transition. Feeding, changing clothing, sleeping, waking—life will never be the same. To the mother, it is a time of devotion, of stress, of anxiety. It is also a time of growing, of daily fulfillment and joy as the child responds more and more to his mother's love. So much takes place during those first few days that there is little time to ponder the mysteries of life, especially the life of this child.

And yet, all that she has been told and all that she has accepted concerning his birth is no doubt somewhere on the back roads of her mind. His birth was unpretentious to be sure. How that fits into the scheme of things might not be clear—royalty, children of substance and stature, are not born in barns. But she is faithful. "And at the end of eight days, when he was circumcised, he was called Jesus, the name given by the angel before he was conceived in the womb" (Luke 2:21, rsv).

How would you like to be the mother of Jesus—Emmanuel, God with us, the one who will save his people from their sins? Impressed with the awesome responsibility that that entails, do you see why Mary deserves our highest respect and admiration?

Dedication

To the handmaid of the Lord, the Law of the Lord is important. According to that Law, every male child is to be presented to him and called "holy to the Lord" (v. 23). It is with joy, therefore, that Mary accompanies Joseph on a visit to the Temple at the time of their purification to dedicate Jesus by offering a sacrifice, "a pair of turtledoves, or two young pigeons" (v. 24), and it is to the righteous and devout Simeon that they bring Jesus for the blessing. He is a man who longs for the "consolation of Israel" (v. 25), to whom it had been revealed that he should not see death "before he had seen the Lord's Christ" (v. 26).

Holding Jesus in his arms, inspired by the Holy Spirit, Simeon offers a prayer that has come to be known as the Nunc Dimittis. Like the Magnificat, it is a cherished part of the Church's liturgical tradition.

> Lord, now lettest thou thy servant depart in peace,
> according to thy word;
> for mine eyes have seen thy salvation
> which thou hast prepared in the presence of all
>   peoples,
> a light for revelation to the Gentiles,
> and for glory to thy people Israel. (vv. 29–32)

"And his father and his mother marveled at what was said about him" (v. 33). But of course, wouldn't you? You may have heard it before, but it never ceases to "set you up." Your son, this baby boy, is the Messiah! Is it possible?

But Mary has no time to ponder these words because suddenly Simeon is speaking again and to her:

> Behold, this child is set for the fall and rising of
>   many in Israel,
> and for a sign that is spoken against
> (and a sword will pierce through your own soul
>   also),
> that thoughts out of many hearts may be revealed.
>   (vv. 34, 35)

On her way home, what were Mary's thoughts? The signals were so mixed. She had heard blessing, promise, and prediction. She had heard that a sword would be pierced through her soul because of her child. Is this something she can bear? The answer, of course, is yes. Love conquers all. Whatever the predictions concerning this child, whatever he is or becomes to others, he will always be hers, her firstborn, her wonderful, wonderful baby boy. Ride all the way to Egypt on the back of a donkey? If it means the saving of her son, she will ride not only to Egypt but around the world.

Perplexity

How would you like to raise an exceptional child? How do you relate to the child that is exceptionally bright and gifted? Those who have, know that it is not always easy. There are advantages, to be sure, but there are also disadvantages. To say that Jesus was an exceptional child is an understatement. "The child grew and became strong, filled with wisdom; and the favor of God was upon him" (v. 40). The record also says that "Jesus increased in wisdom and in stature, and in favor with God and man" (v. 52).

How wonderful to have a child like that! Yes, but not always.

When Jesus was twelve years old, he went with his parents to Jerusalem at the time of the Passover. It was a religious festival, but it was a time of celebration, the celebration of Israel's deliverance from Egypt. Boys and girls and their parents, too, enjoy such times. Feasts can be fun. They do come to an end, however, and then it is time to begin the journey home. But when others are ready to go home, the exceptional child thinks otherwise.

In the hustle and the bustle and the confusion of the crowds leaving the city, Joseph and Mary do not realize that Jesus is not with them. You know how it is—Joseph thinks Mary knows where he is, and Mary presumes that Joseph, as the father, has things under control.

A day's journey out of Jerusalem, they discover that the boy is missing. What to do? You know the frustration, the anxiety. They decide they must return to Jerusalem. There goes the schedule, the extra energy and expense. Who needs that? But that is not all, it takes them three days to find him!

Talk about fit to be tied! You think good people don't get angry? Think again. It did not matter that he was in the Temple, "sitting among the teachers, listening to them and asking them questions," and that, "all who heard him were amazed at his understanding and his answers" (vv. 46, 47). There was an edge to Mary's voice when she said, "Son, why have you treated us so? Behold, your father and I have been looking for you anxiously" (v. 48).

At this point, the average child would probably experience a moment of quaking. The fire in his mother's eyes would more than likely elicit some degree of remorse. But Jesus is exceptional, and his answer, of course, is exceptional, "How is it that you sought me? Did you not know that I must be in my Father's house?" (v. 49).

What do you do with an answer like that from a twelve-year-old? What does he mean? Joseph and Mary didn't know. They were perplexed. And to Mary's credit, she learned to live with that perplexity, she "kept all these things in her heart" (v. 51).

Affirmation

Years have come and gone. Jesus is now an adult and is beginning his ministry as Messiah. There is a wedding in Cana in Galilee, and

Jesus and his mother are there. A crisis develops when the wine runs out. What to do? Mary turns to Jesus, "They have no wine" (John 2:3, RSV). She has come to rely on him. He is her exceptional child that has proven equal to every situation. Jesus' response is abrupt but not discourteous—it is the customary manner of speaking. "O woman, what have you to do with me? My hour has not yet come" (v. 4).

Mary could have been offended. But during the time of Jesus' upbringing, she had learned to trust him. When he speaks in that tone of voice with that finality, you don't challenge him; you obey him. "Do whatever he tells you" (v. 5). This is Mary's affirmation of Christ. She may have found him difficult at times. She may have wondered how to relate to this exceptional child, but she could never deny him. Jesus was the best thing that ever happened to her, and she knew it. Do whatever he tells you, and water becomes wine.

Consolation

We see Mary next at the foot of the cross. The events of the last few days will always remain with her. It is not easy for a mother to see her children suffer. What agony of heart! They have nailed her exceptional boy to a cross. Some of his friends may be standing afar, but she is near. If she could only take him down from the cross, put her arms around him, and treat his wounds! But no, this is not to be. He is the Messiah, and she knows it. If this is God's way of saving the world, let it be. "Do whatever he tells you." The heart still breaks, but she sorrows not as those who have no hope.

Jesus, looking down from the cross, sees his beloved disciple standing near his mother and says, "Woman, behold, your son," and to the disciple, "Behold, your mother!" (John 19:26, 27, RSV). The words of love and compassion are so typical of Jesus. He spent his life healing and making people whole. Now he ministers in consolation to his mother. He provides for her security. The beloved John will care for Mary for the rest of her life.

Reunion

The only other mention we have of Mary, following the Crucifixion, is recorded in Acts 1:14, "All these with one accord devoted themselves to prayer, together with the women and Mary the mother of

Jesus, and with his brothers." It seems quite clear that she remained a part of the believing community until her death.

She was not to see her son again in this life, but she died in the hope that she would see him again in the Second Coming. This has been the hope of the Church since its inception. It is based upon Christ's own promise recorded in John 14:3, "I will come again," and confirmed by the angels in Acts 1:11, "This Jesus, who was taken up from you into heaven, will come in the same way as you saw him go into heaven."

Of that Second Coming, Paul writes,

> For the Lord himself will descend from heaven with
> a cry of command, with the archangel's call, and
> with the sound of the trumpet of God. And the
> dead in Christ will rise first; then we who are alive,
> who are left, shall be caught up together with them
> in the clouds to meet the Lord in the air; and so we
> shall always be with the Lord. Therefore comfort
> one another with these words. (1 Thess. 4:16–18,
> RSV)

Observe with me a scene portrayed for us in Rev. 7:9–12. The Second Advent and the resurrection have taken place. The redeemed of earth with all the angels are assembled around the throne of God and before the Lamb. They are there to worship and praise God for salvation and blessing and glory and wisdom and thanksgiving and honor and power and might.

Imagine that you are there and that Mary is there. While she has seen Jesus, they have not yet met face to face since the Resurrection. Suddenly the eyes of Jesus, the Lamb, fall upon Mary, and at once they move toward each other. He takes her in his arms, and they hold each other in a long and loving embrace. Jesus and his mother are together again.

This is the story of Mary, the world's greatest mother. But it is not just Mary's story, it is your story and mine. Jesus is not our son, but he is our brother. He has filled us all with consternation and perplexity. Jesus has a way of turning us upside down. We are no better than Peter, whom Jesus rebuked by saying, "Get behind me, Satan." But we have also known acceptance, fulfillment, affirmation, and consolation. And we share Mary's hope of a Second Coming, a resurrection, and a glorious, grand reunion.

9. Remember Rahab
David R. Wilkinson

Josh. 2:1–24, 6:20–25; Heb. 11:30–31; James 2:21–26

The story in the opening chapters of Joshua has all the elements for an Ian Fleming double-o-seven spy novel. It's got military conflict, high-stakes espionage, adventure, suspense, a dramatic chase scene, and, of course, a beautiful woman.

This action-packed thriller takes place in the first stages of an ambitious military mission, the conquest of Canaan by the people of Israel. Leading the people into battle is an impressive two-member cast. The field general is Joshua, a seasoned veteran who learned the ropes under the tutelage of his predecessor, Moses. After waiting in the wings for years as the number two man, it's now Joshua's chance to command center stage—sort of the George Bush of the Old Testament.

Only, center stage never belongs to Joshua alone. In fact, he is neither the chief character in the story nor the supreme commander on the battlefield. As the biblical writers take great pains to make clear, Joshua reports directly to the real commander in chief, Yahweh, Lord God of the Hebrew nation.

In the opening scene, the children of Israel are camped opposite the Jordan River from the land of Canaan. God has given Joshua the go-ahead to invade the country, promising that the opposition will wilt before him (Josh. 1:5). Before mapping out his battle plan, Joshua picks two of the best members of his reconnaissance team and gives them orders to check out Canaan, especially Jericho.

David R. Wilkinson is a vice-president at The Southern Baptist Theological Seminary, Louisville, Kentucky, and former director of News and Information Services, Christian Life Commission of the Southern Baptist Convention. He has won numerous awards in journalism and is coauthor of the book *Urban Heartbeat.*

That is certainly predictable strategy. But the twist in the story comes when the two spies meet a lady—or, more precisely, a madam. Her name is Rahab. Her profession is prostitution—harlotry, in biblical terminology. In fact, that's the name the Bible gives her: Rahab the Harlot. Her profession is cited almost as if it were an extension of her name. Can you imagine being introduced at a party? "Hello, I'd like for you to meet Joe the Camel Driver and his wife, Sarah the Sheepherder. And this is Harold the Tent Maker and, of course, Rahab the Harlot. Imagine Rahab's income tax form. Last name: "Harlot." First name: "Rahab." Middle: "the." You could look her up in the business section of the white pages under *H* for harlot.

But back to the story.

When the two spies reached Jericho, they headed straight for Rahab's place. It was on the edge of town, so maybe it was the first place they came to. Or perhaps they noticed the big neon sign out front. Or maybe it was the $2.99 blue plate special advertised in the window.

More than likely, Rahab's place was an inn—a kind of bed and breakfast place with a little something extra.[1] It was that something extra, of course, that gave the place its reputation. It was a place where you didn't need a reservation, they accepted three major credit cards, and you didn't have to answer any questions about who you were, where you'd been, or where you were headed.

Rahab's establishment was strategically located, built across the interior and exterior walls that surrounded the city. It came complete with something every such establishment needs—a rear exit; in this case, a window above the outside wall.

The Bible doesn't tell us why the spies chose this place. It simply reports that they lodged there. The question of whether they came to take advantage of all of the inn's services is left to our imagination. It's certainly reasonable to assume that their visit was purely in the line of duty. Have you seen a cop show yet where the detective didn't meander down to the local bar to pick up a few leads on a case?

In this case, the two spies got more than leads; they got answers. And the answers came from none other than the proprietor herself.

In her particular line of business, Rahab had learned a lot about life—and about truth. Over the years, she had heard about every lie known to women and told by men. In contrast, she knew the truth when she heard it.

Rahab also knew men. She had seen them all and listened to them all. She knew what drove them, what pleased them, and what scared them. She knew their weaknesses, their frailties, their fears. On more than one occasion, grown and powerful men had wept in her lap, confessing things to her they had never told another soul.

Perhaps it was during one of those impromptu confessionals that she first heard about this horde of Hebrews and their Yahweh God. The more times she heard the stories, the more interested she became. And the more convinced she became that the stories must be true.

Sometimes, sitting on the front porch swing contemplating her loneliness, she replayed those stories in her mind and wondered what meaning they might have for her.

Now she was about to find out.

Though the spies thought they might go unnoticed, the word soon got back to the mayor of Jericho that a couple of Israelites had checked into Rahab's place, and it didn't look like the usual one-night stand. Clearly, they were secret agents with hostile intentions.

The mayor hurriedly gathered a posse and sent the men over to Rahab's place with orders for her to turn her guests over for questioning.

Rahab, however, had her own plans. Besides, she certainly owed no loyalty to the mayor. Knowing full well that the spies were hiding upstairs under stalks of flax that were drying on the roof, she acknowledged that she had, indeed, seen the gentlemen in question. But, as luck would have it, they had just left.

"Where were they headed?" asked the sheriff.

"I don't know," deadpanned Rahab, "but I'm sure you can catch them if you hurry."

The sheriff, being more like Barney Fife than Marshal Dillon, thought that made sense, and he and his men disappeared into the darkness.

Rahab ran back up to the roof to announce to the spies that the coast was clear. But now that she had risked her life by hiding them, she was ready to cut a deal with them. While the mayor and his men had guessed why the Israelites were in town, Rahab knew even more.

"I know the Lord has given you the land," she said, meaning, of course, her homeland. "We've heard how the Lord parted the Red Sea for you when you were hightailing it out of Egypt. And not only are you good at running, it seems you've learned how to fight as well. We've heard what happened to those Amorite kings who got in your way.

"We're as good as dead, and everyone knows it. The whole town is terrified. There's not so much as a thimbleful of courage left in the biggest, bravest man in town."

Rahab's description struck a chord with the spies. Years earlier, God had made a promise to Moses. " 'I will . . . put the dread and fear of you upon the peoples everywhere . . . who, when they hear the report of you, shall tremble and be in anguish because of you' " (Deut. 2:25, ASV). Now, God was making good on his promise. He had the Canaanites shaking in their sandals.

The spies put away their notes and turned off the concealed tape recorders. They had heard all they needed to know. Information about the strength of the enemy—fortifications, troop strength and location, supplies, and so forth—is always good to have. But nothing can replace the knowledge that the enemy had lost its courage.

Rahab, however, didn't stop with a mere recitation of the facts. In an amazing statement, this foreign prostitute declared her faith in the God of the Hebrews: "I know these things have happened because the Lord your God is God of all. He is Lord in heaven above and on earth beneath."

In addition to her faith, Rahab also had her wits.

"I know what's coming," she said. "This town is about to be wiped off the map. Since I've helped you, I want you to help me. Pledge to me and to the Lord that you will spare me and my family."

The men agreed but warned that the contract would be null and void if she failed to keep their business a secret. As a sign, Rahab was instructed to tie a scarlet thread or cord in her window above the wall. During the attack, the invaders would then know which house to protect. But, they warned, if one of your family members so much as wanders outside to visit the outhouse, he's history.

Rahab then lowered the men by a rope out her window and advised them to head for the hills where they could hide for a few days until the posse gave up.

The men did just that, and when they returned to camp they issued their report to Joshua. Based on the testimony of a foreign prostitute, they reported that Jericho was easy pickings: "The land is ours for the taking. As for the inhabitants, we have it on good authority that they have already melted before us."

In the meantime back in Jericho, Rahab was getting ready for the great escape. She pulled the shades and hung a "Closed for Remodeling" sign in the front window. Soon the neighbors noticed that her family—including her father, who hadn't spoken to her in years—had practically moved in with her. In the evenings, she would stand at the back window, staring out at the horizon. Before going to bed, she would gently run her fingers down the scarlet thread as it glistened in the candlelight, fully aware that her life was now hanging by that thread.

A few days later, the devastating news came to Jericho that the Hebrews had miraculously crossed the Jordan at flood stage. While an attack had seemed inevitable for some time, the town had managed to that point to take some comfort in the knowledge that the river stood between them and the enemy. Now the city fell into a self-imposed siege. The gates were shut. No one came in, and no one went out.

Then, suddenly, the dreaded army was there. But rather than a full-scale assault on the walls, this strange bunch of Hebrews simply queued up and marched around the city, following some ornate box shouldered by what appeared to be priests. If it weren't a life-and-death matter, the scene would have been laughable. Instead of war whoops, there was a trumpet fanfare followed by absolute, uncanny, unnerving silence. For six days the scene was repeated, and by the seventh day, the panic inside the walls was six times greater than it had been a week earlier. This time the strange processional continued to circle the city—once, twice, three times, four times, five times, six. At the completion of the seventh trip, a mighty roar shattered the silence. And the walls of Jericho shook, cracked, buckled, and fell flat.

Except, that is, for the portion of the wall holding up Rahab's place. While the march around Jericho ended in death and destruction for all her neighbors, Rahab was spared. Years earlier, it had been the Hebrew families who spread crimson blood from the Passover lamb on their front posts and were spared from the final and most terrible plague on the Egyptians. Now, with a crimson thread hung in the window, a Canaanite prostitute and her family experienced another Passover. In fact, the Scriptures tell us that Rahab eventually was welcomed by the Israelites as one of their own (Josh. 6:25).

That's the last mention of Rahab in the Old Testament. According to some rabbinic and early Christian traditions, she went on to marry none other than Joshua and to become the ancestress of several prophets (including Jeremiah) and a prophetess.[2]

It is not until the New Testament that the biblical writers again refer to Rahab. She is mentioned three times. Matthew includes her name in his genealogy of Jesus—one of four women so included (Matt. 1:5). At first, we may be surprised to find her there. But when you think about it, there was a spiritual as well as physical kinship between Rahab the Harlot and Jesus the Savior.

It was Jesus, after all, who throughout his ministry constantly confounded and angered the self-appointed righteous by extending God's grace to people like Rahab—foreigners, prostitutes, tax collectors, lepers, and the like. He was forever telling stories about a kingdom where banquet tables fit for a king were spread before peasants and beggars. Certainly he would have welcomed and understood Rahab's startling confession of faith in God. Jesus had a unique way of recognizing genuine faith, even if its form was unorthodox and unrefined.

The other references are in Heb. 11:31 and James 2:25. Hebrews points to Rahab as an example that we are saved by faith. Amazingly, this Canaanite prostitute is included in Hebrews's great Hall of Faith, right up there with Abraham, Isaac, Jacob, Joseph, Moses, and Joshua.

James, on the other hand, upholds Rahab as an example of justification by works. His message is that faith is required, yes, but real faith finds expression through action. Faith is not really faith until it is put to work. Rahab, he notes, did more than confess her belief in the sovereign God of the universe; she acted upon that faith.

So, there you have it: Rahab the Harlot—saved by faith, saved by works; the real "Total Woman."

If the New Testament writers remembered Rahab in this way, we would do well to remember her, too. She stands as a model of faith. And she serves as a reminder of the mystery, the unpredictability, and the unlimited vastness of God's grace.

There is a thread of mystery woven into God's mercy that we can never fully fathom. Imagine, if you had the power to plan the conquest of Canaan, would you have written a foreign prostitute into the script? Yet that is only part of the irony in the story. The God of the universe, with omnipotent power, chooses an old, childless couple living on the backside of nowhere and announces that they will become the proud parents of a great and mighty nation. That nation, he promises, will have a land, a home, to call their own. Generations later, under the leadership of Joshua, the children of Abraham are poised to take the land by force. And who is going to stop an army led by a God who has brought Pharaoh to his knees with a series of plagues on the Egyptians, paved a four-lane highway across the bottom of the Red Sea, rained bread every morning from the skies, and provided a guided tour across the desert by means of a cloud by day and a pillar of fire by night?

Yet it is precisely there that the story takes another unexpected turn. God may be on the side of the Israelites, but the success of the critical opening battle in this conquest hinges on the word of a foreign prostitute. If Rahab had squealed, the whole story might have ended differently. What if she had gone to the mayor, told him about her conversation with the spies, and a preemptive strike had been planned against the Hebrews just as they were crossing the river?

If we were in control, we would never have written "the Rahab factor" into the story. But Rahab gives us a window into the marvelous mystery of God's grace. It is an astonishing, dumbfounding picture: the Divine teaming up with the human. For reasons we can never fully understand, God has chosen to work with his creation, rather than to dictate and manipulate. That's the way he has chosen to operate since the beginning, even when things go wrong. Since the moment Eve and Adam sunk their teeth into the forbidden fruit, God has been inviting you and me to work alongside him in redeeming and reclaiming his creation.

As the hymn declares, "God moves in a mysterious way His wonders to perform."[3]

But there is more than mystery; there is also an unmeasurable vastness to God's mercy. His mercy knows no limits or boundaries.

"There's a wideness in God's mercy Like the wideness of the sea."[4] That is the message in Rahab's story, and through the life, death, and Resurrection of Jesus Christ, it is the wonderful, glorious, good news of the gospel story.

Perhaps today you feel a kind of kinship to Rahab. Like a prostitute shoved to the edge of society, you feel—for whatever reasons and through whatever circumstances—that life is pushing you to the edge. Maybe it's loneliness or helplessness or boredom. Maybe it's a job you hate, a broken relationship, a sin you think is too ugly to confess. Maybe it's an addiction that only you know about. Or maybe age has caught up with you, and you're feeling worn out and worn down.

The good news of the gospel is that there is no edge, no place beyond the long, loving reach of God's mercy and grace. Like Rahab, taken in by the Israelites, we too can be taken in and given a home. It's a home with a capital *H,* a permanent residence in the everlasting presence of a loving Father. Here and now, as well as in eternity, that home can be found in a relationship with Jesus Christ. It can also be found in the fellowship of God's family, the Church. So we can sing with Darrell Adams, "How good to be a family . . . We're not alone. We've found a home. The family of God."⁵

The wideness in God's mercy is a wideness we are unprepared for and do not deserve. In response to such grace, we sometimes stand humbly alongside Rahab and marvel that God would save someone like *us.* At other times, however, we are tempted to stand opposite Rahab and marvel that God would save someone like *her.*

Therein lies a warning. Too often we're preoccupied with building dams while God's mercy is overflowing the banks. We keep putting periods in the story, only to have the Editor in Chief come along and replace them with commas, colons, and semicolons. We build walls, while the Master Architect is busy designing windows, doors, and bridges. We sing in unison, while the Master Composer fills the air with glorious harmony. Like prison wardens, we think we have a lock on the truth only to find that no sooner has the door clanged shut than the Benevolent Outlaw has backed his horse to the window, tied a rope around the bars, and pulled off another jailbreak. And as he rides away, we hear him say something about the truth setting you free.

So let us be forever cautious about presuming upon God whom he can and cannot save and whom he can and cannot use to accomplish his purposes in the world. Who knows? God just might be in the business of using a woman who dares to respond to his call. Or a blue-collar welder at the Ford factory. Or a toothless old man who calls a park bench his home. Or even a naive, Bible-thumping ultraconservative with a diploma from an unaccredited Bible school.

Grace is not a commodity to be hoarded or rationed. It is to be lavished upon anyone willing to receive it. We ought to celebrate wherever, whenever, and upon whomever it may be poured.

So, there is a two-sided message in Rahab's story and in the larger gospel story. To those who assume they are on the inside—and are bent on excluding others—*look out.* If you try to shut the door on God's mercy, you may be shocked to discover which side of the door you're actually on. To those who assume they are on the outside—and believe they have been cut off from God's grace—*look up.* The good news of the gospel is that God is on a daring rescue mission, and he is ready and able to rescue, reclaim you, and restore you to wholeness. It's a rescue every bit as miraculous as Rahab's.

We don't hear much about Rahab today. I wonder why. In sermons and Sunday school lessons, we often hear about Moses and Joshua, but precious little is said about Rahab. In fact, I thought it was rather ironic that our Southern Baptist Sunday school literature took a detour around chapter 2 and Rahab during a recent trip through Joshua and Judges. It was enough to inspire a sermon!

Today, our children continue to sing that "Joshua fit the battle of Jericho," and so he did. But the walls may never have come tumbling down without the collaboration—and the faith—of Rahab the Harlot.

So today, let us remember Rahab. And in remembering, let us welcome the good news of the gospel—the glorious good news of the wonderful wideness in God's mercy. For, you see, if there is room for Rahab, then maybe—just maybe—there is room for me.

Oh, Lord, we marvel at the mystery and the depth of your mercy and grace. For those who have experienced that grace through Jesus Christ, we pray for hearts of gratitude and lives of obedience and faith. For those who have been standing on the shores of your grace, we pray for the courage today to plunge in and to be washed clean.

Through Christ our Lord. Amen.

NOTES

1. O. J. Baab, "Prostitution," in *The Interpreter's Dictionary of the Bible* (Nashville: Abingdon Press, 1962), 3:932. Josephus also referred to Rahab as an innkeeper; cf. A. T. Hanson, "Rahab the Harlot in Early Christian Tradition," *Journal for the Study of the New Testament* (1978):55.

2. Hanson, "Rahab the Harlot," 58. Also, see J. F. Ross, "Rahab," in *The Interpreter's Dictionary of the Bible,* 4:6.

3. William Cowper, "God Moves in a Mysterious Way," *Baptist Hymnal* (Nashville: Convention Press, 1975), no. 439.

4. Frederick W. Faber, "There's a Wideness in God's Mercy," *Baptist Hymnal,* no. 171.

5. Paul Duke and Darrell Adams, "The Family of God" (Louisville: Windmill Power, 1981).

10. He's Back
William H. Willimon

And behold, Jesus met them and said, "Hail!"

—Matt. 28:1–10

There are those who argue that we are gathered here this morning out of a collective wish projection. Here's how the argument goes: We just can't accept that creatures so wonderful as ourselves should die, that there will be a day when you and I, as well as all those whom we love, will be no more. So we fantasize about some inexplicable reversal of everything we know about life (namely, that it is terminal) that enables people who've once lived and died to live again. We want to live forever, so we project our wish as reality.

Although propagated with great subtlety by philosophers like Feuerbach, I call this the "Tinker Bell theory" of religion. Do you remember how, in the stage version of *Peter Pan,* Tinker Bell for some reason fades away and can be resuscitated only by everyone in the theater closing the eyes and believing very hard in fairies?

"Do you believe in fairies, boys and girls? Say you do," pleads Peter Pan. "Believe in fairies, and they will be true."

Thus, someone has called the Resurrection "the most selfish of all Christian doctrines." We Christians just cannot get it through our heads that we shall die. So we close our eyes and, with the aid of Matthew, we believe in the Resurrection.

Yet that is not at all what we claim to be doing here today, and if nonbelievers are going to dismiss us, they at least ought to do us

William H. Willimon, a Methodist, is dean of Duke Chapel and professor of the Practice of Christian Ministry at Duke University in Durham, North Carolina. He is the author of numerous books, including *Sighing for Eden* and *What's Right with the Church,* and is an editor-at-large for *The Christian Century.*

the courtesy of rejecting what we claim to believe rather than wasting time disbelieving what we don't believe in anyway, right?

Easter is not just about a general resurrection of dead people. It is certainly not about the "immortality of the soul" or "the eternal return of the robin in the spring" or other such pagan drivel. No, Easter is about a dead Jesus—whom we helped condemn, humiliate, whip, nail to a cross, and finally kill; this dead Jesus whom we then took down from the cross, wrapped in linen, and entombed; this Jesus come back to us risen, risen indeed.

And I can't, for the life of me, see why any of us would have wanted, expected, or wished that, because in coming back to us, he came to us not as some disembodied, ethereal "soul" but as *Jesus,* the same one who troubled us before Good Friday and came back on Easter. His appearance had changed; not everybody recognized him at first. Still, once they were with him awhile, they agreed with the women who had run back from the cemetery: He's back. Jesus has come back for us.

And I ask you, If we were wishing for something, would we have wished for that? After all, he gave us enough challenge in the three or four years we knew him, said enough that shook us up, so why would we have wanted *him* back? There are those who claim that the Resurrection of Jesus was a myth propagated by his disciples who had worked themselves up into such grief over his death, who were so pleased by his presence, that they just couldn't bear to let him go. So they got together and imagined that he never really died.

Yet that's not how the story goes. The story says that he was dead. The disciples knew he was dead as dead.

"We weren't really all that near," said Matthew and Mark. "We told the women to go on up to the front where they could see better. But even from where we were, at the back, we could see he was dead."

More than that, the gospels agree that all of his followers accepted his death. On Sunday, the women went out to dress his body with spices (decaying bodies smell, you know). They did not go in the hope that it all might have been a bad dream or that in some way "he will live on in our memories."

It was the first day of the week. People were back at work. The Jesus movement, begun with such promise, was over. None of them expected him back; what is more shocking, none of them appear to have *wanted* him back. Not Jesus. It would have been fine to have had back some disembodied phantom who murmured soothing cliches like "consider the lilies." But they had on their hands again the one who worked into his sermons stuff like, "Go, sell what you have, and give it to the poor," or "Anyone who loves his father or mother more than me is not worthy of me." To have *that* once-dead man back on your hands on a Sunday morning was something else again. Is that why the Risen Christ keeps saying to his astonished disciples, "Do not fear" and "Peace be unto you"? Isn't it interesting that the predominant emotion on the first Easter was not joy? It was *fear.* Earlier they had said, "He's dead. Now what's to become of us?" After Easter, it was "He's back! Now what's to become of us?"

So let's give nonbelievers a break. Their disbelief in Easter is dumb if they are disbelieving in a collectively projected Santa Claus returned to pat us on the head and give us what we want. But that isn't Jesus before Easter. And it wasn't the Risen Christ after Easter. Plenty of folk agreed with the troubled man who shouted, upon the occasion of meeting Jesus for the first time, "Get out of here Jesus of Nazareth! What have you to do with us?"

And if you've been here on Sundays other than Easter, heard the stories of sayings of the pre-Easter Jesus, you know enough to empathize with those disciples who were less than pleased to go out to the cemetery to visit the grave of a dead man, only to be encountered there by the not-at-all-dead post-Easter Christ. They were scared. Scared half out of their wits. He's back.

Wish projection, my eye. The real comfort comes not from believing in the Resurrection of Jesus of Nazareth but from believing that he is gone. Then we could, after a decent period of mourning, proceed right on with business as usual, free now to be as cynical or as naively optimistic or whatever we chose to be, because it really doesn't matter since we're on our own anyway. Now, it's all left up to us to figure out what to do on Monday since our world with Jesus ended on *Friday.*

Let's get back to the good old status quo, back to the comfort of things as they have always been before Jesus, before he intruded into our settled arrangements and conventional judgments. We could go on killing in El Salvador, separating in South Africa, having sex with other people's spouses in Durham, and all of our other death-loving ways, and who would there be to stop us, to judge us, to call our hand?

But if the women are right, if this thing isn't over but just beginning, if it's Jesus again, then—

"Whither shall I go from thy Spirit? Or whither shall I flee from thy presence? If I take the wings of the morning and fly to the outermost parts of the sea" (Psalm 139). Surprise!

If there is one thing we fear more than the death of God, it's the fear of a god who won't stay dead, who keeps following us, hounding us, coming back to us.

They had come all the way out to the cemetery to show some respect for poor, dead Jesus only to be told that he had beaten them back to town and was even now prodding and nagging the disciples, just like the old days.

"He isn't here," said the angel. "He's risen."

I remember, as a student, seeing a play somewhere that depicted a troubled man who had spent his whole life tormented by thoughts of God, by feelings of his own inadequacy, obsessed by guilt. Finally, he determined to end it all, to at last put a stop to the voices and the dreams, the late night visions, and the inner torment. In the last scene he is raving, he grabs a pistol and puts a bullet through his head. There is the explosion of the shot on stage. Then the stage goes totally dark. When the lights come back on, he is sprawled in the middle of the stage, pistol nearby. Behind him now sits a man at a desk who is the first to speak.

"Gabriel, bring me the file on Smith. That's J. A. Smith."

The man struggles to his feet. The man at the desk speaks to him now. "Well, Mr. Smith, so much for your theatrics. Now let's get down to business. We've got all the time in the world." The play ends.

What if the real hell of life is not that we are without God but that we can't be rid of God? What if our business with God isn't over until he says it's over? "If I make my bed in hell, if I take the wings of the morning . . . thou art there."

Herein is our hope, our fear, our hope. He wouldn't leave us be in life, we know that. On Easter, we know, to our surprise (yes, and even sometimes fear), that he has no intention of leaving us be in death. He has come back, will come back whenever we get caught, back against the wall, dead end—whether it be all the dead ways we attempt to deal with death on our own, the dead habits and social arrangements, lies and deceits, or whether it be the death that comes on the last day of your life. He just won't let us be.

"Ya'll go on out to the cemetery. And take these flowers. We'll be on out, soon as it looks safe. Fix up Jesus' grave real nice, will you?"

The angel said to the women, "Don't be afraid. You seek Jesus? Dead, crucified Jesus? He isn't here. He has risen. Go, tell the rest of them, he has risen from the dead. He's gone on ahead of you."

And they ran all the way back, with joy, yes, and also fear, saying, "He's back!"

11. The Tragicomedy of the Gospel

C. Michael Fuhrman

John 9:1–41

One of my favorite outings each summer is to attend a play at the Arrow Rock Lyceum Theater. This repertory theater is located in the quaint little village of Arrow Rock, situated high on a bluff overlooking the Missouri River in central Missouri. Last year, in this annual rite of summer, I saw the most unusual play that I have ever seen, *The Mystery of Edwin Drood,* which is based upon an unfinished work by Charles Dickens. The contemporary playwright, unable to know how Dickens intended to conclude the mystery, has so crafted the play that the viewing audience determines the ending. The narrator and cast interrupt the play just before the final act. They present to the viewing audience the possible suspects for the murder. The audience then votes for the actor in the cast whom they suspect of being the villain. The play resumes, and the cast concludes the play in such a way that the cast member elected by the audience is unmasked as the villain in the final scene.

New Testament interpreters have pointed out that John 9:1–41 is written much like a play in seven acts or scenes.[1] The setting is apparently near the end of Jesus' public ministry. Conflict with the Jewish religious Establishment hangs as heavy in the air as the oppressive heat before a July thunderstorm. At some unspecified street

---

C. Michael Fuhrman is pastor at Northgate Baptist Church in Kansas City, Missouri. He received not only his master of divinity from Southern Baptist Theological Seminary, but his Ph.D. in New Testament as well. Fuhrman has contributed numerous articles to Christian publications, and he has also been pastor of Baptist churches in Kentucky and India.

corner in Jerusalem, the disciples spy a blind man begging. The constant glare of the sun, the dust that sometimes filled the air, and ignorance about matters of hygiene made blindness common in ancient Palestine. The disciples see this man and ask Jesus to convene a theology seminar on the spot: "Rabbi, who sinned, this man or his parents, that he was born blind?" I suppose that it never occurred to the disciples to try to do something practical, like helping. Good preachers that they are, all they can think of is to find somebody to blame—and quick! At any rate, Jesus dissolves the seminar almost as soon as he convenes it. Jesus denies that anybody's sin caused congenital blindness. "Neither this man sinned, nor his parents, but that the works of God might be made manifest in him." Jesus teaches his disciples: God doesn't author human pain. God eradicates it. As David Redding observes, "Lucifer is not God's agent but his spade. God takes advantage of all the harm the devil has done . . ."[2]

Now Jesus stoops to daub in the mud. He spits in the dirt and rolls it around to make a paste. He uses this mud as a salve to smear on the man's eyes. Literally, in verse 6, Jesus anoints or "christs" the man's eyes. What about this? One interpreter has suggested that Jesus mixed in some medicinal ingredients on the sly with the spit paste to give it curative powers. No! Ancient people believed that spittle, especially that of a distinguished person or holy man, held curative properties. Lest we raise an eyebrow too far at what looks to us like Ozark folk medicine, just remember the last time you burned your finger in the kitchen. You instinctively put your finger in your mouth, right? Or you kissed the scratched knee of your granddaughter who had just taken a spill from her bike. Then Jesus tells the blind man to go wash the mud off in the Pool of Siloam. The man can see again. End of scene 1.

Scene 2 opens in verse 8. A curious thing unfolds. Jesus, whom we would expect to perform in the leading male role, is "offstage."[3] In fact, he will remain offstage in our little drama for the next twenty-eight verses, or the bulk of the show. The blind man's neighbors make their entrance upon the Gospel stage. They inspect a man who, for the first time since he was born, can see palm trees bending in the wind, can see the camels padding down the street, and can behold the splendor of the Temple for himself. The neighbors don't know how to react. They can't even agree that it's the same man that they used to see sit and beg. A few neighbors think the now-sighted man is only a look-alike, a double, in Hollywood terms. For the most part, however, the neighbors respond to the man with speculative yawns. End of scene 2.

The villains make their grand entrance upon the stage in scene 3, beginning with verse 13.[4] They bring the ex-blind man to the Pharisees. The somber music begins to build to a crescendo in the background, like in an old Western movie, letting you know that the "exciting scenes" have arrived. Now we learn that Jesus healed this man on the Sabbath. Oh-oh! Here we go again! According to the Pharisees' interpretation of the Law, Jesus had broken the Law twice in healing this man. First, kneading, even of a mud-pack, was forbidden on the Sabbath. Second, it was illegal in Jewish eyes to heal on the Sabbath unless life was endangered. Chronic eye diseases could wait until Sunday for treatment. Scene 3 closes with a battle of syllogisms. Some Pharisees try seizing the logical high ground with convoluted reasoning: Anyone who breaks the Sabbath is not a man of God. This man, Jesus, broke the Sabbath. Therefore, he is not of God. Other, more open-minded Pharisees, willing to consider the testimony of a person who has had an experience with Christ, reason that anyone who cures congenital blindness is a man of God. Jesus performed such a cure. Therefore, he is a man of God. With that, the curtain falls on scene 3.

Before scene 4 opens, we have a brief intermission that allows us to reflect on what we have seen so far. Both the Pharisees and the ex-blind man make a series of confessions regarding Jesus throughout the scenes of our drama. In verse 11, the ex-blind man confesses, "The man who is called Jesus made clay and anointed my eyes . . ." The blind man's understanding of who Jesus is grows all through the drama. In verse 17, he now understands that Jesus is more than a man. He confesses, "He is a prophet." Simultaneously, the Pharisees confess just one verse before, "This man is not from God."

The curtain comes up on scene 4. The Pharisees issued a subpoena to the parents of the man who was born blind to interrogate them down at the police station, so to speak. The frightened parents, with the bright lights shining in their faces, confirm that the man is their son and that his blind condition is congenital, but they testify that they know nothing about how their son's ophthalmologist affected a cure. In an aside to the hushed audience watching the performance of this drama, John informs us that the man's parents gave such a guarded answer because they feared the Jews. Anyone who confessed that Jesus is the Christ became a *persona non grata* at the neighborhood synagogue. Isn't it astonishing? They have grieved with their son every day of his life that he was born blind. He and they have endured the slings and arrows of folk theology of the day that maintained either the parents had sinned or the fetus had sinned in his mother's womb and that God was settling outstanding accounts by sending blindness to the baby-now-become-man. Now, on what should have been the greatest day of rejoicing in their family's life together, is the religious Establishment rejoicing with them at this serendipitous turn of events? No! The religious leaders, in fact, are giving the parents the third degree, stifling the joy that they must have wanted to shout from every housetop in the holy city. Whereas the neighbors respond to the healing of their blind friend with bemused indifference, the man's own parents respond by distancing themselves from their son.

Tellingly, the Jewish leaders are growing in their unbelief. Whereas in verse 16 in scene 3 they concede that Jesus has, in fact, restored sight to this man, in scene 4 John tells us that the Jews now don't even believe that the man had been born blind. Perhaps they felt what you and I have felt when we see somebody throw away their crutches at a healing service in a tent meeting. "They must have been faking it," we say to ourselves. "They surely weren't really lame to begin with."

The fourth scene concludes with the frightened parents retorting, "Our son is of legal age. Ask him how he regained his sight." Stagehands change the set on the stage. The curtain rises on scene 5. The ex-blind man is on the witness stand again. "Give God the praise," the Pharisees' prosecuting attorney tells him, meaning, "Own up; tell the truth, so help you God." Criminals about to be executed were also encouraged to confess in this way, in order to share in the life of the age to come. The Pharisees make another in a series of self-incriminating confessions in verse 24: "We know that this man is a sinner." Now our blind friend grows bolder. He retorts with the testimony of irrefutable experience. "Whether he is a sinner, I do not know. One thing I know, that though I was blind, now I see." The former blind man isn't able to look into Jesus' heart to know if Jesus is a sinner, but he has a lock on the one rock-hard reality of his life: He was blind, and now he can see. The man born blind has just had his life invested with new horizons and new opportunities because of his cure. Hence, unlike his inquisitors, he remains open to new truth and new experience.

"How did he [Jesus] open your eyes?" the Pharisees ask in verse 26. He answered them, "I have told you already, and you would not listen. Why do you want to hear my deposition again? Do you too want to become his disciples?" That's rubbing salt in a wound! The ex-blind man is getting uppity now. Don't you just love this guy? He has such a smart mouth. Sometimes I wonder if mealy-mouthed Christians don't nauseate God—at least just a tiny bit. So often it seems that when people get converted they simultaneously get bland and boring. The blind man didn't get bland. This man has spunk! "Growing in grace" is something other than "maturing in boredom." The Spirit gives the ex-blind man the holy boldness of a smart mouth. He may have been blind, but he was no wimp! Scene 5 concludes with the former blind man making the smartest, boldest confession that he has made to this point in the drama: "If this man were not from God, he could do nothing." Now he is killing them with common sense!

As the curtain falls on scene 5, we are left to ask, Why is it that the Pharisees miss seeing the hand of God at work in the healing of this blind man? The answer is that, because they are so tied to religious institutionalism, bound by dogma, and shackled to their past, they could not and did not recognize the Light of the World even when he walked in their midst. The Gospel of John tells us how the story unfolds. On Palm Sunday this year, we remember that religious intolerance crucified Jesus. Intolerance in the name of God survives down to this very day and not just in people such as the Ayatollah Khomeini or members of the IRA. You will find it also in the legalism of right-wing "Christian" politics, for example. Jesus gives religious legalists fits. Beware of the dogmatism of the devout! For all of the talk that we hear about secular humanism these days, the haunting, daunting fact is that the secular humanists didn't crucify Jesus. A bigger bogeyman called the religious Establishment did—in order to protect its own petty self-interest and dogmatic arrogance.

Simon and Garfunkel were right, you know. "People [even religious, Christian people] hear what they want to hear and disregard the rest." A closed mind is always an ugly and dangerous thing, but baptizing a closed mind is surely the ugliest, most dangerous closed mind of all.

What the devout think they know may shut them off from receiving the new revelation of God in Christ. That's dangerous. It reminds me of the jibe that we often hear in election campaigns. One candidate will say: "It's not what my opponent knows that scares me, and it's not what he doesn't know that scares me. It's what he thinks he knows that just ain't so that scares me!" Sometimes when I look at religious extremists, be they in Iran or Northern Ireland or the United States, the scariest thing of all is not what they know, nor what they think they know, but what they think they know that just ain't so! That kind of closed-minded, rigid legalism strung our Savior up on a cross.

Religion of the man-made variety closes people up and chains them. Christ opens us up and liberates us. It pains us all to admit that both the largest and the smallest people that we have known, both the kindest people and the pettiest, can be found in the Church, at least claiming membership among the people of God. That means we have a mission field here in our pews for people to find the liberating Christ. Nobody loves the Pharisees among us; nobody that is, except Jesus. He died for the sins of legalism as much as he died for sins of passion; as much for the stuffed-shirt preacher as for the woman caught in adultery; as much for the Pharisee as for the tax-collector; as much for the Ayatollah as for Mother Teresa.

Now scene 6 opens. For the first time since scene 1, way back in verse 7, Jesus is on stage. "Well, it's about time," you say. Only Jesus can redeem the mess the religious crowd has created. The closed-minded Pharisees, like religious dogmatists of every generation, assume that they have cornered the market on truth about God. So they cast this ex-blind man, heretic and smart mouth that he is, right out of their synagogue. Note: The person that organized religion casts out, Jesus seeks out. This blind man has lost it all. He has lost his profession as a beggar based on his blindness. He has lost his confused neighbors that he had counted as friends. He has lost his intimidated parents. And now he has lost his membership at the local house of faith.[5] Chrysostom, that great preacher of sixteen hundred years ago, commented, "The Jews cast Him out of the Temple. The Lord of the Temple found him." Now the ex-blind man, whose understanding has grown steadily all through this chapter, from viewing Jesus as simply a man, then to a prophet, and then to a man from God, makes his last and climactic confession. In verse 38 he confesses, "Lord, I believe." When Jesus heals blind people in the first three Gospels, he seems to do so in response to their faith. Faith precedes the miracle. The Gospel of John, however, shows us the other side of the coin, equally true. The blind man believes in Jesus after the miracle. He has an experience of Christ before conversion. It usually happens this way for us. We have, not one, but hundreds of little encounters with Christ. We sense his love in a devout second-grade public school teacher whose Christianity shines through her patience with kids. We experience Christ in the caress of a mother's hand on a child's fevered brow. We experience Christ in the integrity of a Christian friend. Often we experience Christ unaware. Then one day all of these little encounters with the incognito Christ climax in a moment when we want to commit our lives to him. The drama in our text has as its point: We learn from a blind man how to see Jesus.[6] Now, in this second interview with Jesus, the former blind man gains sight in a deeper sense. He begins to experience God's future in his own life, and he throws himself to the ground to worship his Lord.

The climactic scene begins. As dramatists would say, the ninth chapter of John is tragicomedy. It contains elements of both comedies, such as Shakespeare's *The Merchant of Venice,* and of tragedies, such as *Macbeth, Julius Caesar,* or *West Side Story.* The story of the ex-blind man is a plot of comedy, not comedy as in sitcom or Johnny Carson, but comedy dramatically speaking. The plot of life for him moves upward toward well-being, salvation, and inclusion in desirable society. The plot, due to Christ's grace and his own choice of faith, ends happily for him. Not so with the Pharisees. For them, our little seven-act drama is a drama of tragedy. The plot moves downward for them toward catastrophe and isolation and away from happiness and God's kind of life.

Our text thus has a double movement. Even as a blind man is gradually coming, not just to physical sight, but to the spiritual insight that Jesus is the Light of the World, the religious crowd, which on the physical level has no need to consult an opthalmologist, plunges deeper and deeper into spiritual darkness, until in the last scene, in verse 39, Jesus himself pronounces them blind. The blind man and the Pharisees pass one another like two ships in the night, one going up, the other going down. The Pharisees illustrate the truth of John 1:5: "The light shines in the darkness, and the darkness comprehendeth it not." Who, after all, is really blind?

The entire ninth chapter turns on verse 39: "Jesus said, 'For judgment [literally, crisis] I came into this world, that those who do not see may see, and that those who see may become blind.' " People born blind can gain sight. Others born with sight, through nobody's fault but their own, can become blind before God. Their blindness is willful. Some people don't want to see. The coming of Christ means that a sentence or judicial decision—a crisis—is reached. For anyone rejecting Christ, their unbelief becomes a judgment. The Pharisees ask in verse 40, "You're not saying that even we are blind, are you?" Jesus responds, in effect, "Would to God that you were!"[7]

The drama in our text is now history. We can't change it. The drama being lived out in our lives, however, like the plot in *The Mystery of Edwin Drood* is still being written. How will you write the script for the way the play is to end for you? The choices that we make and the values we cherish may move life toward the tragic, toward catastrophe, toward alienation and darkness. Or, thanks be to God, our life stories can be comedies. We can decide for Christ as the blind man did and see our lives move toward wholeness, toward peace with God, and toward meaningful existence. In this theater of the absurd that we call life, the choice is up to us.

NOTES

1. Others have noted the dramatic structure of John 9:1–41. See, for example Robert Kysar, *John's Story of Jesus* (Philadelphia: Fortress Press, 1984), 49. I, however, have developed this idea, including the title, in my own unique way.

2. David A. Redding, *The Miracles of Christ* (Westwood, NJ: Fleming H. Revell, 1964), 98.

3. Kysar, p. 50.

4. The Gospel of John poses a vexing problem to the preacher in that many of its great "purple" passages depict sharp conflicts between Jesus and Jewish leaders and, hence, can be ill-used by people guilty of anti-Semitism. When reading such New Testament passages as this, we should remember at every step along the way that Christianity has produced its own "Pharisees" and that they are as much in error as these about which we read in the Bible.

5. William E. Hull, "John," in *The Broadman Bible Commentary,* edited by Clifton J. Allen (Nashville: Broadman Press, 1970), 9:301.

6. The thought was expressed by Robert Canoy, professor of New Testament at Midwestern Baptist Theological Seminary, in a personal conversation, Kansas City, Missouri, February 8, 1989.

7. Hull, "John," 302.

12. Dirty Work
Jeffrey L. Ruff

Luke 19:1–10

Luke shares a delightful story of a little man who takes a risk, who literally goes out on a limb to see Christ, but who wins the prize of acceptance by the Lord Jesus and inclusion in the family of God.

I almost hate to ruin the story by interpreting it for you, but for a few moments let me share some thoughts. There is a long-standing debate as to the meaning of the announcement Zacchaeus made in response to the crowd's accusations against him.

"Jesus has gone in to be the guest of a man who is a sinner," they all murmured. But Zacchaeus stood up as tall as he could and said to the Lord, "Behold, Lord, the half of my goods I give to the poor; and if I have defrauded anyone of anything, I restore it fourfold."

Now you'll notice that the words of the little man are in the present tense. Presumably he wasn't *at that very moment* performing those remarkably generous acts. So there are only two possible interpretations. One is that though he was speaking in the present, he actually meant he would do these things sometime in the near future. In other words, he was making a kind of pledge. They call that a futuristic present tense. I suspect that is the interpretation you have always heard. It is clearly the most common.

It is, however, not the only possible meaning. Zacchaeus could have been defending himself before Jesus, saying, in effect, "I am not the sinner this crowd thinks I am. I give half of my profits to the poor;

Jeffrey L. Ruff is pastor of Keystone Presbyterian Church in Odessa, Florida. Ruff received his B.A. at the University of South Florida and his master of divinity at Union Theological Seminary in Richmond, Virginia. He is also a musician and composer, and before entering the ministry he was a part-time classical radio station announcer.

and if I inadvertently defraud anyone, I give a fourfold restitution." They call this the customary present tense because it describes what one customarily does.

Without going into all the grammatical arguments, suffice it to say that there is at least as much evidence for this interpretation as the other. I'm not going to say one has to understand the story in this unfamiliar way, but I would like us at least to keep an open mind this morning and think about what Luke's story might mean if that interpretation were the correct one.

What if this were not a story about a notorious sinner who repents, as we've always thought of it, but rather about a man like many of us, who finds himself working in a job that is something less than perfect? Let's call it a dirty job but one that somebody has to do. And what if this vocation of his is the kind of job that brings him nothing but grief from his customers, kind of like that of a government bureaucrat? And no matter how well he does his job or how much he bends over backward to help the truly needy or those who get ground up in the system, he is universally hated, condemned, and rejected by society because of his dirty job. What if Zacchaeus was as much a victim of the system as those poor people who were forced to pay taxes they couldn't afford to pay, only his injuries were not financial but rather personal and, ultimately, spiritual? Could it not be that Zacchaeus was yet another outcast, like the Samaritans or the lepers or the children or the widows, the lost sheep Jesus came to gather back into the fold of God's family?

According to Luke, Zacchaeus was a chief tax collector, meaning he had bid for and acquired a tax monopoly from the Romans. Though he himself was a Jew, it was his business to collect money from the Jews for the Roman rulers through his employees, the tax collectors. Zacchaeus was an ambitious and successful businessman, there can be no doubt about that. Today a typical chief tax collector would wear $500 suits, have a car phone and a fax machine in his BMW, a sizable investment portfolio, and a condo on the beach to unwind in on that rare day off.

But Zacchaeus was an oddity among business executives, for he possessed a profound social conscience. Sure, all of his friends prided themselves in the loose change they dropped in the beggars' cups and the offering plate. But for Zacchaeus it was different. He gave away vast sums of money to the poor. He tried not to cheat anyone, and when he found out that someone was treated unfairly by one of his collectors, he fired the man on the spot and reimbursed the defrauded family fourfold. But he never made a show of it. He did what he did quietly, figuring it was between him and his God.

Still, the people who had not personally benefited from Zacchaeus's kindness hated him for taking their money. All tax collectors are the same, they said. He was treated as a pariah at the Temple. The priests, scribes and Pharisees treated him with respect for his money and position, but behind his back they sneered and spit on the ground, mocking him and making a joke of his shortness. And far too often, deep inside, the truth was, he hated himself. No matter how much he gave away, his conscience wouldn't let him alone. He thought often about quitting and moving to some town where no one had ever heard of him, taking up some harmless vocation like tent making.

Does Zacchaeus's story ring any bells for you? I don't think you have to be a tax chief or an arms dealer or a government bureaucrat to feel the crunch of working in the world while trying to enter the Kingdom of Heaven, that is, of having a dirty job while trying to be clean for the Lord. As one commentator notes, "Zacchaeus' profession points up the problem of accommodating the structures necessary in the secular world to the call that comes from God"[1] No job on earth is ideal or pristine, not in the government, the business community, the service industry, or even the church. (Everyone knows the ministry's clean, right?!) All work is dirty, frought with compromise and ambiguity. And thus the dilemma with which we all must wrestle as people of faith, no matter what our vocation may be, is how best to minimize harm and maximize justice in our daily work. The issue often comes to us in the form of the question, Which is better, a job that allows me to keep all my ideals intact but that gives me little income or influence in the world or a job that yields high rewards and enables me considerable influence but that requires that I sacrifice many of my most cherished values and ideals?

This past week on the television series "thirtysomething," the young couple, Michael and Hope, found themselves on different sides of this issue. Hope is offered a job at a magazine that will force her to compromise her ideals. She turns the job down but admits privately to a friend that she really doesn't see her high ideals making much of a difference anywhere. Michael, on the other hand, holds a party at their home to impress the boss, whom he despises. Hope is disgusted with him for selling himself in this way. Michael responds that he's only doing it to insure a solid financial future for their family. Hope counters that she also sees holding on to one's ideals as insuring a future—though not only for her family but for the whole imperiled earth. What good will a solid financial situation do their daughter, she asks, if there is no safe place for her to live? Michael responds with a question equally troublesome: What good will it do the earth or anyone if, in the name of high ideals, he fails at his vocation and allows himself and his family to lose everything?

Therein lies the dilemma of so many of us. How can I be responsible to God and also responsible to my family and my society? How can I be productive in the worldly sense and also productive of the fruits of the Spirit of Christ? And perhaps there is an even more basic question than these: How can I, as a follower of Jesus, work in human society and still live with myself?

The little businessman who climbed a tree to see Jesus knew part of the answer even before he met his Savior. Give back to God in justice and charity a generous portion of the material blessings he gives to you. Help the less fortunate. Try not to hurt anyone and give generous restitution to those you can't help hurting. Seek justice and abundant life for all. This is what God wants us to do with everything he has given us in the world. He calls us to be good stewards, to take care of what we have, with what we have.

But we're also going to have to accept the fact that none of us are going to be able to avoid sin completely in anything we do in this life. And our consciences, like the crowd in the story of Zacchaeus, accuse us and convict us of our sins. Nothing we do, no matter how generous or brilliant or magnificent or beautiful, can remove from us the stain of guilt. Lord knows we try, and our good works make us feel better for a while, but it never lasts. For our dirty work goes on and on, muddying up our good works and our consciences with them.

We don't really know any other reason why Zacchaeus went out on that limb to see Jesus, other than because he was so short. And I believe it was indeed because he was short—short, that is, like we're all short: smaller than God meant him to be, not in physical stature but in spiritual stature. In his own eyes and the eyes of his brothers and sisters, he was very small indeed. He, like us all, needed to be lifted up, glorified in the sight of God.

And so, perhaps out of a faith he didn't yet understand himself, while yet a sinner, Zacchaeus mounted a tree to see the man who would one day mount his own tree to save all us sinners like him. And for his sake and ours, Jesus went out on his dangerous limb, befriending a sinner for the kingdom, inviting God into his life again. In a sense, Zacchaeus became the first thief on a cross for Jesus to save. Only this time instead of Jesus saying, "Today you will be with me in paradise," he said, "Make haste and come down, for today I must stay at your house"; and then a little later, "Today salvation has come to this house."

The good news is that, while we are yet sinners, Christ invites us into the banquet of God. He covers our sinfulness with the robe of forgiveness wrought on the tree of Calvary. Though we are inextricably joined to the sinful, secular, and unjust world, we are nevertheless assured of our acceptableness in God's family, the family of Abraham, whom God long ago promised would be blessed beyond measure and would itself become a blessing to all the earth.

But wait a minute. Are we saying that there is no work too dirty to exclude one from the saving presence of Christ? That bothers me. Does it bother you? (It bothered the crowd.) I'd hate that some drug lord passing out money to the poor might find solace in this story. It would help if we could draw a line between *necessary* evils like participating in an unjust government that overtaxes the poor and *un*necessary evils like manufacturing and distributing cocaine. But where precisely would we draw that line? If we're all sinners caught in ambiguity and compromise, if grace through faith and not works makes us acceptable to God, than who are we to judge?

Zacchaeus had a dirty job in an imperfect government; but he also had a hunger for righteousness and the faith to go out on a limb and take a risk to have that hunger fed. And what was the risk? Maybe it was the risk of falling and getting hurt or of being seen by others and ridiculed or condemned as unworthy.

But most of all it was the risk of being seen by Christ himself, being gazed upon by the eyes of him who sees us as we are, behind the mask and the games and, yes, even behind the sin, being found out, and then, despite it all, being loved and visited by the Savior. I wonder: Did Zacchaeus climb the tree to see or be seen?

As Jesus said, "The Son of man came to seek and to save the lost." The search goes on amid all the dirty jobs and guilty hearts and small souls and, yes, also amid all the self-righteousness, hypocrisy, and hatred. Some of us are still lost. Will we risk being found, forgiven, and loved? Or will we keep hiding? The choice is always before us.

NOTE

1. E. Schweizer, *The Good News According to Luke* (Atlanta: John Knox Press, 1984), 290.

13. Joseph
Neta Pringle

Matt. 1:18–25

Joseph is always part of the Christmas scenery. We see him leading the donkey, knocking on the door of the inn, or standing solemnly next to Mary. But that's what he is, just part of the scenery.

In a recent book, Jim Dites tells of his youthful pride in being given the part of Joseph in the church Christmas pageant—that is, until he tried to do something with the role. Every time he would try to put some personal interpretation into it, the director would shout at him, "No! No! Just stand there!" It wasn't until he froze in place that she said, "That's perfect."

It wasn't until I found the song we are going to sing later, by Carol Doran, that I realized it was the first carol I knew of where Joseph even has a part, let alone the leading role. Just as I was thinking about all this, I got a book of cross-stitch patterns. There is one for Mary and the child in lovely colors—and Joseph in the background, rather ghostlike in pale, muted shades. One option they suggest is to leave him out altogether. Even in the Gospels, he never says a word.

Tradition says he was old and wise, but who could be wise enough for what he had to face? Maybe he was young and scared, like Mary, trying to figure it all out. After the trip to Jerusalem with Mary and his runaway junior high son, Joseph simply disappears from the stories. We hear no more of him. Did he die? Or was it

Neta Pringle is pastor at Christ's First Presbyterian Church in Hempstead, New York. Pringle received her B.S. at Douglass College and a master of divinity at Union Theological Seminary in New York City. She was also interim pastor of Trinity Presbyterian Church in Paramus, New Jersey.

perhaps all too much, and he simply withdrew into the carpenter's shop.

Poor Joseph. Is he always to stay frozen, silent, and ghostlike, or is there something we can know about him? Matthew describes him as a just man then goes on to tell how he broke the Law. The marriage customs of his day were not so different from ours: a time of engagement or betrothal, then the wedding. Like an earlier day in our own society, that engagement time meant no living together and no sleeping together.

Think what it was like for Joseph to hear that Mary was pregnant. He knew the child wasn't his. Can you imagine his feelings of dismay and betrayal? of anger! The law was very clear about what to do in such cases: a public divorce, with charges clearly announced. Mary would be shamed before the whole village, her reputation ruined. Had they been actually married, she would have been stoned to death for adultery.

In such a case, a just man was not only vindicated in seeking a divorce, it was expected of him. Something in Joseph resists that. In the midst of his own hurt, his own pain, he struggles with other alternatives. The old accepted categories will not work. This situation escapes them. Feelings are not so easily legislated. Justice seems harsh and irrelevant. What else can he do?

Those are the struggles that make us grow up. Those are the questions that shake apart the tidy answers and deepen our souls. If Joseph was not already old and wise, surely he must have been by the time it was all over.

Just as Joseph reaches a decision (he will divorce her quietly, not announce the charges—as if a pregnancy can be ignored!), the angel comes with yet another choice. "Marry her, Joseph. Claim the child as your own." What an outrageous demand! Joseph could have opted out. "Thank you, but no thank you." Instead, he chose to be a part of it all.

It is the same challenge that comes to all of us. Will you be part of what God is about? Will you be a player in the drama? How that choice will come to you, I do not know. I suspect it is most likely to come in those times when, like Joseph, you stew and fret over the right thing to do, when the outrageous choice is God's choice.

Joseph took the least expected option. He married Mary, and he named the child. Jesus. Joshua, in Hebrew. The One Who Saves, "for he will save his people from their sins." Out of his own struggle, out of his willingness to go where God has led him, Joseph names the child, for he understands.

Such understanding does not come lightly or easily. Mary will resist it. Later Jesus' own disciples will have to struggle with it. You and I must wrestle with it. Some will never comprehend.

The child has already saved Joseph from his own shallow justice. His coming has forced Joseph to confront his own dark side, to deal with life on a deeper level. So many in the land will avoid that. They will ask for quick and easy salvation. They will want miracles and signs. They will seek political solutions. None will want to be confronted with their own sinfulness.

Surely, there must be sadness and grief for Joseph as he names the child who will save us from our sins. He must know that such salvation will exact a heavy price.

Above all, Joseph must simply be a father to this child. He must do the best he can to love him, teach him, and, yes, discipline him. That is the gift he will give to Mary's child. Surely that is why God has entrusted this child to him.

The gift of a good father is not given to all God's children. Martin Luther said he had great trouble addressing God as father: His own had been harsh and abusive. For him it was a term that held no warmth, no tenderness. Too often it brought fear. Some of you can understand that all too well. Others of you have fathers known more by their absence than by their presence. Undoubtedly it is Jesus' tribute to Joseph that he addresses God as a little child speaks to his father, "Abba, Daddy." So it is, Jesus gives to each of us the father that does not fail: God, who is all that we can expect, whose love is more than we can ask.

Joseph stands there in the Christmas scenes, silent, hardly noticed, yet if you will listen to him, he will speak to you of the true meaning of this season.

III. DOCTRINAL/ THEOLOGICAL

14. He Is Going before You
Chevis F. Horne

Matt. 28:1–10; Heb. 12:1–2

It was just at dawn—the freshest and most beautiful part of the day—when some women were making their way to the tomb of Jesus. The world seemed to be bathed in the dew of the night. Soon the first light of the day would be lifting the mist from the hills and driving away the shadows from the valley.

When they got there, they were greatly surprised—the stone in the doorway of the tomb had been rolled away, and an angel sat upon it in proud defiance of death.

"Do not be afraid," he said to the women. "For I know you seek Jesus who was crucified. He is not here; for he has risen, as he said. Come, see the place where he lay."

Continuing, the angel said, "Then go quickly and tell his disciples that he has risen from the dead, and behold, he is going before you to Galilee; there you will see him."

The Risen Christ is seen as one who goes before us. We shall later speak of him as our pioneer who crosses boundaries we have not passed over and moves upon frontiers we have not entered.

Going Before

Our text leads us to one of the most exciting doctrines of our Christian faith, namely, the providence of God.

Chevis F. Horne was, for his entire pastoral ministry, pastor of one congregation, the First Baptist Church, Martinsville, Virginia, after which he served as professor of preaching at Southeastern Baptist Theological Seminary, Wake Forest, North Carolina. Dr. Horne is the author of a number of books, among them *Preaching the Great Themes of the Bible*.

The providence of God is seen in several dimensions. As we look back of us, we see his providence. He is like the spring of a stream. He is the source of life. He created us in love and set our feet in paths that go somewhere.

As we look above us, we see the providence and caring of God. He spans our lives in grace like the vast heavens. "As the heavens are high above the earth, so great is his steadfast love toward those who fear him" (Ps. 103:11).

As we come closer to our lives, we see his providence by our sides like a companion that will not forsake us. He is present in the Holy Spirit, who has been called to our sides to be our guide, counselor, and comforter. He is with us to give us strength and to keep our faces turned in the right direction and our feet set in right paths.

But when we think of God's providence, we turn in a special way to the future. God goes ahead of us; he is the end of all our journeying. We believe our years are in his care and keeping. "Our times are in his hands."

The story of Joseph, which is one of the great stories in the world's literature, tells how he was sold into slavery by his jealous brothers and taken into Egypt. Because of his strange powers to interpret dreams, he got the attention of the king and began rising fast in the government until he became prime minister of the land, the second most important position, next to that of the king.

One of the dreams he interpreted told of seven years of plenty followed by seven years of famine. Egypt, the granary of the near East, took steps to meet the lean years. They built large warehouses and stored grain in them. Joseph's family back home felt the pain and privation of the famine and made three trips to Egypt for grain. On the third trip, Joseph made himself known to his brothers. He sent everyone in the room away and was left with his brothers. He said simply to them, "I am your brother Joseph, whom you sold into Egypt." He then wept so loudly that he was heard throughout the court. When he composed himself, he said to his brothers: "And now do not be distressed or angry with yourselves because you sold me here; for God sent me before you to preserve life."

What a wonderful God who can take something as tragic as that and use it for good. He can take evil and bring good out of it; take that which is marred and bring beauty out of it; take a hopeless situation and bring hope out of it; take that which is without meaning and bring meaning out of it. He takes life when it is like a stream at flood time, with its waters overrunning its banks, wreaking destruction on everything in its path, and he brings the swollen waters back into the channel. Through storm and flood he sees the river to its destination.

Jesus had told his disciples that he would be leaving them and they could not go with him. They felt sad in their lonely moment. Jesus said to them, "Let not your hearts be troubled; believe in God, believe also in me. In my Father's house are many rooms; if it were not so, would I have told you that I go to prepare a place for you? And when I go and prepare a place for you, I will come again and will take you to myself, that where I am you may be also" (John 14:1–3).

Once more, Jesus is going before his disciples. No matter how narrow and cramped their earthly quarters, he was going to prepare a place with great spaciousness. There would be room for all. Then he would come back for them. He wanted them to be with him.

The author of Hebrews speaks of Jesus as being a pioneer. In the second chapter, Jesus is spoken of as the "pioneer of their salvation," and in the twelfth chapter as the "pioneer and perfecter of our faith."

In the eleventh chapter, the author made a roll call of the national heroes and heroines of the past, men and women who lived by faith, enduring "as seeing him who is invisible." They were people of whom the world was not worthy. Then in the twelfth chapter, he begins with the image of a Greek race: "Therefore, since we are surrounded by so great a cloud of witnesses, let us also lay aside every weight, and sin which clings so closely, and let us run with perseverance the race that is set before us, looking to Jesus the pioneer and perfecter of our faith, who for the joy that was set before him endured the cross, despising the shame, and is seated at the right hand of the throne of God."

Who made up the cloud of witnesses? Their fallen heroes and heroines mentioned in the preceding chapter. They had not gone far, only up in the bleachers and from there were looking down upon the author and his generation who are the runners. But where is Jesus? He didn't go up into the bleachers. He went ahead of them, and they are admonished to look to "Jesus the pioneer and perfecter of our faith." They are running toward him in the full assurance that Jesus has already covered the territory they must traverse.

The Risen Christ as Pioneer

"He is going before you." He is called pioneer.

Let us make several observations about Christ, who is our pioneer, going before us.

First, he goes before us morally.

In him, we have seen perfect character. He is better than we are, better than we can ever become. There are no dark shadows beneath his eyes, no impurities in his motives, no remorseful memories, no guilty conscience that lashes him without mercy. He is without sin. He was accused of many things but never of sin. He once asked, "Which of you convicts me of sin?" (John 8:46).

John tells us that "God sent the Son into the world, not to condemn the world, but that the world might be saved through him" (John 3:17).

Jesus Christ did not come into the world as judge but as Savior. Yet, while he was not an official judge, there was an inevitable judgment about him. It was the kind of judgment you see in light judging darkness, truth judging falsehood, and love judging hatred. It was moral in nature.

We all know Simon Peter's experience when one day he was in Jesus' presence. He dropped to his knees and cried out, "Depart from me, for I am a sinful man, O Lord" (Luke 5:8).

There is a light in his eyes that exposes the darkness and shadows of my mind, a selflessness that exposes my pettiness and littleness, and a love that exposes the bitterness and hatred in my life.

Further, Jesus goes before us socially.

People mattered to Jesus. He did not let social propriety stand between him and them. He trampled social and religious barriers to get to people. A strange company traveled with Jesus, among them tax collectors, sinners, and prostitutes. He saw worth and beauty in the riffraff, the social outcasts, those who had been rejected by the strict religionists, and those who had been thrown on the human junk heap of the world. There was something to be reclaimed in the most depraved. He loved those the world did not love, those who did not love themselves.

He broke down the last barrier to full social acceptance, which is the dinner table. Jesus called Matthew, a despised tax collector, to be one of his disciples, and Matthew gave a party in his honor. The Pharisees saw this motley group of people gathered around the dinner table, and they asked Jesus' disciples, "Why does your teacher eat with tax collectors and sinners?" (Matt. 9:11). Luke prefaced the three parables of the lost sheep, the lost coin, and the lost son like this: "Now the tax collectors and sinners were all drawing near to hear him. And the Pharisees and the scribes murmured, saying, 'This man receives sinners and eats with them' " (Luke 15:1–2).

We find many surprises in Jesus' parable of the great judgment recorded in the twenty-fifth chapter of Matthew. One of the most shocking is that the questions asked on that last great day will be social, not religious. Did you give food to the hungry, drink to the thirsty, clothe the naked, take in the homeless, visit the sick, and care for prisoners? Yet, nowhere is it suggested that the righteous are saved by their humanitarian deeds. They are not. They are saved the way all of us are—by grace. But the grace that saved them had become graciousness in them. Here is the test of our being saved by grace: Does that grace make us gracious? The test of our spirituality is social in nature; our relationship with God is judged by our relationship with our brother and sister.

When we compare the social concern of Jesus with that of the modern church we should bow our heads in shame. Who can forget that racism made one of its last-ditch stands in the church and that it lingers on in the life of the church? The white Protestant church is one of the most racist institutions in our society.

Again, Jesus goes before us spiritually.

He has blazed a path into the presence of a holy God, and the simplest man and woman can walk that path into that presence. He doesn't have to have a priest or preacher in order to go there. No hands of ordination have to be laid on his or her head.

Here is found one of the most significant doctrines of Protestanism, namely the priesthood of the believer. The believer does not need the help of an official priest, since he by the grace of Christ has become a priest. He is his own priest. But more than that, he has become a priest to his neighbor. I go to God without official aid, but today I do not go alone. I say to God, "I am bringing John with me. He is my neighbor and lives just down the street from me. I am his priest today."

Because Jesus Christ has opened a new path to God, he has at the same time made possible a new way to my brother. I have spoken of social concern, but this is much more than accepting people and affirming their worth, beauty, and value. Because God has accepted us in Christ, we are able to accept each other in a strange new way.

When Paul looked out upon his world, he saw a broken, fragmented existence. But the most intractable situation was the separation of Jew and Gentile. How far apart they were, how elusive, how they hated each other. Paul, in the second chapter of Ephesians, tells how Christ through his death brought together Jew and Gentile in forgiveness, love, and acceptance. It was a miracle of miracles. They were no longer enemies but brothers and sisters in the Body of Christ, which was the Church. Out of the two warring races, God was creating a new humanity.

Finally, Christ has gone ahead of us in our death.

I, like all my brothers and sisters, am mortal. I am always walking into the night of my death. I am going to die, and I know two things about my death. It will come sooner than I expect it; I will not be ready for it. And it will find me with some unfinished task. I will lay aside my tools at the close of a day and expect to pick them up in the morning. But the morning will not come. I will not only leave some unfinished task but also an unfinished life.

Christ has not gone ahead for me only but for my loved ones and my fellow human beings everywhere.

Death brings the most painful loss. I go with a loved one as far as I can. Then he turns abruptly and walks away from me into the solitary way of death, leaving me lonely, grieved, and with insufferable loss. I would have gone further, but I could not. Is there someone who will not only go with him but who stands on the other side of life ready to receive him? Yes, there is. Christ has gone ahead of us, walking through the shadows and darkness of death. He tells us not be be afraid as we walk into the descent of death. He stands on a fairer shore and in the purer light of a new day that will not end. There in the light of that morning, we shall not only see him, but we shall see again the faces of those we have known and loved here.

We fear the future. Yet Easter sets our faces resolutely toward the unknown. It assures us that the great pioneer who has gone before us also goes with us. Don't be afraid!

15. The Bible: Its Diversity and Its Unity

Bruce M. Metzger

Ps. 119:105

During the ceremony of the coronation of a British monarch, the moderator of the Church of Scotland presents a Bible to the new sovereign and says, "We present you with this book, the most valuable thing that this world affords." This statement is followed by words that set forth the value ascribed to the Bible: "Here is Wisdom. This is the royal Law. These are the lively oracles of God." This explanation indicates that the authority attributed to the Bible is ultimately the authority belonging to God. It is, therefore, not an authority intrinsic to the book as a piece of typography, but is linked with the conviction that the book emanates from God. Because God is held to be holy, the Bible, too, is described as "holy," and we speak of the "holy Scriptures" or "sacred writings."

The text of the sermon this evening is taken from the 119th Psalm. This psalm, which is by far the longest psalm in the Bible, is an extended meditation upon the majesty of holy Scripture. In every one except two of the 176 verses of this psalm, there is a reference to the Word of God. Of course, many synonyms are used, such as the Law of God, the decrees of God, the precepts, the commandments, the statutes, and the like. The psalmist makes it clear that our

Bruce M. Metzger is emeritus professor of New Testament of Princeton Theological Seminary and was chair of the translation committee for the *New Revised Standard Version* of the Bible. This sermon was preached on May 16, 1990, at the Episcopal Cathedral in Pittsburgh, when the National Council of the Churches of Christ held a Service of Blessing and Commemoration of the New Revised Standard Version of the Bible.

knowledge of God, as well as our ability to live in this world, is based upon divine revelation. The wonderful truth is that God has spoken and that we have a trustworthy record of these disclosures in the Scriptures. One of the highlights of the 119th Psalm is verse 105, in which the psalmist gives us this memorable statement: "Your Word is a lamp to my feet and a light to my path."

Here the psalmist compares the Word of God to a lamp or lantern such as that which is carried on dark nights in areas where other lights are not to be found. The point of the comparison concerns, of course, the function of the Word of God in showing us the way. It does this by showing both the entrance to the way and the way itself. If at some crossroads we might in darkness turn in the wrong direction, this lamp will show us the true path. As Isaiah says, "If you stray from the path, whether to the right or the left, you will hear a voice from behind you sounding in your ears saying, 'This is the way; walk in it.'"

Furthermore, the Word of God also shows us the end of the way. It will guide us all the way to heaven, where we shall need it no more.

Confronted by this picturesque metaphor describing the Bible, let us now consider more specifically the makeup and the central message of the Scriptures. We look at two aspects of the Bible: its diversity and its unity.

First, there is diversity in that several dozen books are bound together between the two covers of the Bible. These books come from various times and places, spanning centuries of time and traversing diverse countries. It is not surprising that these books were composed in different languages: Hebrew for the Old Testament, with some chapters of Ezra and of Daniel in Aramaic, a related Semitic language; and the New Testament in Greek. There is also diversity as to authorship, with materials coming from a broad spectrum of speakers and writers, including the Song of Deborah in the Old Testament and the Magnificat of Mary in the New. All told, scores of men and women have contributed oral or written materials now incorporated in this small library of books.

Furthermore, there is diversity in the qualifications and backgrounds of these different authors. Here are words from people in such varied callings in life as Moses, who was trained in the wisdom of Egypt; David, who grew up as a shepherd boy; Solomon, reputed to be the wisest of kings. Isaiah was a priest; Matthew, a tax collector; Peter, a fisherman; Paul, a tent maker, and so on.

There is also diversity in literary forms included in the Bible. Here we have law in the Pentateuch, history in the books of Samuel and Kings, philosophy in the book of Job, love lyrics in the Song of Solomon, prophecy in Isaiah and Jeremiah, as well as in a dozen other books in the Old Testament. The Psalms have served as a hymn book for Israel and the Church. In the New Testament, we have books of news—but this is good news, not the kind that grows stale the following week. We also have twenty-one letters written by leaders in the early Church and sent to congregations and to individuals, climaxed by the Apocalypse, or the Book of Revelation, at the close of the Bible.

This is certainly a very great diversity, and we might well expect nothing but confusion among so many pieces from different times, places, authors, and content. But there is another remarkable feature of the Bible, and this is its unity. By unity, of course, we do not mean uniformity but rather an underlying harmony, like that of a musical composition. This harmony has an exultant quality that can be best described as a message of hope and anticipation that comes to a climax in the good news of the gospel. Despite the disparate and diverse parts of the Bible, this underlying unity binds it all together and justifies the bringing of so many portions within two covers of one book.

First of all, the Hebrew Scriptures, which Christians call the Old Testament, can be seen as the preparation for the coming of the gospel of Jesus Christ. Through Abraham, Isaac, and Jacob, God was weaving together a redemptive pattern in which the divine purpose was being disclosed. The biblical designation of God as "the God of Israel" bears witness to the formation of a people through whom God's purposes were both revealed and carried forward in history. Through the pages of the Hebrew Scriptures, prophets spoke for and about God, leading Israel into a fuller understanding of ethical monotheism. Typical of such teaching is the memorable statement of the prophet Micah, "What does the Lord require of you but to do justice, and to love kindness, and to walk humbly with your God?" (6:8). The ultimate purpose of God has been to form a community of the people of God, through whom the nations of humankind should learn justice and be blessed through the worship of Israel's God.

Such is the preparation in the Hebrew Scriptures for the coming of the one whom the prophets foretold would be sent as the promised Messiah. In the Gospels, we have four accounts of the life of Jesus the Messiah, his teaching, healing ministry, death, and Resurrection. Though each differs somewhat from the others, depending in part on the needs of its intended reading public, they unite in telling of the redemptive character of the work of Jesus, disclosed already in his gathering the nucleus of a new Israel in the persons of the twelve apostles. This unifying fellowship with their Teacher was made up of individuals from the most diverse backgrounds and interests. For example, Matthew was a tax collector who, though a Jew, was working for the Roman government. He had, so to speak, sold his soul to the devil and was siphoning off to Roman coffers exorbitant taxes from his compatriots in Palestine. On the other hand, among the Twelve was Simon the Zealot, a Jewish freedom-fighter, ready at the drop of the hat to take up arms against the hated Roman overlords. In modern terms, Jesus had called together into the apostolic fellowship the equivalent of a card-carrying Communist and a member of the John Birch Society!

Following the account given in the Gospels, in the Book of the Acts of the Apostles we see the growth and extension of the Church. Into the fellowship of believers are brought diverse elements of human society, among whom no true partnership had hitherto existed. Individual Jews and Gentiles, masters and slaves, men and women, cultured and unlettered—all these found their unity as members of the Church. In three successive chapters (chapters 8, 9, and 10) Luke presents three vignettes that symbolize the bringing together into the fellowship of the Church representatives of different races, cultures, and continents. These are the Ethiopian treasurer from Africa; the Jewish rabbi Saul of Tarsus in Asia Minor; and Cornelius, the Roman centurion from Europe. Each of these three was brought in a different manner to acknowledge the lordship of Jesus Christ.

It became the function of the Church, as the Body of Christ, to make God's will known among humankind so that the Kingdom of God might come and the divine will be done on earth as it is in heaven. The Book of Acts carries this story forward from Jerusalem, the capital of a small area in the East, to Rome, the capital of the far-flung empire.

Next, in the twenty-one epistles of the New Testament, we have the explanation of the gospel of Jesus Christ as this bears on various needs and problems that arose, whether in different congregations or in the lives of individual believers. Here we have both diversity and unity. Paul is the apostle of faith; Peter, the apostle of hope; John, the apostle of love; James, the apostle of works. But all of them are committed to the same Lord Jesus Christ, who, though he had died, was still recognized as living and active among the members of the growing and expanding fellowship.

Finally, the concluding book of the Bible, the Book of Revelation, sets forth the climax of the gospel of the Lord Jesus Christ, when the New Jerusalem shall usher in peace and harmony for a new heaven and a new earth.

Thus, the unity of the Bible can be summed up in terms of the gospel, or good news, of Jesus Christ: The Old Testament is the preparation for the gospel of Jesus Christ; the four Gospels set forth the manifestation of the gospel; the Acts of the Apostles, the propagation; the epistles, the explanation; and the Book of Revelation, the consummation of the gospel of Jesus Christ. Such is the makeup and the central message of the Bible—its diversity and its unity. It is these Scriptures that serve as a lamp to our feet and a light to our path.

Over the past sixteen years, it has been the responsibility of a committee of about thirty biblical scholars, under the aegis of the National Council of Churches, to attempt to put these disparate Scriptures of the Old and New Testaments into language that is direct and meaningful to people today. The task was certainly not to rewrite the Bible, as some people might allege—far from it. The task was rather to convey the message of the Scriptures in simple, enduring words and expressions that are worthy to stand in the great tradition of the King James Bible and its predecessors. Although at times the magnitude of the work made it difficult for the committee to see the end of its task, all who were privileged to complete the work are now grateful to God.

Looking back over the years of labor, I think that all of the members of the committee have mixed feelings of relief and of regret: relief that the years of exacting toil are over but also regret that, had we taken a few more years for the job, it would doubtless have been better. But there comes a time when one must say, enough is enough! In humility, we recognize that, in view of the ongoing development of the English language and the acquisition of new textual and lexicographical information, our best efforts will some day need to be reviewed and modified.

Meanwhile, this new version seeks to preserve all that is best in the English Bible as it has been known and used through the years. It is intended for use in public reading and congregational worship, as well as in private study, instruction, and meditation. It is the hope and prayer of the translators that this version of the Bible may continue to hold a large place in congregational life and to speak to all readers, young and old alike, helping them to understand and believe and respond to its message. In this way, the New Revised Standard Version will serve as "a lamp to our feet and a light to our path."

16. The Big One and the Not-So-Big One
Ronald D. Sisk

Psalm 121

Susan Saul was in the checkout line at the Marina Safeway. Gus Miklos was driving down Van Ness. Barry Stricker was at SFO waiting to get on an airplane; Alex Hamilton, on the twenty-ninth floor of Embarcadero Center. John Byrd and Linden Moore had each come through the Cypress section of 880 a few minutes before five o'clock. Already there's a T-shirt making the rounds in the city that says, "Please Don't Tell Me Where You Were When the Earthquake Hit."

But the truth is that it is important to us. We are a traveling people here in the Bay Area. Our jobs, our schools, our families, our amusements mean we have to get around in earthquake country. And that bothers us more this Sunday than it did a week ago. Sheryl and I are trying to figure out how to stay off underpasses and out of elevators and parking garages for the rest of our natural lives. The truth, of course, is there is no adequate way to defend ourselves. We've all been reminded this week how fragile human life is. How genuine is the danger underneath us. How quickly the crisis can come. The question is, What comfort can you and I find this Sunday

---

Ronald D. Sisk is pastor of the Tiburon Baptist Church in Tiburon, California. Dr. Sisk has served as director of program development for the Christian Life Commission of the Southern Baptist Convention and is the author of several publications of the Christian Life Commission, including *Alcohol Awareness: A Guide for Teenagers and Their Parents* and *Critical Issues: Nuclear Doomsday.* This sermon was preached on October 22, 1989, the Sunday after a 7.1 earthquake had struck northern California.

after the "Not-So-Big One"? We find it, I believe, in the words of the psalm.

There was another group of travelers, you see, one day so long ago, walking one of the dusty "freeways" of Palestine. They were headed through the mountain valleys up toward Jerusalem for the festival. And as they went, they sang this psalm for the first time. They call this a song of ascents because it was sung as they walked along, trudging upward, always upward, toward Jerusalem on the ridge and the Temple on the top of Mount Zion. Many of us grew up with the King James translation: "I will lift up mine eyes unto the hills from whence cometh my help." So we've tended to think of the travelers seeing the hills as the place of comfort. Later translations tell us that was not true. The hills were the place of danger. Bands of robbers could sweep down on defenseless pilgrims at any moment, steal the offering they were taking to the Temple, leave them injured or dead. Wild beasts waited for nightfall to attack pack animals or raid camps for whatever they could get.

So the travelers raised their eyes to the hills, alright, but not for the sense of comfort and peace you and I get from the profile of Tam. They raised their eyes like the people of Washington looked toward Mount St. Helens raining fire and ash. They raised their eyes like we stood in our homes last Tuesday and looked at our ceilings as they shook above us, like the victims on 880 must have done in that last terrifying moment of their lives. They looked around them like a lot of us have been doing in the shock and sorrow of this week. They wondered when danger might swoop down on them next. And they cried out.

From whence does my help come? How am I going to survive? How am I going to keep safe when danger comes? Isn't there anybody who's going to look out after me? It's been really encouraging this week to hear of the response of so many in the Bay Area to the needs of those hardest hit by the quake. Neighbors helping neighbors. Strangers helping strangers. People going out of their way. People putting themselves into danger to help wherever help has been needed. We can help one another. That is one part of the answer to the psalmist's question. But the singer wasn't really asking about human help. He was really asking the question some of us in the Bay Area have been asking and others of us have been avoiding since Tuesday afternoon at 5:04. He was asking, Where does my help come from when human help comes to an end?

"My help comes from the Lord who made heaven and earth. He will not suffer your foot to be moved." The first way the Lord defends us is to defend us from nature itself. The pilgrims' trails were steep and rocky. Nothing was easier than to twist an ankle or break a leg. "The sun shall not smite you by day nor the moon by night." The way led through the desert. In a matter of hours, searing heat could give way to piercing cold. Those were natural hazards no human could do anything about. Just so, the San Andreas fault was here long before the Miwok Indians ever roamed the hills of Marin or you and I ever ventured into California from wherever we or our parents came from. One thing that's absolutely certain is God did not make 880 collapse as a judgment on those 250 drivers or burn a square block of the Marina built on landfill as a judgment on San Francisco. Jesus asked, "Were those eighteen upon whom the tower fell in Siloam and killed them worse sinners than all the others who dwelt in Jerusalem?" And he answered, "I tell you, *no.*" You and I choose to live here. We want to inhabit these ridges and valleys. We build structures that may or may not be safe. That is our choice, not God's, just as with those tower builders in Jerusalem so long ago. The highway department, they tell us now, has long known the Cypress section would not stand up to a quake of this magnitude. That the quake would come one day, we have known for a very long time. So when natural disaster comes, it is just that, the result of forces that have been in place all along, natural and even impersonal in a way.

Even so, our help comes from the Lord. There is a bigger scheme of things than anything you and I do or don't do. The good news is, even in the face of this week's disaster, you and I have been taken care of. I can't tell you why John Byrd drove home a few minutes before five instead of a few minutes after last Tuesday. Or why Richard Tunnell took an apartment a few blocks down Beach Street instead of in the block that collapsed and burned. Why God seems to look after some of us better than others in times like these is just part of the mystery of grace. My grandmother would have said, "It just wasn't their time to go."

But the psalmist would say it isn't your place or mine to question why we were fortunate and others were not. He would say our place this morning is to accept God's grace, to give thanks to God for taking care of so many of us, to let our thanksgiving move us toward the Lord, just as they let their singing move them step by step closer to Jerusalem. Even in the face of earthquakes, my help comes from the Lord who made heaven and earth. The Lord is my keeper.

"He who keeps you will not slumber. Behold he who keeps Israel will neither slumber nor sleep." There is a second way the Lord defends us, you see: not only from natural disaster, but also from the evil that people do. The worst time for the pilgrims was night, of course. Night, when the travelers huddled nervously together in unfamiliar terrain. Night, when the bandits massed in the hills, and the watchmen strained their eyes looking for moving shapes in the dark. And time after time in the middle of the night, when the watchmen grew bored and heavy-eyed, the attacks came. So it was this week that some climbed into the 880 wreckage Tuesday night, not to look for survivors, but to see if they could rip off car radios. Others ran into downtown Los Gatos and Santa Cruz under cover of dark, not to help, but to loot. One store in the city, so we heard, raised its price on flashlight batteries to $5.00 a piece.

The earthquake is no exception, you see. It simply reveals who we already are. Again and again in this life, you and I will find ourselves under surprise attack from human evil—sometimes evil from outside of us, sometimes things that surprise us from within ourselves. The psychologists have been saying since Tuesday night that we need to expect some surprises from our own emotions in the weeks ahead: depression, irritability, fatigue, and at the same time difficulty sleeping. You parents need to watch for signs of fearfulness in your children. In a very genuine sense, we've all had the world pulled out from under us. We all need to give each other room and time, to be nice to all those East Bay people crowding our Marin freeways come tomorrow morning, to give ourselves time to grieve and heal, to watch the World Series this week and learn to laugh again. Sometimes we disappoint ourselves, you see—sometimes in spite of all we try. And what we need as much as anything is to relax and remember.

You and I have someone watching over us. Someone who doesn't sleep. Someone to protect us when we are attacked. Someone to protect us from ourselves. The pilgrims knew, while they did God's work, God would look after them. We Christians know even more than that. We know it is more than accident so many of us came through last Tuesday so well. We know we have a protector in Jesus Christ many people in our area do not have. But we know even more than that. We know even if it had been far worse for us, even if the epicenter had been in San Rafael, and we'd had a church van full of members on the Cypress structure, and we were meeting this morning on a parking lot next to a ruined shell—even then our God would be with us.

Verse 7 in the King James reads, "The Lord shall preserve thee from all evil; He shall preserve thy soul." Sometimes even to Christians, you see, the worst does come. Scripture says, "It is appointed unto man once to die." That is the way of the world. And much as we try to forget it, that is true of every one of us in this room this morning. But the good news is for those of us who are pilgrims on God's way. For we who give ourselves to Jesus Christ and walk day by day down his roads, our selves, our souls, that which is the life in you and me, can never be lost, never be hurt. And we do not have to be afraid. Come hurricane, come earthquake, come freeway pileup, come old age, come death, come disease, the promise of God in Jesus Christ is the promise of God in the psalmist's song. God will preserve us from all evil. We shall live forever.

So the shaking is settling down now, at least for the time being. Gradually, you and I will go back to the normal everyday pathways of our lives. Someday soon we'll cross the bridges again and go under the underpasses and get in the elevators without so much as a second thought. Well, maybe without a third. But as we do what we can to help the cleanup, let's remember you and I have more to offer people than a few cans of food and a blanket. We have confidence in the midst of anxiety. We have hope in the midst of despair. We have Jesus who walks beside us when we are lonely and carries us when we cannot move forward on our own. Maybe if somebody asks if you were frightened, you could even screw up your courage to say, "Yes, but I knew God would take care of me."

And let us take comfort in the Lord of the travelers. "The Lord will keep your going out and your coming in from this time forth and even for evermore." Several years ago the movie *The Day After* tried to show us what life would be like in America if ever we suffer a nuclear attack. As the movie theme song, they chose the old Christian hymn "How Firm a Foundation." Someone joked this morning that that is the last hymn we should sing today. But we are going to. Every time we face this kind of crisis now, the last two verses of that hymn come back to me. "When through fiery trials thy pathway shall lie / my grace all-sufficient shall be thy supply / The flame shall not hurt thee. I only design / thy dross to consume and thy gold to refine / The soul that on Jesus hath leaned for repose / I will not, I will not desert to his foes / That soul, though all hell should endeavor to shake / I'll never, no never, no never forsake."

So goes the old song of the Church and the even older song of the psalmist. This is the promise of God. As we sing "How Firm a Foundation," will you take advantage of God's promise this morning? Will you lean on Jesus? Will you take your next step on the pilgrim way?

17. God Remembers
Krister Stendahl

I would like to lift up a verse from Psalm 103. "For God knows our frame. God remembers that we are dust." I love that verse. It is so liberating. God knows. There is no shame in being weak and mortal. Weakness is not sin. Weakness does not conjure up guilt, or should not. One of the difficult things with Western Christianity is that it cultivated a kind of introspective conscience which somehow thought that one gave honor to God by describing oneself in utter depravity. Men and women are created in the image of God. In a world full of many tensions, we need to reach back to our common humanity. Remember that the dignity of human beings lies in the fact that we are created in the image of God. The rabbis asked, "Why did God create only one human being, Adam?" "So that nobody should be able to say, 'My father is better than your father.'" To be created in the image of God, there lies our dignity.

But in the Western tradition, we have so overdone the destruction and smashing of the image of God that it actually has very little operative power. And it gives very little dignity. That which in the Western tradition was called "the Fall" and "Original Sin" was understood by the early Christians in a very different way. Actually, there is no term *fall* and no term *sin* in the text. No, here is that ambiguous story where the innocence of human beings passes away,

Krister Stendahl, a native of Stockholm, Sweden, was educated at Uppsala University, where he received his doctorate and served as parish pastor and university chaplain. In 1984, following thirty years on the faculty at Harvard Divinity School, eleven as dean, Stendahl returned to Sweden to serve as Bishop of Stockholm, Church of Sweden. Since his retirement in 1988 he has served as chaplain to Harvard Divinity School. Among his writings are *The Bible and the Role of Women* (1966) and *Meanings* (1984). This sermon was delivered as the Price Lecture at Trinity Church, Boston, in February 1990.

and human beings assume the full dignity of responsible moral life, as they now can distinguish between good and evil. They fell short all right, but that is not the only point. To be able to sin is strangely a sign of human dignity.

The West needs to remember that God knows our frame; God remembers that we are dust, and God is not unreasonable. We have lost the distinction between weakness and sin. I've spent a good deal of time studying the Apostle Paul and his writings. It is striking that Paul never felt guilty about his weakness. That is something which just is and is tragic and for which one needs to seek help. But God knows. God remembers that we are dust. What an exuberance of God to form and sculpture things in the divine image, using as low and passing and brittle material as dust. So fragile. And yet so beautiful. And isn't that our human condition? So fragile. And so beautiful. So dignified by God and yet so vulnerable. God knows. God remembers that we are dust. And, therefore, we are treated tenderly. So let us be tender with one another. We have a tender skin. We are vulnerable. We know that for ourselves, but let's remember that our neighbor also hurts. And let's practice mutual tenderness. God remembers our weakness; let us remember one another's weakness, tenderly. . . .

The paschal mystery and the mystery of Christmas have this in common: They both deal with the interplay, the mixing, the melding and the molding together of the divine and the human. The significance of the suffering of Christ is not the torture as such; terrible to say, the world has invented even more terrible tortures since. The significance of Calvary is rather that somehow it is God who suffers. It is the Son of God, and it is God's self who suffers. The drama is about the human and the divine. The early Christians understood this much better than we do. The first crucifixes for hundreds of years were triumphal crucifixes with a figure of Christ standing in royal garb and royal crown of gold, blessing the cosmos with his outstretched, stung hands. Divine and human. The icons of the Greek church and the Russian church are such that the human form is totally lit through by divine quality; and one sees the divine through the human.

The Gospel of Mark ends the ministry of Jesus, and it may be intentional, with the healing of the blind man, Bartimaeus, before the passion narrative begins. The passion narrative comes to us, invites us to see, to see this mystery, this wonderful mystery which is perhaps the greatest secret of the Christian faith: that God becomes most divine when God becomes most human. Oh, these clever theologians, myself included, who think that they will solve our problems by distinguishing the human from the divine. No, let it sink in: divine and human together.

It is tempting to identify with the figures that surround Jesus, especially in our psychological age. There is a little Peter in all of us, denying, and there is a little Pilate, especially when one looks at the elders, the Establishment, well represented on the vestry of this church. It is so tempting and helpful, and there is nothing wrong in using the image of those who surround Jesus, to identify with them and learn the lessons from them. But the really important thing is to see Jesus. Broken through the prism of the four Gospels, Jesus is wonderful, so far beyond human comprehension that we have to thank God for four portraits that are quite different: Matthew, Mark, Luke, and John. And if you have four portraits of somebody dear to you, you do not make transparencies of them and put the transparencies on top of each other and send light through. That becomes blurred, holy blur if it is Gospels, but blurred. No, you look at one picture at a time, and if the nose is longer on one portrait than the other, your instinct is not to say, Which one has the right measurement? No, you read it as a portrait, as an interpretation based upon understanding and love and devotion. So, too, with the four portraits of Jesus that the evangelists have given us.

Mark, bless his soul, had no apologetic need to pretty up the passion narrative. For Matthew, the passion is cosmic. Luke, however, is the one we always like; he describes Jesus as one should. He also writes the best Greek and appeals to the sentiments of Western culture. It is in Luke that we have the picture of Jesus which we all find self-evident: Here are the words about the good Samaritan and the prodigal son. This is where Jesus says, "Father forgive them, for they know not what they do." And there is the time when he gives the ultimate forgiveness to the criminal, "Today you shall be with me in paradise," after the criminal had prayed the most beautiful prayer I know. For Luke has a sense, a sensitivity, for authentic piety. Remember that prayer, "Jesus, remember me when you come into your kingdom." Is there any better prayer in the world? Not gimme, gimme, gimme! Not even fathoming what I should pray for. Not expecting to get anything, just, "Remember me, Jesus, remember me." And finally the Gospel of John, which excels in expressing the divine quality of Jesus as his last words are words of victory.

You might ask which Gospel reflects the way it really was. I advise you not to be impoverished, not to become poor in your imagination. Let all the drama play before your eyes. Good theology is "poetry plus," rather than "science minus." Let it enrich you.

18. Jesus, the Liberator
Bill J. Leonard

John 9:1–12, 29–41

"Democracy," he said. "Democracy and freedom, that's what we want." He was a Chinese student, standing in the middle of Tianan-men Square in the halcyon days of May before tanks and soldiers toting semiautomatic weapons came stalking. "And what is democracy and freedom?" a reporter asked. "I'm not sure," the student replied, "but whatever it is, we need more of it."

"If this were Harvard or Yale," the intense young Southern Baptist declared, "then we could let students ask a lot of questions. But since it is a Southern Baptist school, what we need is more indoctrination."

Lately, I've thought a lot about those two statements made from either end of the world. And I've asked again, What is this freedom we call the gospel? What of the liberation we say only Jesus can give? Do we want it until we get some of it? Does it frighten us after only a taste with its radical freedom? Are there limits to even gospel freedom? Today let us go looking for liberation in one brief gospel story. In discussing it, I am not offering indoctrination, even if some of you need a little. Like that nameless, perhaps now lifeless student, I am not certain what freedom is, I just know we need more of it.

Today's story is a strange one. One of the strangest, perhaps, in the Gospels. Indeed, it borders on the bizarre. It was the Sabbath—Saturday, you know. God's day of rest from the very beginning. Jesus and the disciples are, Scripture says, "on the way" somewhere and

---

Bill J. Leonard is William Walker Brookes Professor of American Christianity at Southern Baptist Theological Seminary in Louisville, Kentucky. Leonard received his Ph.D. in American Church History from Boston University, has published many articles and has been author or editor of several books.

confront a blind man in their path. Seeing him, the disciples quickly assess his entire life—not on the basis of who he is but what he is. They, like most of us, see his blindness as the thing that most defines his entire personhood. It is as if when you know one thing about anyone, you can say what they are always like. And then they asked the old theological brainteaser, asked frequently no doubt along the way with Jesus and in assorted late-night, apostolic dormitory discussions: Why was the man born blind? Who sinned—the man or his parents? It was one or the other, had to be. After all, God decrees these things for a purpose, and popular Hebrew (dare we say Southern Baptist) religion readily saw such conditions as evidence of sin. Did the man himself commit some fetal mistake? Some interuterine trespass? Or did his parents bring the judgment of God upon him?

But Jesus does not answer their question with some easy response that solves forever the issue we call theodicy—the ancient dilemma of why the innocent suffer and why evil seems to prevail in the world. I really wish he had. I wish he had said, "Yes, God caused it," or better yet, "No, God did not cause it." I wish he had given us a direct answer on who is responsible for all this suffering, then and now. But he does not generalize from this one case to all cases of suffering. Rather, he says, "It is not that this man or his parents sinned, but that the power of God might be displayed in curing him." You asked the wrong question, my friends. What will occur from the blindness is evidence of the liberating power of God. Jesus takes only this case, not all such cases. He addressed this man, not all the disabled. Perhaps one of the great gifts of the gospel (and seminary at its gospel best) is in teaching us to ask the questions differently than we ever did before.

And then Jesus does something very strange, you must admit. He spits. The Son of God spit on the ground and made a paste, the Bible says, and dabbed it on the eyes of the blind man and sent him to the pool of Siloam. Eeee gross! my fourteen-year-old daughter would say. But when he washed off the stuff, the man could see, and the blindness was over. Whatever was it that did that? Is this some magic formula? Some messianic medicine? Or a strange and unpredictable symbol of healing from a liberating savior? Whatever it was, dirt and spit and faith and hope combined, and this guy can see. Thank God. Who's next?

But not so fast. Next thing we know, it turns into a theological controversy of the first magnitude[1]. In fact, it gets pretty nasty.

Fascinating, don't you think, the response of the various protagonists in the story? The Pharisees get into the action rather quickly. For them, the liberation of this lost soul is as bad or worse than the blindness that had plagued the man since birth. They, like the disciples, believed that the blindness was caused by some terrible sin—some divine retribution justly distributed, no doubt. And thus the blind man had a special place in first-century society, and he should know his place. He, like all the crippled, was God's way of reminding the rest of the world of the wages of sin and the judgment of the Divine. And disturbing that place, healing him, implied something about the very nature of sin, about Jesus of Nazareth, and about, ultimately, the living God. All of which the Pharisees were unable to accept.

In fact, all these events made the Pharisees extremely theologically uncomfortable. And thus, they conclude, God simply doesn't act that way. Their God, the true God, doesn't do that kind of liberating. "Now hold on here," we almost hear them say. "Don't you realize that this man was liberated on the Sabbath? Our God doesn't permit liberation on the Sabbath. Therefore, anyone who violates it, even in the name of goodness, disobeys God. Any pagan should know that." There is little concern for the man and almost no joy about his new-found sight, no thought of his life or the gift he had received. All these folks can see is that the healing did not fit their rules; this sort of liberation had no place in their theology. They read the Scriptures. They prayed. They faithfully kept God's Law. They knew exactly how God acts and whom he blesses and when he punishes. Because this healing did not fit their plans, they argued that it simply never happened.

They went first to the man's parents and tried to intimidate them into denying that this was their son. "If this is your son, and you say he was born blind, how is it that he can now see?" they asked. The parents were scared, bewildered, and refused to get involved. "Go see our son," they said. "He is of age. He'll tell you what happened." And they go to the man himself and try to trap him into admitting it was all a fake. And when he lectures them, turns their theology around, they attack his character—"abusively" the New English Bible says.

Taking another shot at this man and his parents, they warn, "Who are you to give us lessons, born and bred in sin as you are? Listen, boy, don't tell us about God. We are the professionals," and were they ever. The Pharisees were nobody's fools. They knew how to deal with upstart theologians and religious rabble-rousers. When reason fails and patience grows thin, when you've tried being nice and patronizing, give them guilt. How dare you talk to us about faith, born and bred in sin as you are? So what if you're liberated now? We know what you used to be. We know where your parents live. We will never let you forget. And grace gets lost in the rules. The Pharisees in the New Testament are not always bad. They are simply too good. Sometimes you can be too good for grace, and that is one of the major points of the story.

In a way, you can't blame the Pharisees. They were simply doing their jobs—protecting the common people from bad religion, guarding the naive populace from the unscrupulous charlatan, upholding the Word of the Lord. Religion has its rules, good religion anyway. And religious tricksters are a dime a dozen. (These days they are a couple of million a dozen.) The Pharisees were responsible for helping people sort out true religion from false, ultimately using certain divinely objective criteria. And no doubt it had worked before with false messiahs, zealots, and other religious fanatics. But when genuine liberation occurs, in front of them, they prefer the safety of old formulas to the gamble of new grace. They bring their objective dogmas to bear on Immanuel.

The hypothesis goes something like this: The Sabbath is God's unbreakable rule. To break the Sabbath is to disobey God. Jesus broke the Sabbath. Jesus disobeyed God. Therefore, no true liberation occurred. Sooner or later, all organized religion acts just like that. It is one of religion's greatest sins. Usually when it does, somebody gets fired, burned, or crucified. It happens frequently in Christian history. Some Baptists demand separation of church and state and religious liberty for all people under God. And the Establishment answers back, Be subject to the higher powers. That is the rule; violators will be prosecuted. Case closed.

Some blacks demand liberation from slavery. And the Establishment says, Slaves obey your earthly masters with fear and trembling, single-mindedly, as serving Christ. To deny divine sanction of slavery is to deny the Word of God. Case closed.

Some women affirm a call to Christian ministry. And the Establishment says, I do not permit a woman to be a teacher nor must women domineer over men; she must be quiet in church. "The bishop must be husband of one wife." The rule is that women must stay in their place. God does not call women. Case closed.

It is a dilemma for all of us. What are the rules? How do we know? What causes sin? Who is from God? When do we cling to the security of tradition, and when do we fling it to the four winds? Who is a prophet, and who is not, and how do you know the difference, and who will tell you? Can we celebrate liberation and salvation when it comes to people we thought were irredeemable in ways we thought God would never act? The Spirit moves where it will, and we never know who exactly it will touch or where. Best to be ready for a surprise. Best to wear our proof texts ever so lightly. Sometimes the only time healing can occur is when it doesn't fit the rules.

And that brings us to the man born blind. We learn a lot about him in this brief text. There is no indication that he asked for healing; Jesus just did it for him. He isn't told to have faith or believe in Jesus; that happens later. Just to wash the paste off his eyes. His friends do not recognize him at first, so he identifies himself to them—it really is me, friends. The Pharisees question him twice, and the second time he displays a sense of humor, even sarcasm before his social betters. "Look," he says—no pun intended—"I told you all I know." Do you want to become his disciples, too? Surely no sinner could do a wonderful thing like this. And when he said that, they decided it was time to throw him out of the church.

It's hard to get mad at a blind man. Even an ex-blind man. Several years ago I was on a program with musician, prophet, poet, blind man Ken Medema. We were at a college somewhere in the American South. (Not a seedbed of radical religion.) The first session, Medema walked to the piano and started singing about nukes and Nicaragua. About peace, justice, and American materialism. And by the time I finally got up to speak to the crowd, he had sung something to alienate almost everyone present. That night, at a rap session, several (very conservative) students (I mean everyone in the whole room) confessed that they were angry with him for his political views and his religious radicalism. Perhaps they also felt guilty about being angry at him because he was blind. What they meant, I think, was that, like the apostles and Pharisees, we tend to judge disabled people by their condition—not imagining that they should have political or theological opinions, let alone controversial ones. Blind people are to be pitied, not to be listened to.

And that's why I love this former blind man in Holy Scripture and Ken Medema as well. They don't take nothin' off nobody. You see, Jesus' liberation may not make all blind people see or all crippled people walk or all speechless people speak or all saved people whole all at once. But they may know liberation all the same. Ken Medema is a liberated Christian person—although he cannot use his eyes, he sees and knows and tells, even when it is dangerous, controversial, and meddlesome. See, you and I need not have everything healed to be liberated by Christ. We need not get it all together to find courage, faith, and grace to speak and act in his name. And if we wait until we understand everything, have every question answered, we won't do anything with the gospel.

And then there's Jesus, who, if you look closely, has a rather minor speaking part—a sort of cameo appearance in this story. He heals the man and then goes off who-knows-where while the blind man gets the center stage and has to face all the heat. But Jesus hears that the man has been expelled from the synagogue and goes looking for him. The text says, "And when he found him." Isn't that great? Jesus asked, "Have you faith in the Son of man?" And the man replies, "Tell me who he is that I should put my faith in him." And Jesus does his own play on words. "You have seen him, indeed it is him who is speaking to you." "Lord, I believe," the man says. And the liberation continues.

And Jesus ends the story by reminding them and us that he really came into the world after all to give sight to the sightless and to make blind those who see. "What?!" say the Pharisees. "Do you mean we are blind?" "If you were blind," said Jesus, "you would not be guilty. But because you say we see, your guilt remains." And so the gospel continues. The people who know they can't see are liberated. And the people who think they see everything, see nothing. It is a wonderful and terrible story. It is our story, isn't it? Annie Dillard sums it up like this (I don't know if I understand what she says, but I sure like it):

> His disciples asked Christ about a roadside beggar
> who had been blind from birth. "Who did sin, this
> man or his parents, that he was born blind?" And
> Christ, who spat on the ground, made a mud of his
> spittle and clay, plastered the mud over the man's
> eyes, and gave him sight, answered, "Neither hath
> this man sinned, nor his parents: but that the works
> of God should be made manifest in him." Really? If
> we take this answer to refer to the affliction
> itself—and not the subsequent cure—as "God's
> works made manifest," then we have, along with

"Not as the world gives do I give unto you," two
meager, baffling, and infuriating answers to one of
the few questions worth asking, to wit, What in the
Sam Hill is going on here?

The works of God made manifest? Do we really
need more victims to remind us that we're all
victims . . . ? Do we need blind men stumbling
about . . . to remind us what God can—and
will—do . . . ? Yes, in fact we do. We do need
reminding, not of what God can do, but of what he
cannot do, or will not, which is to catch time in its
free fall and stick a nickel's worth of sense into our
days. And we need reminding of what time can do,
must only do; churn out enormity at random and
beat it, with God's blessing, into our heads: that we
are created, *created,* sojourners in a land we did not
make, a land with no meaning of itself and no
meaning we can make for it alone. Who are we to
demand explanations of God . . . ? We forget
ourselves, picnicking; we forget where we are . . .
"God is at home," says Meister Eckhardt. "We are
in the far country."[1]

And that is the good news on the way to liberation. It is this: The
gospel transforms everything, but some things even the gospel cannot change. Some questions still aren't answered, but faith is possible nonetheless. The innocent still suffer, and we still wonder why.
The people who can't see, can. And the people who do see, don't.
Most of us are more secure with rules and religion than we are with
faith and liberation. We want answers to all our questions now, but
God doesn't readily oblige. Instead, God comes looking for us—
sending us to Siloam with spit and dust and water and unrequited
love.

NOTE

1. Annie Dillard, *Holy the Firm* (New York: Harper & Row, 1977),
60–62.

19. The Saints: Dogged Blunderers toward Heaven

Carroll E. Simcox

> Let us run with patience the race that is set before us, looking to Jesus the author and finisher of our faith.
>
> —Heb. 12:1–2

"For the saints of God are just folk like me, and I mean to be one, too!" So we say in the rollicking hymn we have just sung. It was my happy privilege to know the man who composed the tune, a gifted and saintly old priest who was once our house guest. At the time, our children were very young, just four and two, and Father John Henry Hopkins was very old; but it was a sight never to be forgotten to see him enchanting them with the manual tricks he could play with a handkerchief. He was not only musically but spiritually fit to compose a song of the saints of God because he knew from the inside what being a saint feels like.

The preacher at this Feast of All Saints must surely try to clarify precisely what a saint is—and is not. The saints are ill served by the stock stereotypes of them, which are miserable and demeaning parodies—cartoons, really. Saints are not goody-goodies. They are not too heavenly to get mixed up in such earthly matters as business and politics and pleasure. When I hear somebody say that we don't need

---

Carroll E. Simcox was editor of *The Living Church* from 1964 through 1977. He served the Episcopal church as a parish priest for over forty years in Minnesota, Vermont, New York, and Florida. Simcox is the author of many books, including *Three Thousand Quotations on Christian Themes, They Met at Philippi,* and *The Eternal You.* He is now affiliated with the American Episcopal Church and lives in Hendersonville, North Carolina.

a saint in the White House—we need somebody who knows how to run the country—I wonder what he knows about saints and also what he knows about what it takes to run the country. Perhaps it's not as much as he seems to think.

Phyllis McGinley is a poet who loves to write about saints. She says, "The wonderful thing about saints is that they were human. They lost their tempers, scolded God, were egotistical or testy or impatient in their turns, made mistakes and regretted them. Still they went on doggedly blundering toward heaven."

Doggedly blundering toward heaven. Just folk like me. With these phrases, I think we're blundering toward our definition of a saint. Somebody has said that a saint is a sinner who keeps on trying. That's a good solid contribution. A saint is a fool for Christ's sake. He's trying something at which he knows he can't possibly succeed while still in this poor, weak, vulnerable, and transient flesh. Who has ever seen a *successful* saint? I'm tempted to stop right here and make this our definition: *A saint is a faithful failure.* But that won't quite do; he's more than a failure. The saint is an aspirant, though not an achiever, who can say with Browning's rabbi:

> What I aspired to be
> And was not, comforts me:
> A brute I might have been, but would not sink i'
>   the scale!

Another line of Browning comes to mind, from his poem "A Death in the Desert": "Man partly is, and wholly hopes to be." Nobody realizes this truth as does the saint, who lives by the hope of becoming at last a full-grown Christian who has put away all childish things.

So here is our definition: *A saint is a Christian in the making.*

Let's be clear in our minds what Christian initiation is. When we are baptized, we are formally, "officially" made Christians, living members of the Body of Christ. God adopts us through holy baptism to be henceforward and forever his own children in Christ. When people tell us that they've already been saved by Christ, I don't want to argue with them, but I hope they know what they mean. If they mean that Christ has so finished his work with them that there's nothing more that needs to be done, that they are already finished products of his grace, I can only say that they are victims of a comfortable but dangerous delusion. In fairness, however, I don't believe that all Christians who speak of their "being saved" as an already fully accomplished fact really mean that. I think they may be confusing salvation, in its final sense, with conversion or the beginning of conversion, which of course means "change"—and for Christians, change into the likeness of Christ.

Karl Barth, perhaps the most influential theologian of our century, said this: "Rightly understood, there are no Christians. There is only the eternal opportunity of becoming Christians." One of the early Christian martyrs, who had lived for many years as a devoted servant of Christ, was brought at last to the arena to be put to death, and he declared, "Now I begin to be a Christian!" Only a beginner? As he saw himself, yes, and it was realism, not false humility. He was thinking in eternal terms of his end, of the true and full consummation of his being, and so must we, if we see ourselves as children—just children—in the family of Christ, and if we believe that our divine destiny is to grow up into the family likeness and character. That family likeness and character is what we see perfectly manifested in the human life of Jesus.

If you see your life and your reason-for-being and your destiny in this way; if you prayerfully strive to live by this self-understanding day by day and moment by moment; if you know that you only "partly are" but you "wholly hope to be"; and if, no matter how often you stumble and fall away from what seems "the heroic for earth too hard," you always pick yourself up and resume your dogged blundering toward heaven—you are a saint: a Christian in the making.

As the New Testament writers use the word, a saint is one who has been baptized into Christ and is *now being shaped* into the likeness of Christ by the Holy Spirit of God. Theologians call this divine operation of shaping us up *sanctification,* and the word *saint* comes from the same root.

The writer of the Epistle to the Hebrews, in a sublime chapter often called the Westminster Abbey of the Bible, calls the roll of great heroes of God's people in the ages before Christ. Whatever their faults and failings, which the Bible records honestly enough, they all lived and died in faith "as seeing him who is invisible." Thus they bore their witness in their generations to their God in whom they placed their whole hope and trust. Then the writer turns to us Christians with this challenge: "Seeing therefore that we are surrounded by so great a cloud of witnesses, let us lay aside every weight, and the sin that so easily besets us, and let us run with patience the race that is set before us, fixing our eyes on Jesus the author and finisher of our faith: who for the joy that was set before him endured the cross, despising the shame, and is now established at the right hand of the throne of God."

We are to *run with patience* this race that is set before us. It is an obstacle course designed and laid out by the very devil. It is well strewn with booby traps, and we are the boobies. We easily blunder into them when blinded and stupefied by our own silly pride and lusts and sloth and cowardice. We need patience of a very special kind if we are to cross this mine field to the end of our course. It is the patience of Christ. As we examine it in the gospel, we see that it is a two-edged sword—active on one edge and passive on the other.

Look first at the active, *fighting* patience of Jesus. As long as he was doing his work up in Galilee, preaching and teaching and healing, he knew he was safe enough from his enemies, who were bent upon killing him. He could have stayed up there and possibly lived out a long and happy life and then died peacefully in his bed, full of years and honor. But when he knew that the time for his last and fiercest fight was at hand, he fixed his face steadfastly, like a flint, to go to Jerusalem where his enemies were ready and waiting and whetting their knives for him. Such was his fighting patience, acting and daring and facing the foe.

Then, on the night of his betrayal, we see him praying in Gethsemane and saying to his Father, "Your will, not mine, be done!" Here is the divine passivity. Essentially, it is the acceptance of what must be, of what cannot be avoided if one is to be faithful to his trust from God. The next day, at noon, we see him stretching his tortured body on the ground, stark naked, with a jeering crowd looking on, to receive the nails into his hands and feet. Here is his passive, *suffering* patience, which must be ours when there is need not to fight but to accept. In the famous "serenity prayer" given to us by Reinhold Niebuhr, we pray for the grace to change the things that must be changed (the active patience) and for the grace to accept the things that cannot be changed (the passive patience). To have both and to use each when needed is to have the patience of Christ. Armed with this, we can run the hard race and fight the good fight and suffer the unavoidable wounds as true soldiers and faithful servants of Jesus Christ trying to be worthy to bear his name.

Now from everything I have said thus far, you might well infer that in my view the Christian in the making, the dogged blunderer toward heaven, has little but trouble and misery on his journey through and that his lot is a lonely and solitary one. Nothing could be farther from the truth; for the saint not only believes in the communion of saints, he shares in it, practices it, lives in it, and in this experience he finds joy unspeakable. A French Christian writer of our century, Léon Bloy, made the arresting statement, "There is only one sorrow—the sorrow of not being a saint." Of *not* being a saint. He knew enough about saints and nonsaints to be sure he was right, and I'm sure he was. Yet it is surprising to hear.

The truth is that we cannot know what real community is like unless we experience it in Christ. Aristotle taught us long before Christ that man is a political animal. He meant that we cannot be fulfilled as human beings except as we experience mutual belonging to one another and for one another as many-in-one. But he did not fully see or sense the reality that we are actually designed and constructed by our Creator not only to *live with* one another in mutual interdependence but to be actually *members of* one another. The full realization of this is given to us through Christ. St. Paul compares our membership of the Body of Christ to the organs of a human body in which all the particular organs (the eye, the ear, the pancreas, the lungs—every single cell) all together constitute one body, one life. Understand that mystery and you understand the communion of saints, for they are the same thing. The truth was well expressed by that wise and wonderful Quaker statesman-saint, William Penn: "They that love beyond the world cannot be separated by it. Death is but a crossing of the world, as friends do the seas; they live in one another still." They live in one another forever because they live in Christ.

In our doctrine of the Church, we make a threefold distinction. The Body of Christ lives in these dimensions: the Church "militant and suffering on earth," the Church "expectant in paradise," and the Church "triumphant in heaven." These are not three bodies but one Body. We know our own struggling selves well enough to know what is meant by "militant and suffering on earth"—militant against the sin that so easily besets us. We speak of the Church "expectant in paradise," meaning our brothers and sisters who have finished their earthly race but who died still uncompleted in Christ, as shall you and I be when we cross over. They are still "expectant," aspiring, still looking forward to the final goal of glorification with the glory of Christ himself. Even now they "in glory shine" because they are more closely with the Lord.

Though they shine in glory, they still must grow, and they need our prayers, and we need their prayers. For the only way that we particular members of Christ can love and help the other particular members is through prayer for them. Such intercessory prayer is the living bond that unites us all in one eternal union. When we pray for others, we need not undertake to tell God what we think he ought to do for them. We simply commend them to the Everlasting Mercy, knowing that God is doing better things for them than we can desire or pray for. Whenever you think of somebody in this life or the next and you simply *direct Godward* your thought of that person, you intercede for him. In the communion of saints, we continuously *think Godwardly* of our brothers and sisters in this holy and eternal family, and we know that they do the same for us. And no soul who lives in this communion can ever for even a moment be unfriended, unloved, unprayed for and alone. This is the joy of the saints. It is the highest joy we can know short of the final beatific vision of God himself, which we shall share with all saints in the Church "triumphant in heaven," if with the patience of Christ we persevere to the end.

So let us with good heart and holy hope press on in our dogged blundering toward heaven. Our names are written there—and we are expected.

20. An Hour's Work and a Day's Pay

L. Alan Sasser

Matt. 20:1–16

For as long as the Christian faith has been in existence, there has been a tension between righteousness that comes to us as a free gift and righteousness that is earned.

The first kind, we have learned to call grace. Grace, as you know, is the unmerited favor of God. As the Bible says, God is never-ceasing in his mercy extended to us. He has loved us with an everlasting love.

God's grace, freely given, lavishly bestowed upon us, is what makes us the crown of creation. We have worth and value because we are made in the image and likeness of God.

Grace says, "You are the salt of the earth." And, "You are the light of the world." It's not necessary to achieve saltness or lightness; it is already your possession.

Grace says reality is sometimes different from appearance. Remember the story of the Pharisee and the tax collector and the prayers they offered at the Temple? By all appearances, it was the Pharisee who should have been accorded recognition.

After all, he was the obviously religious character. Nevertheless, it was the tax collector's prayer that God heard and responded to with affirmation. Grace.

L. Alan Sasser is pastor of Greystone Baptist Church in Raleigh, North Carolina. A graduate of Wake Forest University, Sasser holds a master of divinity degree and a Ph.D. from Southeastern Baptist Theological Seminary.

Remember the story of the younger son who left home and squandered his portion of inheritance in irresponsible behavior? He left behind at home a father and an older brother.

By all appearances, the older brother should have been accorded a pat on the back for being a good, trustworthy son and rewarded for his steadfast loyalty. It was the returning prodigal, however, who got shoes for his feet, a ring for his finger, and the fatted-calf feast. Grace.

Here's the truth: It's not grace if you have to work for it. It's not grace unless it's free. It's only grace when it comes unsolicited and unmerited. And the righteousness that is grace's by-product is the kind the Bible says makes us Christians.

Then, there's that other kind. Righteousness that is earned is what we call works. There is no grace in it. Moreover, it is rarely gracious.

Works righteousness takes the form Russell Baker described in his excellent autobiography, *The Good Times.* Speaking of his relationship to his mother, he says,

> My mother, dead now to this world but still roaming free in my mind, wakes me some mornings before daybreak. "If there's one thing I can't stand, it's a quitter." I have heard her say that all my life. Now, lying in bed, coming awake in the dark, I feel the fury of her energy fighting the good-for-nothing idler within me who wants to go back to sleep instead of tackling the brave new day. . . . She has hounded me with these same battle cries since I was a boy in short pants back in the Depression. "Amount to something!" "Make something of yourself!" "Don't be a quitter!" On bad mornings, in the darkness, suspended between dreams and daybreak, with my mother racketing around in my head, I feel crushed by failure. I am a fool to think I amount to anything. A man doesn't amount to something because he has been successful at a third-rate career like journalism. It is evidence, that's all: evidence that if he buckled down and worked hard, he might some day do something really worth doing.

There is no joy in works righteousness. It is purely and simply a matter of accounting. Over in the left-hand column are all my good deeds, good thoughts, good words, and good intentions. Over in the right-hand column are all my bad deeds, bad thoughts, bad words, and missed opportunities. Line them up side by side.

If the left side stacks up more favorably than the right, then I am righteous. But if the right side holds the numerical edge, then I'm sunk. Given the human bent to sinning, pervasive as it is, we're all sunk. Works righteousness is what it is called. The Bible condemns it from cover to cover. But almost all of us have been, or are now, its victims.

Jesus spent the better part of his ministry trying to help his followers move away from a life pattern of works righteousness and toward a life pattern of grace. One of the ways he did it was by telling them, and us, stories of grace. I read one of them as our text for today. The scholars refer to it as a kingdom parable.

All that means is that it is describing to us in the literary form of a short story what life is to be like in the Kingdom of God. If you'll look in the upper left-hand corner of your worship bulletin, you'll notice that we are in the liturgical season of Kingdomtide just now.

Kingdomtide is part of Pentecost. Its observance began on the Sunday before Labor Day and continues until the beginning of Advent. It's the time during the church year when we give attention to the themes of life in the kingdom.

One of those themes is grace. What is God's grace like? How is God's grace extended humanward? And what is our proper response to God's grace?

Take another look at the parable. At first reading, it seems puzzling and disconcerting. It is about a farm manager who goes into a village to enlist day laborers to gather his crop.

He gets some of them first thing in the morning, offering to pay them a fair day's wage. Later in the morning, he signs on another group. Still later, about the middle of the afternoon, he recruits some more. Then, only an hour before quitting time, he signs on a few more and works them alongside the others.

Nobody quibbles about this apparent idiosyncrasy until it's time to settle the accounts. Now, you need to know that Jewish Law mandated payment to the laborers at the end of each working day. Deuteronomy 24:15 says, "Each day, before sunset, pay him for that day's work; he needs the money and has counted on getting it."

Hired hands back then lived on the edge of poverty, and this kindly provision of the Law protected them at least a little. The fact is, day laborers still live on the edge of poverty, and we who are employers, supervisors, managers, and owners have a special responsibility to those for whom a minimum wage is their only source of income. But that's another sermon.

Jesus probably told this story in the late summer, about the time of the grape harvest. Usually, the grapes were at their peak during August and early September. By the middle of September, the rains came. Then it was a race with the weather to get the grapes gathered.

So calling in extra laborers at all hours of the day was not as far-fetched as it might first appear. But the problem arose, as I said a moment ago, when it came time to settle up for the day.

The group that had signed on at five o'clock and worked one hour got exactly the same pay as those who had been picking grapes all day in the hot sun. And those all-day workers chafed. "Unfair! Unfair!" they said. "We've been working since early this morning, and you're not paying us any more than you're paying these who've not even broken a sweat."

To which the farm manager gave what to us has to sound like a curious response:

> Friend, I am doing you no wrong. Did you not
> agree with me for a denarius? Take what is yours
> and go your way. I want to give to this last man the
> same as to you. Is it not lawful for me to do what I
> want with my own things? Or is your eye evil
> because I am good?

Now, let me interject at this point a word of explanation. The Bible does not claim to be something it is not. It is not an economics textbook. It is not a line-item guide on how a businessman should set up his payroll.

Moreover, a parable, which is what we're dealing with here, is a made-up short story intended to drive home a point. The point of this story is that God is so good that he pours out his blessings upon us, not because we merit them, but because he loves to demonstrate his goodness.

And the word for this is—what?—*Grace!* This little short story is not really about wage and hour laws or management and labor relations. It is about the extravagant goodness of God.

"The parable does not mean that the Kingdom is a realm of complete equality or that good fortune is bestowed at the expense of faithful labor, or that God's verdicts are arbitrary."[1] No, this parable is one little piece of a much fuller and richer biblical presentation of the grace of God.

When you see it in its larger context, it makes even more sense. Jesus told it in response to a question asked by Peter in the previous chapter. Matthew 19:16 and following relates the story of the encounter between Jesus and the rich young ruler. You remember that incident. Jesus challenged the rich young ruler to become his disciple by turning away from the false security of his material possessions and radically trusting God.

It didn't happen. And then Peter said to Jesus, "We've left everything to follow you. What, then, will there be for us?" That was the question: "What's in it for us?"

And Jesus responded with the parable of the farm manager and the day laborers, the point of which is that no matter what your lot in life, God's mercy and love—God's grace—is sufficient.

We need to understand that we cannot see God's grace if we look at it through jealous eyes. The laborers who had worked the full day received the wages they had been promised when they began to work. But because they were feeling envious of those who got the same thing for less hours, they couldn't be happy with their own.

Sometimes we get to feeling sorry for ourselves and thinking that our lives are more trouble-plagued than the next person's. Once in awhile we court the notion that somebody else is a greater recipient of God's favor than we are.

But when that happens, we need to pause and reflect. You might not really want to trade your 80,000-plus-miles Ford for her new Mercedes. You might not really want to move from your $100,000 home to his $250,000 neighborhood.

It is impossible to know what difficulties plague the other person. Behind that smiling facade may lurk problems and pains beyond your imagination.

The proper response to life is gratitude—always. Be thankful to God for what he has given and pray that he will be as lavish toward others who may be facing hidden trials of which we have no knowledge.

My guess is that most of us would have to confess, if we would be honest about it, that we operate less in the realm of grace and more in the realm of works. I know that in my own life, this is a constant struggle.

Ever since I was a child, I've lived with the conviction that Russell Baker articulated so well. If I am ever going to amount to anything, then it is only going to come through my own good works.

So, working sixty- and seventy-hour weeks, ignoring my body's cries for exercise and relaxation, making excuses for not spending either quantity or quality time with family—these became my way of "amounting to something."

Then, I had a heart attack. And among other things I am learning from that experience is the truth that I am still here, not because of anything I have done, but because of God's grace.

God's grace gives us even late-in-the-day opportunities to be recipients of his spontaneous, generous, lavish love. And it beats the stuffing out of any works righteousness you or I can earn on our own.

St. Paul said it like this: "Forgetting what lies behind and straining forward to what is ahead, I press on toward the prize. . . ." The old spiritual translates that "I ain't what I ought to be, and I ain't what I'm gonna be, but thank God, I ain't what I used to be."

Grace.

NOTE

1. George Buttrick, *The Parables of Jesus* (New York: Harper and Bros., 1928), 162.

IV. ETHICAL

21. The Things That Make for Peace

Elizabeth Achtemeier

Jer. 8:8–13; Luke 19:41–44

It is characteristic of our Lord, according to the Gospel writers, that when he walked this earth, he shared fully in all of the actual conditions of human life. Jesus was born, like we were. He knew our hungers and thirst and temptations. He experienced our loneliness, our sufferings, our sorrows. He knew the joy of family and friends and even the triumphs of earth's little successes. And yes, he died, as we shall die, and was buried in a grave. He experienced human life as it actually is. And so it is that Jesus also shared our longing for peace.

Luke tells us that when Jesus approached Jerusalem, on his final journey to that city, and came down the descent of the Mount of Olives on the east, he wept over Jerusalem, crying out, "Would that even today you knew the things that make for peace." It is a cry that we know, isn't it? For we gaze out over the cities of the world and wish that they, too, knew such things—Beirut and Johannesburg, New Delhi and Kampala, Manila and Managua, and yes, Moscow and Washington and, still, Jerusalem. Everywhere throughout the world, peoples long for peace—for an end to the bloodshed, the hatred, the suffering, for a return to quiet and security and normality, where children can grow up and adults can work and old people can live

Elizabeth Achtemeier has served as adjunct professor of Bible and homiletics at Union Theological Seminary in Virginia since 1973. She is the author of several books on preaching, including *Creative Preaching, Preaching as Theology and Art,* and most recently, *Preaching about Family Relationships.*

out their days in tranquility. "O Jerusalem, Jerusalem," we cry out with our Lord, "when will you know any peace?" And Jerusalem is, for us, every city, and the cry is a universal cry.

As a result, we all have set out in our time to try to be peacemakers and to seek the things that may bring peace on the earth. If we can just halt the arms race, we think, or ban the bomb or force South Africa to give up apartheid; if we can just feed the starving and share the wealth and properly manage the earth's resources; if we can only spread literacy or democracy or methods of population control; then, then we can do away with the awful specter of death that haunts humanity. And so church bodies make peacemaking their first priority, and bishops issue pastoral letters. Demonstrators surround nuclear installations, and government leaders confer together. Literature pours out from the presses, and a million seminars are held every day round the world. But the killing continues, and young people die, and death lurks still outside every door. And Jesus weeps still, "O Jerusalem, Jerusalem," sharing our longing for peace.

Is it not time, therefore, good Christian friends, to note more closely what our weeping Lord says about his Jerusalem and about ours as well? "Your enemies will besiege you and surround you and hem you in on every side," he says, "and they will not leave one stone upon another in you." And then he gives the reason why that ancient capital of the Holy Land would be destroyed by the Romans in A.D. 70: "because you did not know the time of your visitation"—that is, because you did not acknowledge that God had visited you and that you were responsible for trusting and obeying him.

Jesus thinks that peace on earth depends on our relationship with God! And he is only echoing that song that the angels proclaimed on the night of his birth in Bethlehem. "Glory to God in the highest," sang the heavenly host to the shepherds abiding in the fields, "and on earth peace to those with whom he is well pleased." Peace is given to those on earth with whom God is well pleased. Peace depends on our relationship with our Creator and sovereign Lord.

At the beginning of the prophetic visions of Zechariah in the Old Testament, there is a marvelous scene in which the Lord God sends his angelic messengers to patrol the earth, to scout out its condition. And they report back to the Lord God that "all the earth remains at rest." And when we read those words, we think, Oh, how wonderful, all the earth at rest—the guns quiet, the arms stilled, the sounds of battle faded forever. But then, amazingly, in the vision, God rouses himself from his holy dwelling and sets out to disturb that rest. And he himself declares war against the enemies of his people, for earth's tranquility has been won by injustice and oppression, in defiance of his will, and it is, therefore, as John Calvin called it, "an accursed happiness." "Do you think I have come to bring peace on the earth?" Jesus asked, "No, not peace, but a sword," for there can be no peace except it is based on trust and obedience to our God. And so, as in our lesson for the morning from Jeremiah, we cannot reject the Word of God and then claim "peace, peace, when there is no peace" with our Lord. The earth will never know quiet and security and goodness except it stands right with its Maker, for he will upset every accursed happiness that is not based on his will. As Isaiah puts it, "Let them make peace with me, says the Lord, let them make peace with me."

You are probably thinking at this point that you have before you one more enthusiastic preacher who wants to take all the problems of this weary planet and give them that simplistic solution that you can hear from so many TV evangelists—"God is the answer," and if we will just trust him, everything will come up roses. But maybe, just maybe, good Christian friends, Jesus' view of the way to peace is instead a realistic assessment of our human nature. For who are we anyway? Did we create ourselves, each with our unique finger-prints and talents and gestures and consciousness? Did we order the universe, with its intricate ecology, its perfectly balanced interlock-ing of multitudinous life forms? Do we have a purpose that spans all time from stone age to space age and beyond and that steadily plans and prompts the movement of all nations toward one goal of a kingdom on earth? You see, we are not independent centers of self-will who need rely on nothing and no one beyond us. No, we are creatures—the creations of a loving and good Creator who wants us to have abundant life and who has made the world and who is shaping human history to give us that life. And we each were given our individual gifts from him to further that loving purpose, with responsibility always to the one who made us for how we conduct ourselves.

But we have forgotten that, haven't we? We have forgotten that we can never be understood or ever understand ourselves except in relation to our God. And so now we have struck out on our own and decided to follow our own purposes and to run the world according to our own competing wills. And the result has been the chaos of which we read every morning in the newspapers.

But we are not responsible for that chaos, we think. No, it's the system—the system that is wrong. And if we can just fix the system—by reshaping our politics or economics or communications—we can create the peace we long for. And yet, we have the uneasy feeling that we are helpless to do just that—that we are, indeed, a race of impotent human beings trying to manage virile weapons, as one historian put it (Raymond Aron), a race that always manages to come up with new and more imaginative ways of annihilating itself. When Captain Robert Lewis, copilot of the *Enola Gay,* looked down on Hiroshima, he asked in horror, "My God, what have we done?" But, of course, we did what we always do if we can get away with it: We kill one another—and we don't worry about what God thinks of it either.

In his play, *The End of the World,* Arthur Kopit has one of his characters say, "So I sometimes think, now it's all over and we're up there in the big debriefing space in the sky, and the good Lord decides to hold a symposium 'cause he's curious: How did this thing happen? And everybody says, 'Hey, don't look at me. I didn't wanna do it!'" We have struck out on our own—haven't we?—and shed our responsibility to the God who made us. Our Scripture lessons tell us that we shall never have peace as long as we reject our God, because, you see, our God will never settle for less than his abundant life for us, and he knows we cannot have that life except we obey and trust him. Therefore, O Jerusalem, your enemies "will not leave one stone upon another in you; because you did not know the time of your visitation."

If we want to correct that, then our New Testament lesson is also very clear about where to find our God and how to know his will for our lives and thus become peacemakers in our time and place. God comes to us, as he came to Jew and Gentile in first-century Jerusalem, in the person of Jesus of Nazareth. God saw our helplessness before the power struggles and selfish strife of this maddened world. He saw his children wounded, maimed, his lovely earth turned into desolation. And the sight of the suffering and bloodshed and ruin grieved him to his heart. And so God gathered up all his love, all his yearning for life for us, all his purpose for peace and joy, all his words about how to find wholeness, and incarnated them there in his beloved Son and sent him into our situation. And he said to us, "Here, here is your Prince of Peace, the one who can command peace to the nations. Here, here is the one who, if you follow him, can bring light to those who sit in darkness and in the shadow of death. Yes, here is my beloved Son to guide your feet into the way of peace." In Jesus Christ, God visits us, and the question of whether we each will contribute to peacemaking now has to do with whether or not we will live by the truth of that visitation. What shall we do with Christ? Acclaim him as he rides into Jerusalem, crying out with the disciples, "Blessed is the king who comes in the name of the Lord," but then deserting him at the end? Shall we join the mob who wants to crucify him and thinks to be done with him forever, and then simply return to our preoccupation with our own warring wills and ways?

Well, one thing is certain: If we will confess that God has visited us and visits us still in Jesus Christ, then it is going to change the way we work for peace, because it is going to change the way we live our personal lives.

We have some friends in California, who have been very active in the peace movement. The wife converted to Buddhism because she admired some members of that religion who set out to walk from Los Angeles to Washington, D.C., in a plea for peace. And every year the husband sent us a Christmas card, asking that we work for an end to war. But they had trouble in their home. The children went astray, lured off by one or another California fad. The husband had an affair with his secretary. And finally, the news came that their marriage had ended in divorce. And yet, when the husband met my spouse the next year at a conference, his first question was, "What are you doing for peace?"

You see, the peace that trust and obedience to Jesus Christ bring us is very personal, isn't it? Our Lord does not ask us, How many antinuclear demonstrations have you participated in? And he does not question us about whether we are willing to walk from L.A. to Washington, D.C. No, he asks, Are you willing to take up your cross daily and follow me? Are you willing to live by my commandments, no matter what it may cost you? Are you willing to forgive and be reconciled with your husband or wife and thus make peace in your home? Are you willing to spend the hours and give the constant attention it requires to bring up your children in the nurture and admonition of the Lord? Jesus does not command us to love all people on earth. Rather, he gets down to the nitty-gritty of decision by commanding, Love your neighbor! There is what we can do for peace. Not, do you just feel emotional sympathy for the nameless multitudes miles away? But, are you willing to minister to the need of a neighbor whom you do not like very well? What? He is constantly borrowing from you? Then give him more than he asks. What? She is always taking up your time and intruding into your affairs? Then go the second mile and let her know you think she is important.

I had a student in one of my classes at Union Seminary in Richmond, Virginia, where I teach, who used to be a pharmacist. And he told me one day that he decided to come to seminary, after ten years of pharmacy, because he could no longer stand to sell so many tranquilizers. Could that be one of the things the matter with our peacemaking—that in our own personal lives we are seeking the peace that comes from pills and that such an effort is, as Jeremiah says, an attempt to find "peace, peace, when there is no peace"—no peace with God? Oh, yes, if we decide to work for the things that make for peace, by confessing God's visitation of us in Jesus Christ, then it is going to mean a change in the way we live our personal lives.

Let's face it, friends. You and I, by our own individual efforts and by our cooperative work with peace movements around the country, are not going to ensure peace on all the earth and goodwill toward all human beings. Yes, we should constantly work to avert nuclear holocaust. Yes, we should try to disarm all nations. Yes, we should feed the hungry and minister to the poor and win freedom for the captives. But if we do all those things with no regard for how we ourselves are living, and if we think to bring peace on earth, with no recognition that we are responsible to God in Jesus Christ, then all our efforts will end in failure. Human beings, by their own efforts, cannot bring in the Kingdom of God, and, finally, peace on this earth depends on the working of its sovereign Creator. Our only hope and our only trust are that God in Jesus Christ will fulfill his promise and will, indeed, finally command peace to all nations.

If we do trust our God, however, who has visited us in Jesus Christ, and if we do live our lives in responsibility to him, then we can also be assured that there will, indeed, come a day—there will, in fact, come a time—when God's peace will truly come on this earth, even as it is in heaven, for the Prince of Peace has been born into our lives and is now at work to bring in the fullness of God's peaceable kingdom.

You see, our New Testament lesson does not end with Jerusalem about to be destroyed and our Lord weeping over its destruction.

The story continues, the history goes on, first to encompass our killing, with the fairest man of all humankind put to death on a cross by our madness. But then there is that first day of the week, at early dawn, with some women come to his tomb, the stone rolled away, his appearance on the road to Emmaus, and Jesus Christ risen in glory. The Prince of Peace lives, the victor over all our warring evil and the sure guarantee that God will finally guide all the earth into the way of peace. In the words of the psalmist,

> Steadfast love and faithfulness will meet;
>   righteousness and peace will kiss each other.
> Faithfulness will spring up from the ground,
>   and righteousness will look down from the sky.
> Yea, the Lord will give what is good,
>   and our [earth] will yield its increase.
> Righteousness will go before him,
>   and make his footsteps a way. (Ps. 85:10–13)

It is not an idle dream, good Christians. It is the sure outcome of God's work on this earth, because Jesus Christ lives, and he wants life for us, and he cannot be defeated.

But in the meantime, in the meantime, God in Christ can turn us all into peacemakers—instilling in our hearts his love for our neighbors, giving us the power to forgive one another, reconciling husband with wife, parent with child, and all of us to himself so that the peace we live out is, indeed, his peace, in whatever little corner he has placed us. If we trust him and obey his commandments, we can, indeed, know and live out right now the things that make for peace. O Jerusalem, O Christians, do not turn away from this time of your visitation! Amen.

22. A Kind of Loving, for Me
BACCALAUREATE SERMON FOR A PUBLIC HIGH SCHOOL
Walter J. Burghardt

Isa. 40:29–31; Psalm 138

The next fifteen minutes could be painful for you. I don't know
you, except that you seem to "soap" your way out of "The Young
and the Restless." And you don't know me, except that I obviously
stem from a wrinkled stage of humanity. Your pop and rock are not
my mix of music, and my *Swan Lake Ballet* is not likely to turn you
on. We speak a different language, dream different dreams, march
to different drumbeats. And still I shall speak what just might speak
to your hearts; for this afternoon I echo Rod McKuen when he
sings,

> I make words for people I've not met,
> those who will not turn to follow after me.
> It is for me a kind of loving.
> A kind of loving, for me.[1]

At this crucial stage in your growing, as you move from adoles-
cence to young manhood, young womanhood, what is the "kind of
loving" I want to put into words? My springboard is the musical
Godspell, a prayer that goes back to the thirteenth century, a prayer

Walter J. Burghardt, a Jesuit priest, currently is
theologian-in-residence at Georgetown University and is editor in
chief of *Theological Studies.* He has received honorary degress from
many American colleges and universities and is the author of a
number of books, including *Preaching: The Art and the Craft, Lovely in
Eyes Not His,* and *Grace on Crutches.*

with three powerful points: "Dear Lord, these three I pray: to see more clearly, to love more dearly, to follow more nearly." See . . . love . . . follow.

I

First, see more clearly. Today, as in every age, there is a great deal of blindness around. We oldsters—all too many of us—close our eyes to what we do not want to see, what might shake us, shiver us, upset our comfortable life-style, cause us to "toss our cookies." We read that one out of every four children in this "land of the free" is growing up below the poverty line; we read . . . and turn to the comics. We read that in Soviet Central Asia "thousands of infants die within 12 months of birth," that "countless others suffer more slowly, weakened by the heat and infected water, the pesticides from the cotton fields, a diet built on bread and tea and soup";[2] we read . . . and turn to the style section. We read that teenagers are turned on to drugs by the millions, and we shut our eyes; we suggest that our children "say no," and we get "bombed" on our more civilized cocktails. We read that each year in the United States 1.6 million unborn humans are destroyed in the womb, and we close our eyes to everything save my right to choose. We see on prime time a feast of violence and sex, Rambo and porno, and we shrug our shoulders; you can't *prove* it affects our children. We see single parents forced on welfare because it pays more than our shameful minimum wage, and we argue that if they weren't lazy they could find a good job. We see how insider trading and junk bonds can butcher our national and personal budgets, and all too many shake their heads in admiration: "Wish I had thought of that!" And so on into the night.

Graduates of 1990: Don't grow up with blinders! Grow up with eyes wide open, with the peripheral vision you reserve for sports and the opposite sex. Get rid of those cataracts that lay a haze over your understanding. Don't see just what you want to see, what will justify your idea of a "good life," your rosy existence. Open your eyes beyond your backyard, your front lawn, your class, your college, your city, your country—beyond the Redskins and the Caps, beyond Eddie Murphy and the Grateful Dead. Open your eyes wide to *all* your sisters and brothers, black and white, yellow and brown—especially the pimped and the prostituted, the coked and the angel-dusted, those who hunger for bread or justice, for a tomorrow that might be less inhuman than today.

II

But seeing more clearly is not enough. Once you see more clearly, then love more dearly. Not easy. For one thing, *love* is a word much abused. We use it for the sacred covenant between husband and wife and for the unbuttoned promiscuity of "Miami Vice" and the movie channel. We use it for the touching first meeting of adolescents' eyes and for the one-night stands on "Love Boat." We use it for St. Francis of Assisi in love with birds and beasts, with sun and moon, and for every form of sexual abuse. We use it the way Amy Grant sings "Love of Another Kind," and we use it in the new filth that rages through rap and rock.

Genuine love is tough to squeeze into a definition. But if you want to test genuine love against its counterfeits, ask yourself time and again, Where is my focus? on myself or on the other? on my satisfaction or the other's advantage? Am I only a consumer, a taker, a sponger, a leech? Or is my mind-set, How can I help? How much can I give?

Real love is not puppy love; real love is a tough love. It's the tough love that enabled the mother of Detroit Pistons' Isiah Thomas to bring up nine children in an asphalt jungle. It's the tough love that lit up the Potomac in 1981, when Air Florida crashed against the Fourteenth Street Bridge, bodies were flung into the river, a helicopter kept dropping its rescue doughnut, and one drowning passenger kept lifting onto the doughnut one after another people he never knew till the doughnut came down one last time—but he had disappeared beneath the icy waters. It's the tough love that impelled a young nurse-friend of mine to tend an AIDS-afflicted stranger when many a doctor would not go near him. It's the tough love of the Franciscan brothers in Springfield, Illinois, who give their lives for grown men with IQs from zero to thirty-five. It's the tough love of black Sister Thea Bowman, who never let brain cancer slow her wheelchair as she covered the country to bring hope and love to others, as she kept repeating, "I'm too busy to die." But she did— two short months ago.

Such is the mind-set your less fortunate sisters and brothers expect of you. You are gifted beyond the ordinary. The vast majority among you will grace college campuses, some of the country's most prestigious—some even more glamorous than Georgetown! And there you can move either of two ways. You can opt for success 1990 style. I mean, you can roar into the great grade rush with the three goals declared by Harvard freshmen four years ago: (1) money, (2) power, (3) fame. You can decide that in life's game the race is to the swift and the savage, that the meek will never "inherit the earth" (Matt. 5:5), that the gentle only ask to be stepped on, that love is for losers. Or you can echo St. Paul:

> If I speak in the tongues of men and of angels, but
> have not love, I am a noisy gong or a clanging
> cymbal. And if I have prophetic powers, and
> understand all mysteries and all knowledge, and if I
> have all faith, so as to remove mountains, but have
> not love, I am nothing. If I give away all I have,
> and if I deliver my body to be burned, but have not
> love, I gain nothing. (1 Cor. 13:1–3)

III

See more clearly, love more dearly. One need remains: Follow more nearly. Put more concretely, you need role models. I'm sure you have them, whatever you might call them. TV ads live off them, off your hero worship. For flying through the air with the greatest of ease: Michael Jordan. For stealing ninety feet of turf: Ricky Henderson. For a real man in your life: Kevin Costner. For a vibrant woman: Madonna. For a group to turn you on: Red Hot Chili Peppers.

I am not about to laugh at such role models; I refuse to knock them. They can be important for certain stages of your life, for aspects of who you are. I simply submit that at this turn in your life the people you need to follow after should be such as touch your deepest desires, your dearest dreams, people who inspire you to give yourself totally to a cause, to life at its richest, to others.

I mean Martin Luther King, Jr. Whatever your color, here is a man you can follow with your whole mind and heart. Not reproduce every individual thing he did, every single march. More importantly, follow his dream that one day "all of God's children, black and white, Jews and Gentiles, Protestants and Catholics, will be able to join hands and sing, 'Free at last! Free at last! Thank God Almighty, we

are free at last!' " And work for that freedom, not like another ram-
paging Rambo, but without violence, with only the kind of love that
is stronger than death. The kind of love that destroyed Dr. King's
flesh and, from his death, raised up free men and women. The kind
of love that made a white society weep for its racial sins.

I mean Mother Teresa. Whatever your religion, here is a woman
you can follow with all your soul and strength. Not follow her to
India; not pick up from Calcutta's streets 54,000 homeless and watch
23,000 of them die in your room; not ask for the unborn and newborn nobody wants; not even physically cradle the AIDS-infected.
Rather, the conviction that each person whose path you cross—
however outrageously he or she looks or talks or smells—is a child
of God, shaped in God's image; that the standard of genuinely
human living is not the millions you amass, the power you control,
the fame that flings adoring teenagers at your feet, but the way you
treat the least of your sisters and brothers, how well you can walk in
the shoes of the less fortunate.

For those of you who claim to be Christian, I mean, above all
else, a man who was crucified between two thieves two thousand
years ago. I mean the Jesus who wrote and sang, lived and died the
best-selling, longest-lasting pop of them all: "Greater love than this
no one has, to lay down life itself for friends" (John 15:13).

For those of you who follow the faith of Abraham, you who lost
six million brothers and sisters in the Nazi Holocaust we Gentiles
prefer to forget, you whose forebears have been tempted to conclude that "God died in Auschwitz," I give you the remarkable rabbi
Abraham Joshua Heschel:

> To meet a human being is a major challenge to
> mind and heart. I must recall what I normally
> forget. A person is not just a specimen of the
> species called *homo sapiens.* He is all of humanity in
> one, and whenever one man is hurt we are all
> injured. . . . To meet a human being is an
> opportunity to sense the image of God, *the presence*
> of God. According to a rabbinical interpretation,
> the Lord said to Moses: "Wherever you see the
> trace of man there I stand before you. . . ."[3]

For those of you whose eyes are fixed on Islam, by all means
follow "the Prophet." But follow him "more nearly." In harmony

with your sacred Koran, submit yourself completely to the one and only God; worship him alone and live according to his law; don't be distracted by the idols of this world: riches, social position, pride, greed.

Am I giving the back of my hand to excellence? Not at all. I simply want you to grasp what human excellence really is. Am I denouncing money, power, fame? Quite the contrary. I simply want you to ask yourself a three-letter word: Why? Why money? Why power? Why fame? Money to line your own pockets, build a million-dollar condo, buy sex and crack, or to lift your sisters and brothers from the grime and grit of the slums? Power to lord it over others, muscle your way into the corridors of the mighty, or to give power to the powerless, hope to the hopeless? Fame to swell your ego or fame to let the less privileged get to know you, to learn from you, to profit from your love?

A final word. St. Matthew's Gospel has a fascinating parable (Matt. 25:14–30). A rich CEO goes off on a business trip. Before leaving for Dulles, he gives each of three employees a fair amount of money to invest. On his return, he asks an accounting. The first two have done fabulously at the stock exchange: Their investment has doubled. "Well done, gentlemen!" Up comes employee number 3. "Sir, all of us know you're a hard man to please. I was afraid; so I hid your money; here it is, exactly what you gave me." The CEO blows a final fuse: "You worthless piece of garbage! Out you go into the darkness!"

What is the Gospel telling you? That to live the way God wants you to live, you have to risk. I mean, expose yourself to loss or injury, to disadvantage or destruction, perhaps even to death. You have to take chances. The critical question you must decide is, What's worth living for, risking for, dying for? How much are you willing to risk for your dream? Will you play it safe, always punt on fourth down and one? Or will you "go for broke," invest everything you have for a dream that grabs you, a dream shaped of love, a dream that just might make your little world more human?

A recent award winner at the Cannes film festival has a loser-friendly lover, Lula, claiming that the "whole world's wild at heart and weird on top."[4] That may well be. But from all I hear about you, I have high hopes that you may tame some of the wildness at the world's heart, humanize some of the weirdness at the top. In any event, now you know why

I make words for people I've not met,
those who will not turn to follow after me.
It is for me a kind of loving.
A kind of loving, for me.

NOTES

1. Rod McKuen, *Listen to the Warm* (New York: Random House, 1969), 112.

2. *Washington Post,* 22 May 1990, A1.

3. Abraham Joshua Heschel, "No Man Is an Island," *Union Theological Seminary Quarterly* 21 (1965–66):121.

4. See the review by Richard Corliss, "Unlaced and Weird on Top," *Time,* 4 June 1990, 79.

23. The Distorted and the Natural

SERMON FOR LENT I

Allan M. Parrent

Luke 4:1–13

From the Gospel appointed for the first Sunday in Lent: "And Jesus, full of the Holy Spirit, returned from the Jordan, and was led by the Spirit for forty days in the wilderness, tempted by the devil." This is the first week in Lent. Its theme is temptation, and nothing is more tempting to the Church than to be in step with the spirit of the age, to be relevant. That is not a bad thing in and of itself. It is, in fact, commendable and imperative, lest the Church become that backwater of irrelevance it is sometimes accused of being by its cultured despisers. But it is commendable only until the compulsion for relevance or accommodation to the culture become controlling, only until the Church begins to substitute the zeitgeist for its own vision and tradition. As Dean Inge of St. Paul's Cathedral warned years ago, "When the church marries the spirit of the age, it will be left a widow in the next generation." There is a difference between a dialogue with the spirit of the age from a sure foundation and the temptation to relinquish the Church's theological and ethical birthright for the pottage of relevance. There is a difference between making Christianity intelligible to the culture and the temptation to make it merely palatable.

Allan M. Parrent, who holds a Ph.D. from Duke University, currently serves as professor of Christian ethics, associate dean for academic affairs, and vice-president at Episcopal Theological Seminary in Virginia. Dr. Parrent writes and speaks frequently on ethical issues.

I. The Temptation to Distort

Temptation is, among other things, an urge or attractive inducement not necessarily to do evil but to act out of character or out of keeping with our real identity and self-understanding. Jesus, led into the wilderness after his baptism, knew that kind of temptation. Temptation is to feel drawn to behave in ways contrary to our vision of the highest good or contrary to our prior commitments. Jesus also knew that kind of temptation. To succumb to such temptation, either individually or institutionally, is in some fundamental sense to act unnaturally. It is to distort what we essentially are and know ourselves called to be. So before we succumb to such temptation we may, consciously or unconsciously, simply adopt as our own the conventional views of what is good or right or natural. We may narrow our vision of truth to accommodate to the spirit of the age. And, eventually, we may forget that there is a difference between them.

Flannery O'Connor, a writer who wrote explicitly out of a Christian vision, was one who understood the basic difference between what is natural and in accord with ultimate reality and what is a distortion. She also understood the difficulty of conveying that difference to a world that was itself distorted. She once wrote, "The novelist with Christian concerns will find in modern life distortions which are repugnant to him, and his problem will be to make these appear as distortions to an audience which is used to seeing them as natural." Now that's not a bad definition of evangelism—to proclaim the truth that distortions are, in fact, distortions to an audience used to seeing them as natural and also to set forth the vision by the light of which the distinction can be made.

O'Connor wrote about sin and redemption. Her characters were backwoods misfits, the physically malformed, profane Bible salesmen, and others who have been referred to as "rural grotesques." She was often asked why southern writers seemed to have such a penchant for writing about freaks. Her reply was inevitably, "It is because we are still able to recognize one. To be able to recognize a freak, you have to have some conception of the whole person." In order to recognize distortions, we must have some conception of the natural. In order to recognize what is deformed, we must have some conception of wholeness. In order to identify what is ignoble or base, we must have some conception of what is noble or virtuous. In order to recognize wrong, we must have some conception of right. In order to recognize evil, we must have some conception of the good. If we have no criteria for making these distinctions, we have no basis for making moral judgments except personal whim, and that of course only makes us slaves to our passions. Without more ultimate criteria, we have no basis for moral decision making and action except our own advantage.

II. Three Examples

I'm sure I am not alone in believing that in our culture we are accustomed to seeing and adjusting to much that, from any sound Christian social vision, is distorted. It is one thing to recognize deformity, to work to change what can be changed, and to live with the perennial imperfections of what Niebuhr called "proximate solutions to insoluble problems." The temptation, however, is to accept the distortion as natural and normative. On this day when the Episcopal church remembers its first black priest, Absalom Jones, we need to remind ourselves that the Church itself at one time accepted the gross distortions of slavery and segregation as natural and normative.

I will give you three other examples.

An example from the business world: A few years ago there was a best-selling self-help manual entitled *Success!* It is a book on how to make it in the business world. In the first chapter, the writer establishes his norms: "It's OK to be greedy. It's OK to look out for #1. It's OK to be Machiavellian if you can get away with it. It's OK to recognize that honesty is not always the best policy." Success, he says, means getting over worrying about the moral content of what you do, because "morality has very little to do with success." Success is form, not substance; it is chauffeurs and private dining rooms, not quality of work or serving neighbor needs. Success is getting to the top of the ladder by any means available and feeling comfortable about it. Far from identifying such things as deformities, the book embraces them and calls them natural, right, good. It was on this nation's best-seller list for months. There is within the classical Christian tradition a different vision for economic life. It has to do with serving our neighbors through our vocations. It has to do with sharing in God's creativity by producing and distributing goods and services to meet human needs.

An example from the political world: The vocation of politics, which Luther correctly described once as one of the highest callings a Christian could undertake, provides an unlimited number of examples in which distortions are accepted as natural and normative. One example is the concern in political campaigns for marketing an image that sells, rather than for the values that should shape our laws and social arrangements.

Another is the emphasis on how government can best serve me and my group rather than on the civic virtues required to maintain a functioning democracy that will best serve the common good. For example, few even question the moral legitimacy of the query, "Are *you* better off now than you were four years ago?" We are not unaccustomed to seeing a complete inversion of what civic virtue means in political life. Apparently, many even accept the inversion as natural. There was a time in our recent political history, for example, when a strong man was one who succumbed to White House pressure to commit crimes, and a trustworthy man was one who could be relied on to lie to a grand jury. In that kind of distorted moral universe, corruption becomes virtuous and integrity becomes a refuge for scoundrels. There is within the classical Christian tradition a different vision for political life. It has to do with justice, the common welfare, and the cultivation of civic virtue.

An example from education: Several decades of value-free education have given us a generation that is unaccustomed to reasoned moral discourse and uncomfortable with moral argument. We are no longer able as a society to engage in careful moral reasoning, precisely at a time when sensitive moral imagination is most sorely needed.

When value questions are ignored because values are considered to be based only on subjective feelings or private opinion, then moral reason is ruled out of public discourse and only technical reason remains. The key questions of life then become technical and utilitarian. Will it work? Will it succeed? Is it cost-effective? Is it efficient? Will it get me what I happen to want at the moment? As the ultimate questions, those are insufficient, to say the least, especially in an age of electronic listening devices, in vitro fertilization, nuclear-tipped cruise missiles, and perpetual life-support systems. The problem is that portraying such functional questions as the bottom-line questions seems so natural to those who have been educated to see them as natural. There is within the classical Christian tradition a different vision for the life of the mind and a different understanding of the relationship of facts and values.

III. Jesus' Temptation in the Wilderness

The question Lent poses in these and other areas of our lives, such as marriage or sexual behavior, is, How do we respond to the temptation to accept the cultural norm as normative, the common as natural, the expected as the obligatory? In fact, how do we tell one from the other? How do we respond to the temptation to make every action open to being redescribed as good or natural or loving, thereby making it possible, for example, to equate adultery with love?

Here we can turn to the Gospel account of Jesus' temptation in the wilderness. You recall the nature of the temptations.

1. "If you are the Son of God, command this stone to become bread." Jesus could, of course, fulfill both his own legitimate physical needs and popular messianic hopes by such an action. But he replied by quoting God's words to Israel in another wilderness, "Man shall not live by bread alone."

2. "I will give you the authority and glory of the kingdoms of the world if you will worship me." Certainly a little pragmatic obeisance to the prince of this world would be a small price to pay for the prize of the very kingdoms Jesus had been sent to win. But Jesus again replied by quoting from the wilderness Torah: "It is written, you shall worship the Lord your God, and him only shall you serve."

3. "If you are the Son of God, throw yourself down from the pinnacle of the Temple, for it is written, he will give his angels charge over you, to guard you." Here was a chance to prove Jesus' messiahship to himself and others, and to test and prove God's power and faithfulness. But Jesus for the third time quoted God's words to Israel in the wilderness: "You shall not tempt the Lord your God."

IV. Three Questions

The first question is, What is Jesus doing here? That might be answered in a number of ways. But one thing he is doing is discerning and declaring the difference between what is distorted and what is natural. He is separating the distortions of popular messianic expectations from what he discerns as natural, that is, from what the Father called the Son to be and do. He is separating the spirit of the age from the Spirit of the Lord.

The second question is, Why did Jesus act as he did? For at least two reasons. First, Jesus had an identity. He knew who he was. His response to temptation was a "natural" response, given his understanding of his unique identity and vocation. He acted "in character." His being determined his doing. At his baptism, a voice from heaven declared, "Thou art my beloved son; with thee I am well pleased." In the wilderness, that identity was examined and questioned. The temptation was to understand his identity and mission in ways that were both seemingly reasonable and devilishly attractive. But he rejected alien ideas of messiahship because he identified himself as the radically obedient Son of God in the wilderness, in contrast to Israel, the disobedient children of God in another wilderness. Knowing his identity, then, he had a perspective and a foundation from which he could discern what was distorted or out of character and what was not.

The second reason Jesus acted as he did was that he had a tradition, a tradition that informed his actions, nurtured him, and also freed him. Jesus' criterion for his action was clearly not success, popularity, image, self-interest, or power. Rather, it was the authority of his tradition and his faithfulness to it. Now, *tradition* is often seen as a bad word, sometimes deservedly so. But those Old Testament prophets with whom Jesus identified at Nazareth were traditionalists all the way, calling Israel back to its roots and seeking to distinguish distorted tradition from the real thing. Just as they did, Jesus put himself under the authority of Scripture and tradition and, thus, under the authority of God. This gave him a firm foundation on which to stand.

My musical tastes do not run particularly to jazz, but I do admire the ability of a good jazz group to improvise without getting completely lost. If a jazz group is to be free to do what it is intended to do (i.e., improvise), it must first understand and internalize the basics, the tradition. And somebody—the bassist or drummer—must hold the line and keep the improvisation rooted in musical reality. Otherwise, we have not music but chaos. Jesus the Improvisor was first Jesus the Traditionalist.

The third question is, What gospel is contained in this story for us, and what are its implications? The gospel is that in Christ we, too, have an identity. Like him, we have been called by God and given a special identity in baptism. We have been named Christian, sealed by the Holy Spirit, and marked as Christ's own forever. In one of our baptismal prayers, we ask for three things: that the Holy Spirit will sustain us, so that we may act in "character" and in keeping with our identity; that we will receive discerning hearts, so that we may distinguish the distorted from the natural; and that we will have the courage and will to persevere, so that when tempted we can say with Luther, "I have been baptized." The gospel tells us that these baptismal gifts are free and available.

Finally, the implication of that gospel is that we, too, have a tradition and that we who bear the name *Christian* are called to pursue what have been called "the intimations of our tradition." We are part of the historic Christian community and its tradition. The Church is the primary bearer of that tradition, and Scripture is the primary voice within it. By tradition, I do not mean frozen dogma or practice. Rather, I mean a continuity of faith and experience, always reforming but also always rooted in "that which we have received," not in "that which we have invented." When it needs correcting, the best source for the corrective can most often be found in the tradition itself.

All traditions can, of course, become idolatrous. That danger seems rather moot, however, in what used to be called mainline Christianity and in a denomination that was the subject a few years ago of that famous *Harper's* article entitled "Trendier than Thou." The gospel not only gives us our identity in Christ; it also calls us to the task of pursuing the intimations of the classical Christian tradition for the economic, political, social, sexual, familial, and all other arenas of contemporary life. Without it, we have no sure way of recognizing distortions in a world that thinks they are natural and no clear basis for resisting the temptation to call them good.

24. Caught in the Act
James Ayers

Gal. 6:1–10

I thought I would remember. I didn't think I'd have any trouble with it at all. I wanted to quote from the song from the musical *The Fantasticks.* Not everyone knows the show itself, which is about a girl and boy growing up next door to each other and the efforts of their fathers to raise them right and eventually to get them to fall in love with each other. But everyone remembers the song that came out of it, "Try to Remember." Well, as late as yesterday evening—after the library was closed, of course—I still couldn't remember how one of the couplets in it goes. I called a bunch of people on the phone, and they couldn't remember either. Several of us agreed that this is the kind of September worth remembering, but we still couldn't come up with the right lines.

And then, I remembered.

> Try to remember the kind of September
> When grass was green and grain was yellow.
> Try to remember the kind of September
> When life was sweet and oh, so mellow.
> Try to remember when hearts were so tender
> That love was an ember about to billow.
> Try to remember, and if you remember, then
>   follow.

Try to remember. Try to remember back to where you had so many plans and so many hopes. Try to remember back to when you felt the fire blazing within you, when all the days burst forth with

---

James Ayers is pastor of First Presbyterian Church in Waltham, Massachusetts. He received his master of divinity degree from Gordon-Conwell Theological Seminary. Ayers is well versed in seven languages and has held many teaching and pastoral positions.

color and the world burst forth with love. Try to remember back to how you thought life was always going to be. Why hasn't it ended up that way? Try to remember. Because, you see, you might not remember. It could be that it happened too long ago, that once upon a time you felt all those things, but now it's been too many years. Maybe you don't remember, anymore. All that's left is this wistful notion that it might have been nice. Maybe even that's fading. All of it's really too far gone even to remember anymore.

The other song I remember from the show is the one the two fathers sing about the trials of raising children. Kids are so unpredictable. Gardening is better, they say. It's reliable: You know you're going to get what you planted. But you never know for sure how kids will end up: maybe the way you planned, maybe not. "Plant a radish; get a radish, not a Brussels sprout," they sing. "That's why I like vegetables: You know what you're about."

You can never tell about other people. You want to believe the best about them. You want to believe that their intentions are good; you want to believe that they are sincerely trying, to the best of their ability, to do what's right. And then something happens. You weren't planning to check up on them, exactly, but you run into them at the wrong moment, and there they are, caught in the act. No way of pretending it didn't happen. No way to figure out some rationalization about how things can still go on the same. What do you do?

What you've got to do, Paul says, is restore them, gently. It's easy enough to cut them down, to gossip about them, to humiliate them. Instead, you've got to help put them back together. You've got to help bear their burden for a while, until they can bear it for themselves again.

There's no shortage of people doing things wrong, being angry or self-centered or jealous or spiteful, right out in public where you can't help catching them right in the act. When that happens, it's no particular trick to be angry or self-centered or jealous or spiteful right back. It's not much effort just to write them off either: to blow the dust away, to judge them and condemn them, and to tell everyone else—just in passing—about how bad they are and how bad they treated you. But we who identify ourselves as followers of Christ must do something else instead, Paul says. We have to figure out how to restore them. We have to figure out how to make things right again. We have to figure out how to help them bear that burden, so that the pain and wrongness of what they did can be wiped clean.

Why must we do this? There is a reason, Paul says. Don't be deceived about this. God cannot be mocked. You're going to reap what you sow. If you live your life a certain way, that's the kind of person you are going to end up being.

We usually read those lines as a warning to people who consistently practice what we might call an evil life-style. If you go on living your life in a destructive way, don't be surprised if it ends up destroying you. "You reap what you sow," we mutter, shaking our heads at how someone's life has gone wrong, at the obvious consequences of the way they were living.

I think it's true enough that there are often bad consequences to the bad choices we make. But Paul's idea includes more than just that. "You reap what you sow," also means that we will find good consequences resulting from our good choices. And it means—and this is maybe the hardest part—it means that there will be blah consequences resulting from our blah choices.

We don't have control over every detail in our lives. Far from it. And yet to quite a large extent, we decide what kind of people we are going to be. What you plant in your life is what's going to grow there. If you plant a radish, you're going to get a radish, not a Brussels sprout. You can't make that kind of decision for your kids; you can't decide what kind of people your children will become. But you can decide "what kind of people" you yourself will become. If you want the ground to bring forth wheat, you have to plant wheat; it's no good planting crabgrass. If you want roses, then you have to plant roses. Scattering dandelion seeds just will not do it.

And yet a lot of the times we miss this. We go from day to day as if each day's choices didn't make much difference. "I want to make my decisions my own way, for the time being," we say to ourselves. "Not forever; but for the moment I'd rather make my own rules as I go along. Later on I'll probably change. I'll be different then."

Usually, we blame this on teenagers, don't we? "Don't worry, eventually I'm going to be hardworking and responsible. But until then I want to be able to go places and do things right on the spur of the moment. I want to have the freedom to have fun, instead of always having to worry about schedules and responsibilities."

But it isn't just the teens. It's all of us. Right now, we are each of us making choices about who we are. Right now, I'm caught in the act of being who I am. Right now, I'm caught in the act of sowing—

wild oats?—sowing, or planting, the kind of person that I am and that I'm going to be. Don't be deceived. God cannot be mocked. What we plant and cultivate right now is the kind of person that we will be.

Think about this for a moment. How often do you run into someone who says, "When I grow up, I want to be a mean and spiteful person. Miserly. Jealous. Greedy. I want to be the kind of person who always makes sure I get what I want, even if you've got it now, even if I have to step on you pretty hard when I take it away from you. When I grow up I want to be able to do whatever I want whenever I want to. If I feel like being ugly to people, I just will, just because I don't want to bother trying to be nice." Or someone who says, "I want to be an angry person. Vicious. Malicious. I want to be someone who holds a grudge. I want to have a memory that is supremely ready to remember what you did wrong and ready to put you on the rack for it all over again, ready to put in the knife and give it a good hard twist. That's what I'd like to be."

No one talks as if that's what they want. But a lot of us get caught in the act of becoming that kind of person. Why are there angry people? or jealous people? or bitter people? Did they say, "That's what I want to be when I grow up"? No. When they try to remember the fires of September of passion and hope from days gone by, it wasn't filled with longings for vindictiveness or spite. They dreamed of a life filled with love, joy, peace, patience, kindness, goodness, faithfulness, gentleness, and self-control. That's what they dreamed of. But those weren't the choices they made. And they got caught in the act of making those other choices over and over again. And what they kept on planting in their lives came to the harvest: They became the kind of people that they had cultivated themselves to be.

What happens when you run into someone like that? Most of the time we want to run the other way. But what we have to do instead, Paul insists, is figure out how to restore them.

How do we do that? Sometimes we might respond with something as simple as asking, "What would it be like if the two of you could be friends again?" Or, "If you could see God work one change in your life over the next few months, what would you pick?" Don't take words like these as a formula, though, or as a magic spell that makes everything better. Questions like these may well help the process of bringing healing and grace in the midst of brokenness, but it doesn't happen in just a few moments. There's no easy answer, no canned sentence, no one thing that you can memorize and do by rote.

It takes work and commitment. It won't ever become automatic. But we could decide that we want to learn how. And perhaps we could learn to begin by asking the question, "Lord Jesus, in this situation that is so painful and torn, what do you want me to do?" That might put us on the right track. And maybe, if we decide to ask that question regularly and honestly, maybe the answer won't be so hard to hear.

Take a look again at this section we read for the morning lesson. The passage keeps talking about how the people in the Church need to relate to one another. When someone is caught in the act of some sin, restore them gently. Carry each other's burdens. Don't deceive yourself about your own actions; don't deceive yourself about the consequences of your own actions. Don't get tired of doing good to each other; instead, do something special whenever you have the chance and particularly among these people in the family of believers. There's even a verse about making sure you pay the preacher well.

But this all points us toward the fact that there is a reason why Paul puts this admonition about "you reap what you sow" right in the middle of this passage about how people ought to treat each other in the Church. It's because whether or not you choose to be a reconciler has a direct effect on what kind of person you are going to become. When someone does something wrong, when they've become demeaning or demanding or dishonest, when they've gotten caught in the act of making that kind of choice so often that they've become that kind of person, when they are caught in the act of making that kind of choice toward you, at that same moment you are being caught in the act of making a choice of your very own. Will you choose to be a person who works for reconciliation? Or will you choose to be a person who responds to their bad choice with a fair share of anger, bitterness, and spite of your own? Or will you choose not to care one way or the other—if they want to be ugly, I'll just let them be ugly? Don't be deceived. God cannot be mocked. You reap what you sow. What you plant in your life is what's going to grow in your life. If you cultivate a response of anger and bitterness, that's the kind of person you will become. If you plant an attitude of not caring what they do, you will harvest an uncaring personality for yourself. But if you make the choice of being a reconciler, if you make the effort to plant in your life what will please the Holy Spirit, if you cultivate within yourself the attitude that says, "In Jesus Christ, all of us are one, and so I will work to restore this person in gentleness and love"—if you decide to plant that in your life, then that's what's going to grow. You will become the kind of person who knows how to treat others better than they deserve. You will become a person of compassion. You will reap a life where you get to see all the fruit of the Spirit growing to fulfillment—in you.

I have an expectation that each of us is going to get caught in the act today. Sometime in the next few hours it's going to happen: You are going to realize that someone you know is falling short of what they're supposed to be. They aren't behaving the way you would expect a follower of Jesus to behave. At the moment that you see that they're doing it wrong, you're caught in the act: in the act of choosing what kind of person you are going to be. Someone who retaliates. Someone who doesn't care. Or someone who restores and reconciles. Don't be deceived. God cannot be mocked. You will reap what you sow. When you get caught today in the act of choosing what kind of person you are going to be, choose wisely.

25. Is Sex Ever Safe?
Richard Groves

Gen. 3:6–12, 16

I

Has it ever happened to you that, in the course of a conversation, a word you use every day or a phrase you hear all the time suddenly sounds new to your ears, as though you had never heard it before, and because of its newness you realize for the first time how peculiar the word or phrase is? That happened to me recently when I was participating in a meeting with the chaplains at Wake Forest University. They were planning a panel discussion in which they were going to present their views on the meaning of sexuality. In the course of the meeting one of the chaplains used the phrase *safe sex.*

We hear the phrase *safe sex* frequently—in public service announcements encouraging people to "take precautions" lest one or other of the partners contract a sexually transmitted disease or in commercials advertising products that will enable people to take such precautions. But for the first time, the phrase struck me as curious. Safe sex. As opposed to what—unsafe sex? Dangerous sex? Is sex dangerous?

Students at Wake Forest University are being given precisely that message—that sex is or can be dangerous. Beginning in the fall, 1989, every first-year student is being required to have a fifteen-minute conference with a counselor for the purpose of learning ways to avoid contracting a sexually transmitted disease (STD, for those of you who wish to keep up with the latest acronyms). The students

---

Richard Groves, who holds a Ph.D. from Baylor University, is pastor of Wake Forest Baptist Church in North Carolina. Groves is also president of the Southern Baptist Alliance. He has published many articles in *The Christian Century* and other magazines and journals.

are being given a brochure published by the American College Health Association. The brochure is titled "Making Sex Safer." On the back of the brochure is a listing of various amorous activities, ranked according to whether they are "dangerous," "risky," "less risky," or "safe."

Is sex dangerous? If so, can it be made safe? In an effort to answer these two questions on the basis of the biblical revelation, I propose that we turn to the marvelously provocative tale of the Garden of Eden, narrowing the focus of our attention to the relationship between Adam and Eve, as a man and a woman, from the beginning of their being together—the creation of Eve—to their expulsion from the garden.

What will such a narrowing of our focus accomplish? The Garden of Eden story can be understood as a tale told to explain why certain features of life are the way they are (e.g., why snakes crawl on their bellies, why women give birth in such pain, etc.). That being the case, the story would seem to serve the purpose of explaining some things about human relations and human sexuality. For example, why is it that when a man and a woman come together in marriage they become united in such a deep, powerful, mysterious, spiritual way? Why is it that in ways they do not understand their sexual union both feeds and is fed by their spiritual union? Why is it that it is not always like that? Why is it that sometimes sex and spirit becomes separated, and sex becomes either shallow and superficial or abusive and coercive? The story was written, in part, to explain why things are the way they are between human beings. That being the case, an investigation into the ancient tale might help us to answer the question, Is sex ever safe? Let us, then, return to the Garden of Eden.

II

Adam was created of dust and the breath of God, according to the ancient story, combining within himself matter and spirit, the earthly and the divine. It is a wonderfully tantalizing image—dust and the breath of God—giving expression to the intuitive grasp the Scripture writers had of both the glory and the frustration inherent in human nature. The glory is that, though we are dust-born and dust-bound, nonetheless there has been breathed into us the very breath of God. That is what amazed the psalmist:

> When I look at thy heavens, the work of thy fingers,
>   the moon and the stars which thou hast
>   established;
> what is man that thou art mindful of him,
>   and the son of man that thou dost care for him?
> Thou hast made him a little less than God,
>   and crowned him with glory and honor.
>
>   (Psalm 8: 3–5)

Dust animated by the very life of God. That is our glory. Our frustration is that, though it is the very breath of God which animates us, nonetheless we never get over being dust. "God has put eternity into our minds," wrote the author of Ecclesiastes, "but not in such a way that we can understand what God has been doing from beginning to end!" (Eccles. 3:11). Shakespeare knew the glory and the frustration, the agony and the ecstasy. "What a piece of work is man! How like a god—the beauty of the world; the paragon of animals . . . [the] quintessence of dust" (*Hamlet* 2:2). Thus was Adam created.

However lofty the concept was, however impressive the design, nonetheless the divine pronouncement on Adam was, "It is not good—it is not good that the man should be alone." So God created the woman. Out of the man's own body, the woman was created. "Bone of my bone and flesh of my flesh," a Hebrew cliché we find elsewhere in the Old Testament. Its meaning was similar to our own cliché, "my own flesh and blood," which we do not mean literally but which, because of its potential as a literalism, speaks powerfully, if crudely, of the oneness we feel with those to whom we are related. The image suggests in mythological terms that the desire woman and man have for one another is a longing to overcome their separateness and to reestablish their lost unity.

So Adam and Eve were together in the garden. The nature of their being together is captured in yet another powerful phrase: "They were naked yet without shame." There is a relationship between physical nakedness and honesty, openness, and truthfulness that has been seen by many peoples and has been preserved in language. We speak of the "naked truth," by which we mean truth that is unadorned, truth that is not disguised, truth that is presented just the way it is. "Naked yet without shame," then, speaks of the intimate relationship between Adam and Eve. They were "naked," that is, they were completely open and honest, totally truthful with one another. They were ashamed of neither their bodies nor themselves. The baring of their souls was symbolized in the baring of their bodies.

To be stripped of every layer of pretense, every defense mechanism, every self-protective device—the glib one-liner, the knowing laugh, the smug smile, the haughty expression—and to be seen by another human being in one's "nakedness" can be a terrifying experience. But it was not so in Eden. For sin had not yet entered the lives of Adam and Eve; trust had not yet turned to distrust; security had not yet turned to insecurity; love had not yet turned to fear; and intimacy—the modern catchword for openness based on love and trust—was the most natural way to live. There was no risk involved. Adam and Eve were in no danger of being hurt. They were not vulnerable. Intimacy was easy in Eden.

The Church has traditionally viewed this earliest stage in the relationship between Adam and Eve as a time of innocence. Dreaming innocence, Paul Tillich called it. It was not the "real world," the one we know. Intimacy is not easy in the real world, which is the only world in which human beings have ever lived. Intimacy is the courage to risk openness in a post-Eden world. Wherever it occurs, it is a victory over sin. But we are getting ahead of ourselves.

Sin entered the lives of Adam and Eve. And when sin entered, everything changed. "They knew that they were naked." But they had known that before. What was different? Now they were ashamed. It was not simply that they were embarrassed—shame is more than being embarrassed. It was not simply that they felt guilty—shame is more even than feeling guilty. They were ashamed. Shame—that uniquely human emotion. Self-disgust. Self-loathing. Humiliating disgrace.

"They sewed fig leaves together and made themselves aprons." The purpose of the aprons was to hide themselves from one another. They had bared their souls as well as their bodies to one another, and in the state of innocence, that was safe. But in a state of sin, they weren't sure it was safe anymore. They were not sure they could risk being vulnerable. Better in such a state to hide one's self than to take a chance revealing one's self.

When they found they could no longer trust one another, the nature of their being together changed as well. They were still together, but a wall of distrust had been built between them, a wall they would henceforth have to work to scale if they were to find each other, for it could never be torn down completely. When God asked Adam how it came about that he had eaten of the forbidden fruit, he pointed to Eve, the one of whom he had once said, "bone of my bone and flesh of my flesh," and said, "The woman . . . gave me of the fruit of the tree. . . ." He did not even call her by name; she was "the woman." His sin was her fault. In their sin, they became divided against one another. They no longer spoke of "us"; now they spoke of "you and me." They were together, but they were no longer in union with one another.

But that was not the final state of the relationship between Adam and Eve. God meted out the punishment for their sin. Eve's punishment was that she would desire her husband, but he would dominate her. The Bible doesn't say so, but that was Adam's punishment, too—that he would dominate his wife. For any superior/inferior relationship between human beings—whether between masters and slaves, employers and employees, or husbands and wives—demeans and diminishes one as much as the other. (Let all those who believe that male domination is divinely ordained please note that Adam's dominance over Eve was not the intention of God; it was the consequence and the evidence of their sin!)

One way to talk about sin is to say that it is the separation of the physical and spiritual dimensions of life. It is stripping the physical realm of any spiritual meaning or significance, so that the physical realm becomes barren. It simply is what it appears to be and nothing more. For Adam and Eve, the physical and the spiritual became separated. And when sex and spirit are separated, sex either becomes superficial, "casual," "recreational," or a means of domination, intimidation, threat. For Adam and Eve, it became the latter. The loss of their spiritual union—the loss of the trust that had made "naked but without shame" possible—meant that from that time onward their relationship would be characterized by being cautious and wary rather than by being free and open; by protecting their vulnerabilities rather than by relaxing in their loved one's acceptance; by hiding from one another rather than by being open with one another. They would continue to relate sexually—the next chapter tells of the birth of their children—but it would never again be the same.

So at the conclusion of the story, we see Adam and Eve walking out of the garden, expelled by God, forever to wander the earth looking for Eden, the mythic garden of bliss. Adam, we might imagine, walks a good ten feet ahead.

III

Let us return to the two questions we asked at the outset of this sermon. First, is sex dangerous? Most assuredly, sex has the potential for being very dangerous. It was not so before sin entered the story. But it is so now. And we cannot go back. We live post-Eden. We live in a world in which everything is infected by sin, especially our relationships with other people, most especially our sexual relationships.

Of course, the notion that sex is dangerous is not news to anyone. Older generations in every age have used danger as a way to keep younger generations sexually inactive for as long as possible. But what is the nature of the danger? Is it AIDS? Is it some other sexually transmitted disease? Is it pregnancy? Of course, it is all these things. And we would be foolhardy if we were to say otherwise. The terror and the devastation wrought by AIDS and the twin perils of abortion or unwanted children are shredding the very fabric of our society. But the possibility of disease or pregnancy is only part of the dangerous potential of sex. The greater danger—greater in the sense of the number of people who can be and are being hurt—is the violation that becomes possible when people are completely open with one another and, therefore, vulnerable to one another. There are no statistics to indicate the number of wounded, for humiliation drives us inward and renders us unlikely to share our shame, but the anecdotal evidence is staggering.

Second, if sex is dangerous, can it be made safe? That depends. If sex means having intercourse, that and nothing more, then "taking precautions" will make sex safe. And I would be irresponsible if I did not say that I am in favor of safe sex in this limited sense. But if sex, by its very nature, is more than that, if it is inextricably wed to our spirituality as well as to our physicality, if it has to do with the question whether we will be naked with or without shame, then the answer to the question, Can sex be made safe? is no, not completely, not ever. Sex was safe in Eden. But nothing is safe after Eden. That being the case, we run the greatest risk of all when we think we have made sex safe simply because we have "taken precautions"! And that is the danger of having fifteen-minute conferences about safe sex! All you can do in fifteen minutes is talk about sexuality in its most superficial sense and safety in its most limited sense. If we wish to talk seriously about safe sex, we will undergird conversations about mechanics and products with concern for values and spirituality.

In the final analysis, love and trust are the only precautions we can take that will make sex in its deepest meaning safe. For love and trust create an environment in which we are free to be ourselves, to relax, to let down our defenses, to be vulnerable.

"Oh, I can see it coming," I hear you say. "We finally got to the 'only in marriage' part." No, I'm not saying that. I'm saying *more* than that. I am saying that, even in marriage, sex has the potential for being dangerous. Talk to an abused spouse, if you don't think so. Sin separates the physical from the spiritual inside marriage just as it does outside marriage. And sex becomes superficial or coercive, shallow or threatening, inside marriage as well as outside marriage. Love and trust, which make "naked yet without shame" possible, can never be taken for granted, not even in marriage, especially not in marriage. They must be tended like the most delicate flowers. When they are so tended, they create a garden that is not Eden but that is, in its own way, even more beautiful.

May God grant that in our most intensely private lives the physical will always be understood in light of the spiritual. May God grant that we will understand that, just as a loaf of bread is not merely a loaf of bread, it is the Body of Christ, which is broken for us, and just as a cup of wine is not merely a cup of wine, it is the blood of Christ, which is shed for us, even so, our body is not merely a body, a mass of needs and desires that demand to be fulfilled, it is the "temple of the Holy Spirit within you, which you have from God" (1 Cor. 6:19). May God grant that Paul's admonition might not be so much pious talk but rather the ultimate statement of the unity of all things physical and spiritual: "Glorify God with your bodies" (1 Cor. 6:20).

26. God and the "L-Word"
Howard W. Roberts

Isa. 61:1–11; John 8:31–59

During the 1988 presidential campaign, the "L-word" became a hot political issue. The L-word is *liberal,* and the term was used to label Mike Dukakis as bad for the country. Regardless of your political persuasion, what happened in this campaign is what happens too often in life. We hang labels on people who are different than we: the difference may be philosophical, cultural, religious, racial, sexual, educational, or political. Once the label has been attached to an individual or a group, we dismiss their perspective, their right to be heard; we even discount them as people. T. B. Maston, one who experienced verbal attacks especially as a champion of racial justice, called this "libel by label."

The term *liberal* has been used by many as a derogatory identification. Liberal has been a catchall word to label anybody and any organization that is different than we. Too often being different is feared as a threat to our existence because another perspective is being offered. Walter Horton, an American theologian, wrote in 1938 concerning the condition of the German church, "With the advent of the Third Reich, the term 'liberal' became a criminal accusation to level at anyone."

Liberty, liberate, and *liberal* are derivatives of the same Latin root word, *liber,* which means "free." *Liberty* means freedom or release from slavery, imprisonment, captivity, or any other form of arbitrary control. *Liberty* also means the sum of rights and exemptions pos-

---

Howard W. Roberts is pastor at Broadview Baptist Church in Temple Hills, Maryland. A graduate of Southern Baptist Seminary and Southwestern Baptist Seminary, Roberts is the author of five books, including *Learning to Pray, The Lasting Words of Jesus,* and *U-Turns Permitted.*

sessed in common by the people of a community or nation. *Liberate* is a verb meaning to set free, to release from slavery or enemy occupation. In chemistry, it means to free from combination in a compound. *Liberal* means progressive, free-thinking, fair-minded, magnanimous, abundant, generous, lavish, extravagant. It means free and unconfined, not restricted to the literal meaning; favoring reform or progress as in religion or education; specifically, favoring political reforms tending toward democracy and personal freedom for the individual. *Liberal* implies tolerance of others' views as well as open-mindedness that challenges tradition and established institutions. You and I are neither liberal nor conservative but combinations of the two. We are liberal when it comes to what we expect our employers to pay us and conservative when it comes to spending what we earn. Brooks Hays said, "We're both liberal and conservative like the old dog. He's liberal when he chases a rabbit. He's conservative when he buries a bone." Individually and collectively, we are both liberal and conservative.

Carl Sagan, popular scientist, has said it well:

> What we're talking about has little to do with the
> simplistic distinction between "conservatives" and
> "liberals." Conservatives wish to conserve
> traditional institutions. Not all . . . but some. Who,
> knowing the difficulty of designing workable
> political institutions, would oppose preserving what
> works? Liberals (from the Latin word for freedom)
> advocate liberty . . . the maximum possible liberty
> in a functioning and just society. . . . Who, knowing
> the history of tyranny and the charitable imperative
> of the world's great religions, would oppose such
> values? Conservatism and liberalism are not
> mutually exclusive alternatives. Clearly, we need
> some of each. Our problem is to find the right
> mix.[1]

When it comes to being liberal, God is the only purist. God goes to extravagant, liberal extremes for life to be filled with meaning for us. Whatever methods God used to create the universe, it is created to be free. This freedom in the universe in seen by scientists as they acknowledge that the universe is expanding.

> So all we know is that the universe is expanding by
> between 5 percent and 10 percent every thousand
> million years. . . . The present evidence therefore

> suggests that the universe will probably expand
> forever, but all we can really be sure of is that even
> if the universe is going to recollapse, it won't do so
> for at least another ten thousand million years,
> since it has already been expanding for at least that
> long.[2]

This illustrates God's creativity, extravagance, and liberal tendencies. One universe, one planet, one star, one kind of rose, one kind of grass, one kind of tree, one race of people, one color in the rainbow, one shape of snowflakes would have been enough. But being the liberal God is, no two snowflakes are alike, and we cannot count the galaxies in this universe, much less determine how many universes there are. To use the word *liberal* in its proper meaning and context, God is the only genuine liberal there is.

God is so liberal that we have been created in God's image. That means we have been created free. God's liberality encourages and urges us to relate freely out of love to God and one another. God also is so liberal as to permit us to use our freedom to destroy the environment, fellow human beings, and ourselves. We have done enough damage to the ozone layer of the atmosphere in this century that if we stopped the damage now, centuries would be needed for the atmosphere to heal. When we reject God and all that God does for us, how does God respond to us? Like some rigid, tight-fisted, angry tyrant? No. At those times when we have done our worst to God, God is liberal, and God's liberality breathes fresh air into our collapsed lungs and liberates us. God gets in a hurry like the father of the prodigal son and comes running down the road to meet us, hug us, clothe us, feed us, and throw a party in our honor. I tell you, it is liberal attitudes like these that bring good news, heal broken lives, throw open prison doors, and tell captives everywhere, "Free at last! Free at last! Thank God Almighty, you are free at last!"

The fact that God forgives us when we sin is evidence that God is liberal. Were God conservative, there would be a limit on God's forgiveness, like the seven times that Peter asked about. But Jesus' liberal response was that only when we forgive another seven times seventy have we gotten started in the process of forgiveness, and only then are we approaching being like God. Part of what blocks our liberation and liberality is that we will not forgive ourselves. To fail or refuse to forgive ourselves is to hold ourselves higher than God and thus indulge in the sin of a perverted form of pride.

We could summarize Jesus' ministry with the statement "Like God, like son." In the ministry of Jesus, God is identified, described, and experienced as an all-inclusive love, letting the sun fall equally on the Catholics and Baptists, the Arabs and Jews, the Contras and the Sandinistas, the citizens of the United States and the Soviet Union. Much is said today about the need for us to go deep into the Word, but our genuine need is for the Word to go deep into us. The standard for interpreting the written Word of God is the living Word of God, the liberating Christ. As we experience the liberating Christ, we are called to become co-liberators with him. We are to be the redeeming people of God.

Jesus restores the humanity of people, and different interpretations of the eschatological situation result in very different life-styles. John the Baptist's life-style was that of an apocalyptic ascetic, while Jesus was seen by people as a "glutton and a drunkard, a friend of tax collectors and sinners" (Luke 7:34). It was the festive table-sharing at a wedding feast or the royal banquet of a king that characterized Jesus and his liberation movement.

For the liberating Christ, it is party, party, party. It is party time because when we have done our worst, shut God out, God draws a circle that includes us all. Everyone is invited: Jews and Gentiles, slaves and free, men and women, people of color and people who have no color, Republicans, Democrats, and Independents, liberals and conservatives. God is the eccentric host who, when the Yuppies, the Wall Street brokers, and the religious leaders turn out to have more important things to do than to come live with God, God goes out to backwater towns, skid row, Fourteenth Street, Lafayette Park, the heat grates, welfare lines, soup kitchens, and South African townships and brings home the motliest menagerie of human beings imaginable or unimaginable. There they are landlord and tenant, Samaritan and Jew, Soviet and American, moderate and fundamentalist, conservative and liberal seated at the food-laden table in the great hall. The candles are lit; the glasses are filled. At a sign from the host, the musicians in their gallery strike up "Amazing Grace." What a party!

It was the liberating, party-going, party-giving Christ who said, "If you obey my teachings, you are really my disciples; you will know the truth, and the truth will set you free" (John 8:31–32). We often only quote half the statement, "You shall know the truth, and the truth will set you free." That is to state a half-truth. We have hung that half-truth shabbily over institutions of learning to imply that education brings salvation. It is hung over the entrance to the CIA headquarters in Virginia and gives the double, contradictory message that spying, trickery, and deceit are avenues of liberating truth. We hang it in our minds with the superficial understanding that if we can get the facts, then we will have the truth. We have wrapped it around our hearts with the belief that if we can get enough people to hold the same doctrinal beliefs, then our beliefs will be correct, life will be secure, and our struggles will be over. But Jesus said that it was the discipline of obeying his teachings that would enable people to know the liberating truth.

Labels on canned goods and cereal boxes serve a good purpose. They communicate what the contents are and what ingredients are used to make the products. But labels cannot properly and accurately be used to identify people. It is impossible to list all of the ingredients that go into making people. We are too complex. The plethora of influences in our lives include parents, extended family, church, culture, the teachers we had, and what was affecting them as they taught us. No label can capture all of these variables. To use labels is to stereotype people and turn them into objects.

Jesus was too liberal for the religious crowd of his day. The religious leaders smeared Jesus with the "S-word." They called him a Samaritan. Samaritan was synonymous with everything wrong in life. A Samaritan was a foe of Israel, a breaker of religious law, and a heretic. The word meant half-breed heretic with an illegitimate ancestry. Were they making a reference to their views about Jesus' birth when they called him a Samaritan? We cannot possibly know. When the religious leaders said, "You are a Samaritan," they labeled Jesus and libeled him with their label.

They did exactly what many people do when they are frustrated by the expansive spirit of another or when they run out of arguments. The challengers of Jesus in their rage and fury could think of no meaner or damaging thing than to hurl this label—"Samaritan!" When the label did not work to quiet Jesus, they picked up stones to throw at him, but Jesus hid himself and left the Temple (John 8:59).

As threatening as all of this was to Jesus, he did not tone down his liberal attitude and actions. Actually, he seemed to become even bolder with his liberation policy. When he was dying, Jesus asked that his murderers be forgiven. That is liberal. Saint Theresa of

Lysieux wrote to her sister, "If you are willing to serenely bear the trial of being displeasing to yourself, then you will be for Jesus a pleasant place of shelter."[3]

Mark (12:41–44) records the popular story known as the widow's mite, and Jesus commented for all to hear, "I tell you that this poor widow put more in the offering box than all the others. For the others put in what they had to spare of their riches; but she, poor as she is, put in all she had—she gave all she had to live on" (Mark 12:43–44). This woman's extravagant response to God is expressed through her generous gift. She had experienced God being liberal to her, and she was liberal in return through her giving, not because of how much she gave, but because of how little she kept for herself. She was the liberal while the rich men who gave many more dollars than the widow were the conservatives because of how much they kept for themselves. It has been suggested that, if you want to know what people value, examine their cancelled checks. But that will not give you the whole picture. That will tell you for what they spent their money, but it will not tell you how much they kept for themselves. The generous, extravagant, liberal people give themselves and all that they have for the interest and benefit of others. Evidence of God's extravagance is that everything God created was for all people to enjoy. God harbored nothing.

Luke (7:36–50) records another incident that demonstrates Jesus' positive response to another woman who was liberal and extravagant. This woman came in off the street to the house of Simon the Pharisee. No one, except Jesus, paid any attention to her until she poured expensive oil on his feet. Then Simon concluded Jesus wasn't much of a prophet if he permitted this "sinful" woman to touch him. With the label "sinful woman," Simon dismissed the woman as nobody. But her liberal, extravagant gift was in response to the liberal Jesus she had seen and to the liberation that she had experienced through her awareness and encounter with Jesus.

Notice that in the context in which Jesus made his liberating truth statement, people in the audience immediately responded that they were slaves to no one. Often when the truth shines on our need to change, we bristle, claiming we are slaves to nothing. Such reaction is a cue that we protest too much and affirms the insight that you shall know the truth and the truth will make you mad before it sets you free.

What is freedom? We often claim freedom to mean being able to do whatever we want, but soon we realize that such an approach is fraught with constraints. Socrates questioned, "How can you call a man free when his pleasures rule over him?"[4] And Goethe observed that none are more hopelessly enslaved than those who falsely believe they are free.[5]

Adlai Stevenson once noted that there are two great flaws in many modern Americans' concept of freedom: We have assumed that freedom means a common viewpoint, while in truth freedom rings where opinions clash. We have confused the free with the free and easy.[6]

If there is a grain of truth in the Gospels, then everyone mentioned in the Gospels who at first appeared to be free—the religious leaders, the government officials, and the socially elite—are the ones who were bound and gagged, locked in solitary confinement. Those who appeared to be enslaved—the lame, the lepers, the tax collectors, the unclean, and the prostitutes—were the ones who found themselves set free.

People, all people, were created in the image of a liberal, liberating God. But all of us have locked ourselves behind bars. We are prisoners in a world that God created to be free. Prisons dehumanize, and their numbers are legion. They have names like Lorton and Prince George's County Jail. Prisons are addictions like alcohol, drugs, work, church, religion. There also are the prisons of poverty, racism, sexism, nuclearism, communism, and capitalism. These prisons hold people captive inside and out. Some are locked out of life because they are being dehumanized by the power others wield over them. The power brokers are dehumanized by the power and control they wield over fellow human beings.

There are some ways a Christian should always be called liberal: a liberal love for God and love for neighbor; a liberal action in helping those in need; and a liberal financial commitment to Christ and his Church. Don Harbuck was an outstanding Baptist minister who spoke out against racism when most people were saying nothing about the cancer that eats away at relationships. As a result, Harbuck was labeled a liberal. Speaking at a Baptist national summer assembly, he said, "I've been accused of being a liberal, and today I want to confess to it. I've lived all of my life on the basis of one liberal idea. I learned it from my mother: 'God loves everybody.' If you don't think that's liberal, just go out there and try living it, and you'll soon find out."

The disciple of Christ seeks the truth wherever it may be found. When the truth of Christ is experienced, there is an openness, a graciousness, a friendliness, a liberation that comes from Christ, who saw the best in those who were condemned by the conservative Pharisees. We cannot proclaim the love of God to people who are being mistreated without addressing the gospel to the vile of the mistreatment they are experiencing. The gospel of the Kingdom of God has no place for sociohuman neutralism or detached piety. We need to identify and align ourselves with those who are dreaming of human acceptance in society and who are striving to be free partners in a free universe. With God as our Creator and Christ as our Redeemer, we are called to be liberal, liberated, and liberating. With God as our parent and Jesus as our brother, we are invited to be the liberal, liberated, liberating children of God.

Wherever and whenever we will permit the liberal, liberating, loving God to dwell with us, comfort us, and confront us, we will become liberal, liberating, and loving ourselves. We obey the words of Christ. We know the truth, and the truth liberates us. We announce good news, release those held captive, open the prison doors, and heal the broken-hearted. When God's liberated people become co-liberators with God, then justice rolls down like water and mercy like an ever-flowing stream.

NOTES

1. *Parade,* 27 November 1988.
2. Stephen W. Hawking, *A Brief History of Time* (New York: Bantam Books, 1988), 45–46.
3. *Collected Letters of St. Therese of Lisieux,* translated by F. J. Sheed (Kansas City: Sheed and Ward, 1949), 303.
4. Socrates, in *Great Dialogues of Plato,* edited by Eric Warmington and Philip House (London: New English Library, 1956), 379.
5. Van Goethe, quoted in *The International Dictionary of Thoughts,* edited by John P. Bradley, Leo Daniels, and Thomas Jones (Chicago: J. C. Ferguson, 1980), 307.
6. Stevenson, in Bradley, Daniels, and Jones, eds., *International Dictionary of Thoughts,* 308.

V. PASTORAL

27. Your Religion: Method or Motive—Which?

Donald Macleod

Isa. 46:1–4
Isa. 46:4: "I have made . . . and I will carry."

One day Prof. George Adam Smith, that great Old Testament scholar of the late nineteenth century, was seated in a London train beside a young clergyman who was about to set sail as a missionary to Africa. The particular field to which he was going was noted for its tropical diseases that kept any white person's life in jeopardy almost every hour. Dr. Smith tried to reason with the young man that if he must give his life in service to Christ, why should he throw it away on that dark continent? Why not serve Christ in some more civilized area where he might be assured of a long lifetime of commitment and duty, rather than going into a jungle where disease might cut him off without a moment's notice? But the young clergyman turned to Smith in an attitude of deep seriousness and said, "Christ loved me and gave himself for me, and I—can I hold back?"

Contrast this attitude with that of a young Hindu who described the exercise of his religious life in this way: "I get up at four o'clock in the morning, and I go through my religious exercises until nine o'clock; then I go to business until five o'clock, and during those hours, God alone knows what I do. But I become religious again at five o'clock and remain in this attitude until bedtime."

Donald Macleod was born in Nova Scotia, Canada. Dr. Macleod was the founder and first president of the Academy of Homiletics and until 1983 was Francis L. Patton Professor of Preaching and Worship at Princeton Theological Seminary in Princeton, New Jersey. He is the author of ten books in the field of preaching and worship.

Here are two pictures that have to do with motive and method in religion. In one, religion lifts a young man seemingly out of himself and carries his love and faith to their fulfillment upon the far frontiers of life. In the other, religion appears as a matter of checks and balances that are fitted somehow conveniently into the day's account. Moreover, these attitudes confront you and me with important and searching questions, so that we are made to ask ourselves, Is my religion something that lays claim upon me and lifts me out of the narrow shell of self and makes me one in will and purpose with the mind of God? Or is my religion something I hug closely to myself and cut and trim in order to fit it into the pattern of my own conveniences and desires—something I lay down or pick up at will? Or as Henry Sloane Coffin once asked, "Is your religion a load or a lift? Is it dead weight or is it wings?"

Our Scripture text takes us away back to the sixth century before Christ was born, when the children of Israel were still in slavery under the proud and heathen Babylonian Empire. There, in the capital city, stood the nation's gods, their idols on their gilded pedestals—Bel, Nebo, and Amon—with their fierce faces and starey eyes, while blind and superstitious people brought their gifts and made their pagan sacrifices. Then suddenly on their northern borders appeared the massive Persian armies under Cyrus, the rising conqueror, and a shudder of panic swept across the Babylonian plains. Now, the first impulse of the people was to get the gods out and move them into a place of hiding, and in this forty-sixth chapter of Isaiah, we find a vivid word picture of their mad scramble to load the idols on the backs of oxen and to hurry them off into a place of safety. And the prophet Isaiah is witnessing this ridiculous scene, and turning to his fellow captives, he spoke a message from the God of Israel, "I have made . . . and I will carry."

What a contrast! Here were these pagan Babylonians carrying their grotesque and useless gods out from the line of danger, but the living God of Israel, who had cradled the nation in the land of Egypt and had marched majestically with them through the centuries, was still undergirding his people and carrying them upon the wings of a destiny of his own choosing. A time of crisis was upon them, but the gods of Babylon could do nothing, poor senseless things that had to be carried away upon a cart. No wonder Isaiah mocked them as he spoke a word from the God of his people: "I have made . . . and I will carry."

Now this graphic account is not a dead issue away back among the musty chapters of ancient history. It comes alive for us in our own day and poses three important questions for us to consider.

Do You Carry Your Religion, or Does Your Religion Carry You?

It seems somewhat incredible, yet it is quite true that for some people today religion has become a burden to be carried. Like the ancient Babylonians, they groan and sweat under the dead weight of the gods they have strapped to their backs, and hence, religion has become for them a matter of exacting drudgery without joy or radiance or inspiration. Oh, yes, they will repeat the creeds, but simply because it seems to be the thing to do. They go through the motions of the Ten Commandments simply because some ancient Law once required it. Their name is on the role of every organization in the church and community simply because they feel it is their duty to have it there, and constantly they become worn out from running to and fro trying to keep up a record, as if numbers, dates, and appointments were everything. And this is the type of religion many people are carrying laboriously every day, and it gets a person nowhere spiritually; it saves nobody; and it is almost useless when some harrowing crisis is upon them.

But the God of Israel rebukes us kindly but firmly and says, "I have made . . . and I will carry." What a difference would occur in our spiritual makeup if we were to stop carrying our religion and were to allow our religion to carry us! One day a friend asked John Wanamaker, the great American businessman, this question: "How do you find time to run a Sunday school for a thousand boys and girls in Philadelphia in addition to the business of your stores and your work as postmaster general and all the other obligations that are laid upon you?" And Wanamaker replied, "Why, the Sunday school is my business! All other obligations are just things. Forty-five years ago I decided that God's promise was sure—'Seek ye first the Kingdom of God and his righteousness and all these things will be added unto you.'"

There is the matter in its clearest perspective. It is a matter of our religious conviction; that something we believe in and have staked our very life upon; that something that grips us and lifts us and carries us along. Listen to Jesus: "I must be about my Father's business." "I must work the works of him who sent me while it is day." Always he was carried by the strong conviction that God's love and purpose were everything and that they would carry him to the most dazzling spiritual victory this world could ever know.

This brings us to one of the many controversial issues facing us in America today: namely, the whole matter of Bible reading and prayer in the public schools. Now, it is elementary to say that a Christian teacher can make a religious impact upon young children in a hundred ways other than by reading ten verses of Scripture or reciting a few lines of a prayer before class work begins. And by the same token, an unbelieving teacher can make Bible reading and prayer into a farce by a sarcastic remark or a shrug of cold indifference. Our concern must be with those parents who are all too anxious to carry their religion and to deposit responsibility for it into the lap of the public school, as if these schools were intended to be the custodians of American religion.

Religion is not just another academic subject to be studied objectively like geography or Latin or physics; nor is it a vague general philosophy that can be summed up in the homely maxim "Be kind to grandmother and the cat." Our crying need in our religious life today lies in the shaping of our Christian convictions. And this can be done best within the Christian community, namely, the church, and particularly the church in your home and mine. Do you carry your religion and make it someone else's business? Or are you carried by strong convictions, not generated by frothy emotions, but based—as John Calvin put it—on an "informed faith" that is under the constraint of the ends and aims of God's kingdom?

Do You Handle Your Religion, or Does Your Religion Handle You?

The story is told about a little girl in Edinburgh, Scotland, who was saying her prayers just prior to leaving on a three-week vacation down in London. And someone overheard the last sentence of her prayer, which went this way: "And now God I'm going down to London, and I'll not be able to talk to you for three weeks, but I'll get in touch with you as soon as I get back!"

Now, in a way, that is what these Babylonians were thinking as they carted away their gods. After a few weeks, the national crisis would likely be over, and their old gods could be dusted off, straightened out, and put back upon their pedestals so all would be well again. This is symbolic of the danger of our handling our religion instead of our religion handling us. And we see it happening every day. I remember, in the little highland Scottish church where I was brought up as a boy, there was an elderly lady who attended regularly and who was known as a fussy old dogmatist. Indeed, some called her "an Old Testament Christian." On arrival, she had under her arm the handles of her religion, the several things she believed in to the neglect of some equally important others: the absolute literal interpretation of the Scripture, a hard legalistic theory of the Atonement, and a clear notion—as Reinhold Niebuhr phrased it—of "the temperature of hell and the furniture of heaven." And these handles were all wrapped up in a dusty old package called the closed mind. And Sunday after Sunday she would spin the package and fondle these objects and then put them away until next Sunday when it would be safe to parade them again.

Or there was a situation in one of our large cities when a serious harm was being done to the soul of that city's life, but Christian people decided it would be expedient to remain quiet and cover their convictions with a mental blackout until the embarrassing period was past. Do we also handle our religion, or does our religion handle us?

Once there was a stingy millionaire in New York City who was asked to contribute to a fund to erect a statue in honor of George Washington. But he refused nastily and sharply and growled, "I always keep George Washington in my heart!" To which the indignant collector promptly retorted, "I don't think the father of our country would care to be in so tight a spot!" Your religion and mine will handle us when at its essence it is a spiritual experience of the living, moving, redeeming Christ who can transform our littleness into greatness, lift our narrow visions into broader horizons, and lead us out from narrow preoccupation with ourselves into the fellowship of those radiant souls whose God undergirds them with his everlasting arms.

Do You Use Your Religion, or Does Your Religion Use You?

Rudyard Kipling has a poem entitled "Mulholland's Vow." It is the story of a man who worked on a cattle boat and whose job it was to take care of these animals in the dark hold of the ship away below the decks. One day at sea a terrific storm descended upon them, and Mulholland was almost killed as he worked among these lunging and plunging beasts in the darkness of the hold. In the midst of it all, however, Mulholland made a bargain with God that, if he'd bring the ship and the crew safely to land, he would give up his life of hard drinking and swearing and become a preacher. Well, the ship did get to port, and Mulholland resolved to keep his vow. As he walked away from that wretched boat, he began to think how wonderful it was going to be as a preacher: always to be clean, well-dressed, and comfortable among respectable people and never again to be wet, dirty, and cold. But suddenly God stopped him in his tracks and said, "Mulholland, go back to the cattle boat and preach my gospel there!" From a clever design to use his religion to gain social acceptability, Mulholland was to find that real religion takes over a person and uses him or her for God's glory and not their own.

And this business of using religion can be our weakness, too. Let's face up to it: There is a type of religion that is popular among far too many of us today, and it is anything else but Christian. Its heresy is that, instead of acknowledging God as the end of all our living, believing, and loving, it uses God for selfish and material ends. It says to us, Try God and you will have peace of mind, as if peace of mind were the be-all and end-all of the Christian faith. The end of our religion must be that all of us be used to the glory of God's name, and peace of mind comes as one of the by-products. A president of a liberal arts college was addressing the graduating class, and his final remark was, "Be Christian and you'll always be successful!" Is personal success ever to be the litmus test of the abundant life? Ask Jesus, and he will answer, "He who saves his life shall lose it, and he who loses his life for my sake and the gospel the same shall save it." Ask St. Paul, and he will answer, "Love suffers long and is kind. . . . Love seeks not her own."

In an address before Harvard University, Paul Tillich deplored our tolerance in America of a civil religion that accommodates itself to the popular mores of contemporary society and uses it to undergird and justify modern culture and our American way of life. This uses religion, and the inevitable result—Tillich warned—is the perversion of all true religion. How long, then, shall we go on hoping that God will always be on our side and agree to do for us what we most desire for ourselves?

But real Christianity says to us, Commit yourself to God 100 percent, and maybe he will send you to the slums of New York or

Chicago or Washington, there to spend a nameless life in the name of him whose love can never die.

One day someone asked William Booth, the founder of the Salvation Army, to explain the success of the great movement he began. And this is what he said:

> I'll tell you a secret. One day I caught a vision of
> what Jesus Christ could do to the poor and
> underprivileged in the slums of London, and I
> made up my mind that God would have all of
> William Booth there was. And if there is any power
> in the Salvation Army today, it is because God has
> had all the adoration of my heart, all the power of
> my will, and all the influence of my life!

Do you use your religion, or does your religion use you? You see, you and I cannot get away from these questions. And if we see anything at all in our Christian faith, we see a cross. And as we look at it and learn its meaning, its claim burns itself into our very being, and the only adequate response we can give lies in those oft-quoted lines by Isaac Watts:

> Were the whole realm of nature mine,
> That were a present far too small;
> Love so amazing, so divine,
> Demands my soul, my life, my all.

28. Not All Saints, But Surely Some Saints

ALL SAINTS' DAY, NOVEMBER 1

W. Sibley Towner

Ps. 24:1–6; Rev. 7:2–4, 9–12; Matt. 5:9–12

All Saints' Day is not circled in red on the pocket calendar I carry. In fact, it is not mentioned at all. But not to worry! I've got a saint on my mind. She is St. Thérèse of Lisieux, whose life has recently been made by Alain Cavalier into a tender, sensitive, horrifying film. The film tells the story of a young woman out of whose profound conversion experience grew the vocation of a nun. As a religious, she sought to imitate Christ. For her, this discipline was not centered in solidarity with the diseased and marginal people of the world. No, true spirituality consisted in joining Jesus in martyrdom and death. In the years before her early demise, while she was still a young woman, she wrote in her journal,

> From my childhood I have dreamt of
> martyrdom . . . but I don't want to suffer just
> one moment. . . . I want to be scourged and
> crucified. . . . Like St. John, I want to be flung into
> boiling oil. Like St. Ignatius of Antioch, I want to
> be ground by the teeth of wild beasts. With St.
> Agnes and St. Cecelia, I want to offer my neck to

W. Sibley Towner is professor of biblical interpretation at Union Theological Seminary in Richmond, Virginia. Dr. Towner has taught at Princeton Theological Seminary, Yale Divinity School, and the University of Dubuque Theological Seminary. He is the author of many articles and several books, including *How God Deals with Evil* and *Daniel* in the *Interpretation Bible Commentary* series.

the sword of the executioner. . . . My heart leaps
when I think of the unheard tortures Christians will
suffer in the reign of anti-Christ. I want to endure
them all.[1]

The cinematographer shook the audience by showing the face of
St. Thérèse full of joy when she awoke on her last Good Friday to
find a hemorrhage of blood running from her mouth onto her pillow.
It was not so much the blood itself, which we viewers realized was
caused by tuberculosis rather than by extreme spirituality. No, it was
her spirit that was so disturbing—for hers was a spirit that could have
given all of us great gifts but that instead linked spiritual greatness
with suffering and, above all, the shedding of blood.

Though we Calvinists and other Protestants have been just as
outspoken as traditional Augustinian Catholics in expressing our
dubiousness about the virtues of the flesh, we join most other modern Christians in feeling that people like St. Thérèse go too far in
denying the world. Think about St. Lucy, too! Talk about low self-
esteem! When she received a message from a secret admirer praising
her beautiful eyes, she took them out and sent them to him—and is
pictured by medieval artists as a lovely young woman with eyeballs
on a kind of stalk that she holds in her hand.

Maybe saints of this sort concentrated too much on the beatific
vision they imagined awaits holy people in heaven. Maybe they read
the Book of Revelation as if it were an album full of glossy pictures
snapped in the city of God instead of what it really is—a clarion call
to vigorous living now. The picture in today's first lesson is a lovely
and dramatic one, to be sure. There they are—the saints "from all
tribes and people and tongues standing before the throne and
before the Lamb, clothed in white robes, with palm branches in their
hands, and crying out with a loud voice, 'Salvation belongs to our
God . . . !' " (Rev. 7:9–10). Maybe the traditional bleeding saints
erred in the direction of trying to rush God, trying to crowd God
toward the gates of the New Jerusalem. Maybe they needed a vision
at close quarters to set alongside the distant one, in order to keep
alive a sacred passion for the world around them.

The throne of glory never lacks for saints. It's this poor world
that needs them! The cry goes out today, We need worldly saints!
We need good and holy saints who believe in the world and who will
move around in it with boldness and love.

Oh, not as bawdily as some of the more worldly saints of old were wont to do. Not like St. Frisewide. She is one of those wonderful Saxon saints that hang around the edges of the Church of England. Outside of Oxford, I don't think she is venerated very much. But if you happen to be there on October 19, you can join the solemn procession to her tomb in the floor of Christ Church Cathedral, marching to the verses of "Jerusalem, My Happy Home." Indeed, if you happen to be a barren woman, you can even drink water from the well the good saint dug beside the parish church in Binsey, if the sexton will you get you some, and hope to become fertile. A potent, worldly woman indeed, St. Frisewide, whose unfortunate princely lover at a moment of excess was struck blind by lightning. She was into blood, too, but it belonged to other people.

No, I mean worldly saints more like Ireneus of Lyon (ca. 130–200) who, though he was never shot through with dozens of arrows like St. Sebastian or roasted on a grill like St. Lawrence, won his palms by making lavish use of the Hebrew Bible in his struggle against the gnostic rejection of the world and the flesh and is famous for this teaching: "The glory of God is the glory of people fully alive."[2] I mean someone like St. Dominic (ca. 1170–1221), the founder of campus ministries, who saw the need to preach the gospel in the new urban centers and their universities and founded an order dedicated to that end; or someone like his contemporary, St. Francis of Assisi (1181–1225), who sent his deeply reverent and ecologically sensitive friars our into a world, every inch of which is loved by God.

But rather than name more names, let's go back to the Gospel lesson for today and ask, What kind of saintliness does *Jesus* have in mind when he stands on the mountain in Moses' place and delivers nine new guidelines for Christian faith and practice? Look at the way in which these Beatitudes are formulated in Matthew 5. Each and every one of them begins with a brush stroke on the canvas of the Christian life as it is lived in the world here and now. "Blessed are the peacemakers . . ." (Matt. 5:9). Stroke! The world needs to see *now* that reconciliation is preferable to endless enmity. "Blessed are the poor in spirit . . ." (v. 3). Stroke! The world cries *now* for people whose loyalty is undivided and who can incarnate the love of Jesus with everything they've got. "Blessed are the merciful . . ." (v. 7). Stroke! The world can be infused *now* with the quality of mercy.

But Jesus does not neglect the future, either. Indeed, in the second clause of each of the Beatitudes, he lays the groundwork for exalted visions of the completion of God's work of blessing in the world. "Blessed are the merciful, for they shall obtain mercy"—now and in the future. "Blessed are the pure in heart, for they shall see God" (v. 8)—now and in the future. There is nothing wrong with taking bearings on a distant object ahead as one tries to steer over rough terrain. But even better is a pair of markers, one near at hand and one distant. In the Beatitudes, Jesus gives the saints those pairs—the shape of worldly discipleship here and now and its full manifestation on the horizon of the future.

Many forces have led pious Christians in the past to renounce this physical world and to look at it as something to withdraw from. In his book *Imaging God: Dominion as Stewardship,* [3] the Canadian theologian Douglas John Hall lists sources of this ambiguity, such as the historic Christian stress on individual rather than community salvation; the reality that most Christian groups were born as sects that looked to the nurturing of their own circles rather than to the world as a whole; the keen awareness of early Christians that this world was about to end and be replaced by the eon that is to come; the influence of Hellenism, with its dualism between bad matter and good spirit. But above all, thinks Hall, Christian world-denial arose from selective reading and misreading of the Bible, particularly those texts that contrast this eon with the future eon. The fact is, says Hall, that the most significant figures in modern Christianity—people like Bonhoeffer, Thomas Merton, Martin Luther King, Mother Teresa, Dom Helder Camara—"are almost without exception individuals who have had what may be termed a 'conversion to the world' " (p. 37).

My friends, if you have a conversion to the world, don't worry. You can still be a saint. If you start to marvel at the delicate way the world hangs around the sun at the edge of our galaxy; if you revel in the cool light of the full moon and watch with fascination as the luna moths come to sniff the exotic scent and sip the nectar of the night-blooming moon flowers; if you love the black-and-orange terrapins that sneak around the garden taking a single bite out of a tomato here and a cantaloupe there; if you fall in love with the beautiful, upright, sweet-smelling, and smart creatures who are our human kinfolk, don't worry. You can still be a saint! God doesn't speak ill of the world nor call into question the warm affection human beings feel for it. God has no quarrel at all with those worldly saints who cherish the creation and really live in it as long as life endures. "God so loved the world," says the Fourth Evangelist, "that God gave God's only son. . . . God sent not this Son into the world to condemn the world, but that the world might be saved through him" (John 3:16–17).

Oh, there are things that need saving in the world, all right. Right relationships break down. *People* are fatally ignorant of the God who made them. In their hatred of themselves and of God, *people* destroy parts of God's handiwork. But *God* loves the world. That is the core of the gospel message. God neither seeks nor desires to condemn it.

And God needs saints today, true and worldly saints who work with bright eyes and eager hands, with all their physical powers intact, with all of their blood circulating in their veins, all of their tissues and sinews and capillaries fresh and vibrant and ready for action in the world they love.

Some of them will have to give their blood, too. Like Archbishop Romero, some may even have to spill it right on their altars. But, O God, if there must be sacrifice, let our blood, like Jesus' blood, be shed not for the sake simply of sanctity but for the safety of your sons and daughters and your sweet, small creatures, that they may all have life and have it more abundantly. Amen. Amen.

Let us pray.

O God, for millennia now your servants, the saints, have studied your Word in search of your direction for their choices. Sometimes they have done it in desert places; sometimes in cold stone libraries where the books were chained to the desks; sometimes in furtive glimpses at the pages hidden in cracks above their bunks at Auschwitz. Now it is our turn, Lord, to draw energy from you and to follow where you take us. Give us the strength to be worthy of so goodly a heritage.

In the name of Jesus we pray. Amen.

NOTES

1. St. Thérèse of Lisieux, *The Story of a Soul,* translated by John Beevers (Garden City, NJ: Image Books, 1957), 154.

2. Quoted by Matthew Fox, *Original Blessing* (Santa Fe, NM: Bear Publishing, 1983), 307.

3. Douglas John Hall, *Imaging God: Dominion as Stewardship* (Grand Rapids: Eerdman's, 1986).

29. When Life Crashes In
William Powell Tuck

Jer. 15:10–21; John 16:31–33

With his head buried in his hands, tears began to flow. A river of tears poured out as Jeremiah vented his innermost feelings. "O God, O God, where are you? Why do you seem so distant from me? Oh, if I had never been born." In his private, personal journal, which was not written for other eyes to see, Jeremiah had recorded his innermost feelings of distress and turmoil. "O God," he wrote. "I sat alone, isolated, without anyone caring or knowing where I am." In his journal, his feelings seem to leap out. He records feelings of aloneness and anger, frustration and failure, dejection and despondency, despair and doubt, hatred and hostility, ridicule and rejection.

"O God," he writes, "where are you in the midst of all my turmoil? I have done what you asked me to do. I responded to your call. I have preached your message, and yet instead of the people receiving it, I have received only rejection and ridicule. God, where are you?" Isolated and alone, Jeremiah struggled with his personal feelings. God's heaven seemed to be made of brass. "I pray to you," he said, "but there seems to be no response. Where are you, God? My words seem to echo off the walls of Jerusalem, rebounding and ringing around in my head. The words I pray to you come back like the hot breath of the desert wind that throws stinging sand against my face. There is no response. O God, why do you not answer me? Are you too busy? Are you too kind and understanding, or do you

---

William Powell Tuck is currently pastor of St. Matthews Baptist Church, Louisville, Kentucky, and has served as professor of preaching at Southern Baptist Theological Seminary. Dr. Tuck is the author of several books, including *The Way for All Seasons.*

not care? O God, why do you not answer me? Why do you leave me in my aloneness?"

Jeremiah had responded to God at a very early age. Some scholars have conjectured that it might have been at the age of fourteen. He answered God's call to preach his message to the nation of Judah. For forty years, he proclaimed the destruction of Israel. "Judgment would come from the north, and they would fall," he preached. But year after year went by and nothing happened. No enemy came, and no destruction fell upon the people. Jeremiah wanted to get married and have a family, but God said that the end was coming soon and told him not to get married. He was instructed not to engage in social functions. But the end did not come quickly. Jeremiah waited and waited. While he waited for God's judgment to fall, he was rejected by his friends, the political leaders, and the religious leaders. Even his own family plotted to put him to death. They couldn't understand his strange behavior. What were they supposed to make of him?

Jeremiah recorded his personal confessions, and out of his agony cried, "I sat alone." This is the aloneness of a leper, who is isolated from all the rest of society. In his aloneness, Jeremiah longed to sense the presence of God. Too often we think that the ancient prophets always walked in unparalleled fellowship with God. We assume that they always felt the strength of God's strong arm by their side at every moment. But Jeremiah in his honesty tells us that this was not always true for him. There were times when he was caught in the floods and storms of life, which swept him away from his foundation. He reached for the bottom but could not find it. He groped and searched for a word from God. He reached the point that he questioned his calling, purpose, his message, and even God. "Where are you God?" he cried. "I sat alone."

Jeremiah, however, is not the only one who has had that kind of experience, is he? You and I have known those kinds of feelings, haven't we? If we are honest, we have to admit it. Have there not been times in your life when you have felt alone and wondered where God was in your pain, rejection, ridicule, loneliness, despair, and depression? Have there not been moments in your life when you, like Jeremiah, have cried out to God and said, "I sit alone"?

W. H. Auden, in one of his short ballads, writes about a young man named Victor who has been betrayed by his wife. Here are the words the poet recorded:

Victor walked out into the High Street
He walked to the edge of the town;
He came to the allotments and the rubbish heap
And his tears came tumbling down.
Victor looked up at the sunset
As he stood there all alone;
Cried: "Are you in Heaven, Father?"
But the sky said "Address not known."[1]

There are times in your life and in my life when we ask, as Jeremiah did, "Are you in heaven, Father? If so, why don't you do something? Why do you not respond to my need, my prayer, my despair?" Jeremiah had experienced rejection. The people had rejected his message and him, and he sat alone in his despair.

Like Jeremiah, we have all known rejection at some time or another, have we not? Do you recall the first time you tried to get a date with the young lady you had seen at school? You placed your call to her with great hope, but back came her response, "I'm sorry, not interested." Or you may have sat on the other end of the line waiting for someone to call, and the call never came. Or you may have been the young man who raced to the end zone; you were wide open, and the football hit you right in your arms. You had the winning touchdown in your hands, but you dropped it! Later you had to go back to the locker room, and you felt the coolness of your teammates.

Some have known the rejection of losing a job. You have a sinking feeling. After years of hard work, you are no longer wanted or needed. There is an awful sense of rejection that comes in your life like a dark cloud. Some of you know the feeling of rejection that comes when sides are chosen on the sandlot, and you are the one— *you are the one—you are the one* who is always chosen last. Rejection comes in many shapes and forms, and like Jeremiah, we are too familiar with it. Some of you have experienced it when your marriage failed. You have sensed it when people did not like your ideas or thoughts. Or at work, you have noticed the coolness with which you are met. Rejection has come into your life, and like Jeremiah, you feel like you have sat alone.

People laughed at Jeremiah and mockingly said, "You have preached that destruction was coming upon us soon. It has been thirty-eight years since you began preaching that line, Jeremiah, but nobody has come yet. You are a fool!" He became an object of ridicule to them.

Like Jeremiah, many of you have also known ridicule, haven't you? People have sometimes made fun of something you have said or done or the way you look, talk, or walk. I will never forget an experience I had in elementary school. I had been asked to read aloud. While reading, I came across a word I didn't recognize. I probably should have known it, but I didn't. It was a small word— *awe.* I mispronounced it. To this day, I can still feel the ridicule I experienced from my teacher as well as the class.

We have all been ridiculed in some way or another. If you were thin when you were young, people may have teased you and called you "Skinny," "Bones," or "Beanpole." If you were heavy, they might have called you "Piggy," "Fatty," or "Porky." If your teeth protruded, they might call you "Beaver" or "Bucky." If you wore glasses, you were designated as "Four-eyes." Unfortunately, we have all known words of ridicule. Sometimes children can be devastating in the stinging words they say to each other!

A young girl, who was in the fourth grade, came home from school one day, and her mother knew something was wrong. It wasn't until later that she discovered a note that had been written to her daughter by another girl at school. The note read, "Dear Janet, You are the stinkiest girl I know. I wish to God you would die. Nobody likes you. You are a big fat ugly girl and nobody wants you around. Since I don't think you will die, let me make some suggestions. Play in the street. Drink poison. Cut your throat with a knife. I hope to God that you will die soon so that we can all breathe fresh air."[2]

How would you like to get a note like that? How would you like to live with the hurt that would bring to you? For a young child wanting acceptance from her friends, this would be a devastating blow. Ridicule may touch our lives at many ages and in many forms.

Jeremiah also knew loneliness. He felt isolated from other people and especially God. Jeremiah had no support group. His family and friends had rejected him. Only one loyal person, his scribe, stood by him.

But you have known loneliness, too, haven't you? You have known the loneliness of going off to a new city and a new school. There you have had to make new friends and a whole new way of life. It has not been easy. Some of you have known the loneliness of putting your husband or wife or parents in a nursing home. Some of you know the loneliness of eating Thanksgiving or Christmas dinner alone. Some of you know the loneliness of looking across a table each night and seeing an empty chair where a loved one used to sit. I read about a woman living alone who would wait at night to hear the announcer say his closing words before she would turn the radio off and go to sleep. She waited to hear him say, "And I wish to you all a very good night." John Milton said that God proclaimed loneliness as the first thing that was not good. "It is not good for man to be alone." Who among us has not felt loneliness at some point in his or her life?

Jeremiah thought he was a failure. He had preached God's message for thirty-eight years, and he had received only rejection and ridicule from his listeners. He thought he had failed God. But finally God's message was vindicated. We have all known some kind of failure at times. Who has not experienced failure at school, work, or in some relationships with people?

Like Jeremiah, we have also known suffering, haven't we? Sometimes we have felt pain that comes from hurt and isolation. Some of you have suffered with loved ones for a long time as they have slowly died with cancer. Others have watched their children suffer and die from cancer, leukemia, or other dread diseases. Many of you today bear heavy burdens of one kind or another. You know suffering and its harsh reality. You know too well its pain and hurt. Like Jeremiah, you have poured out rivers of tears. You have groped and searched for an answer. "Is there any hope?" you ask.

What does God say to Jeremiah? Instead of offering him comfort, he gives him a challenge. God says, "Jeremiah, you have been preaching to the people to repent, turn, and come back to me. Now, what I want you to do is listen to your own preaching. Repent. You turn back to me, and if you turn back, in your turning back to me, you will find strength and support." God does not give him an easy answer. It was not a new answer. There was no new word, but it was the old message that pointed him to examine his own preaching. "Listen to what you have been preaching," God said. "Turn back to me. You repent, and you will find that I am here to sustain you."

It is easy, isn't it, to worship God on a bright, beautiful day? But . . . can you bend your knee to God in the freezing cold, zero weather? Can you bend your knee to God when the temperature is 110°? When your house is on fire, can you worship God? When your ship is sinking, can you worship God? Is God still a strong force in your life when life is hard and the waves of difficulties beat upon the ship of your life? When the storms rage and crash around you, is the presence of God still strong in your life?

That great hurricane of a preacher, Arthur John Gossip, a Scottish minister, experienced the sudden and unexpected death of his wife. After many weeks of struggling with his grief, he was finally able to return to his duties. The first time he entered the pulpit, he spoke about the death of his wife. He said, "Some people asked me, 'Why didn't you fling away from God?' In heaven's name," he said, "fling away to what? Those of you in the sunshine may believe, but those of us in the shadows must believe."

Fling away to what? When you come to the shadows of life—when you come to dark moments and difficult days—that's when you need to reach out and feel the presence of God. Turn. Turn back to God and discover that he is there closer than the very breath within you. Feel his presence. He wants to sustain you.

God spoke again to Jeremiah. "Distinguish between the artificial and the real. Separate the superficial and artificial from the genuine and vital." Ah, what a needed word for us today. Too many of us have been hooked by sentimental and artificial religion. When our religion is only artificial, and we experience the storms of life, we find ourselves sinking. Many people think that God is someone they can manipulate and control. These persons have bought into the religious lie that the religious life is basically the "get-rich-quicker" life. If you are religious and say the "right words," God will make you rich and happy. Or if you just think positive thoughts, everything will be all right. When difficulties come into your life, this superficial religion crumbles and is not able to sustain you.

I knew a woman who always had easy answers for everybody else's difficult problems. If somebody became ill, she had a quick, pat answer for it. If somebody had trouble, no matter what it was, she thought she could solve it by quoting some verse of Scripture. But one day her husband came down with cancer and slowly died. She had to reach back then and see if her sentimental, artificial religion could sustain her. She discovered that only a genuine faith could undergird her. When she sat alone, her faith was tested to see if it was strong and real or only artificial talk.

God spoke further to Jeremiah. "If you will turn to me and separate the genuine from the artificial, you will become my voice. You will be my spokesperson. You will be"—the words literally are— "'my mouth.' You will be my mouth to proclaim my word to the people." Had Jeremiah been tempted to tell the people what they really wanted to hear? After preaching God's message and being faithful so long, was he later tempted simply to give the people whatever they wanted and not be true to what he understood the message of God to be? God told him that "if you will turn to me, you will receive strength and support." Only if Jeremiah preached God's genuine message would he continue to be God's voice. The real word of God always takes on fleshly form.

Most of us first "saw" God through other people. We saw through their lives a genuine faith that turned us toward God. We all get tired of seeing people whose religion is artificial and a sham. They have religion only on bright days. We look for "living epistles" whose Christianity has invaded their whole lives.

I know a couple who was very faithful and active in church. He had served as a deacon. They both had taught Sunday school, served on committees, and worked with young people for years. They were considered by many an ideal Christian young couple. Their eighteen-year-old son went off to college. The first week he was at college, he was killed in a tragic accident. Everybody undergirded them with support. Many wondered how they would face this tragedy. But they faced it bravely and courageously, with the strength of God undergirding them. Years later, this was the couple that I asked to talk with others when they had to walk through a dark valley. They had a genuine faith that sustained them in their times of difficulty. Now others would listen to them and be helped by them. Their faith in "the dark night" of their soul had enabled them to be a "voice"—a genuine spokesperson for God.

God told Jeremiah, "If you will do these things, you will be like a bronzed wall. You will find that your words will be vindicated. I will fortify and sustain you." God for him would not be like a Palestinian wadi, a brook that had water only in spring time. God would be a living, raging stream that always gave him support and encouragement. Centuries later, Jesus told his disciples, "I am alone, yet I am not alone." He had the certainty of his Father's presence.

Jeremiah found that in his aloneness he was not really alone. And neither are you nor I. There is nothing—absolutely nothing—that can separate us from the presence of God. God is ever present to sustain us. All we have to do is turn and recognize that he is present to undergird and support us. When life crashes in, turn like Jeremiah to God, and you will discover that God is already seeking to nourish you, nurture you, love you, and sustain you. You do not have to bear it alone. He is there to support you. I pray that you will find him.

NOTES

1. W. H. Auden, *Collected Shorter Poems 1927–1957* (London: Faber and Faber, Ltd., 1966).

2. James Dobson, *Hide or Seek* (Old Tappan, NJ: Fleming H. Revell, 1974), 21.

30. The Servant of the Lord
Pavel Filipi

Behold my servant, whom I uphold, my chosen one, in whom my
soul delights; I have put my Spirit upon him, so that he might
pronounce judgment on the nations. He will not cry or lift up his
voice, or make it heard in the street; a bent reed he will not break,
and a dimly burning wick he will not quench; he will pronounce
judgment according to the truth. He will not fail or be discouraged
till he has administered judgment on the earth; and the coastlands
wait for his law.

—Isa. 42:1–4

Sisters and brothers, we are now in the season of Advent. It is a time
when we remind ourselves with a new clarity that God's redemption
has not yet been completed, and that God's kingdom has not yet
been finally established. We are still living in hope and expectation.
We are a Church that is waiting for its Lord. In the same way, the
Church of the Old Testament was a Church that was waiting. And

Pavel Filipi is a member of the Faculty of Protestant Theology,
Evangelická Theologická Fakulta University Karlovy (Charles
University) in Prague, Czechoslovakia, where he teaches practical and
ecumenical theology. This sermon was preached on the first Sunday
of Advent, 1989, at a time of great upheaval in his country. "Every
day," he writes, "people went out to the streets of their towns and
cities to demonstrate—loudly—their wish for more profound changes
in the whole structure of the society, the government, and other
leading institutions. As you know, we finally succeeded without any
bloodshed. This was the context of this sermon—and of course the
question was in the air of what would happen to the representatives
of the old structures, who lost all their authority and sometimes even
integrity." Professor Filipi served as pastor of the Evangelical Church
of Czech Brethren (United Protestant Church) and still takes part in
many activities of his church as well as of the *oikoumene* both in his
country and abroad.

what sort of Lord is it that we are waiting for, along with the Church of the Old Covenant? What will he be like, that "servant of the Lord" who is supposed to set things right and to restore proper order to God's damaged creation? Let us hear what the prophet Isaiah has to say about him.

He is the Lord's servant, the one that the Lord has picked for this task, chosen, armed and equipped with his Spirit. He is not a self-appointed savior of humanity who has decided on his own initiative to save the world. (Plenty of these self-appointed messiahs have been seen throughout human history. But usually when they had finished, the problems were even greater than before.) He is God's Chosen One. That means that he did not attain his position as Savior of humanity with the help of the army or of a powerful political party, but neither was he elected to it by a democratic majority. Human society, it is true, needs to have people in leading positions who have the respect and trust of the majority. But God's damaged creation can only be put right by the Lord's servant, selected, chosen, authorized, and empowered to do so by God himself. In the New Testament, he assumed for himself definitively the title *Christ*, which means "the anointed one," so as to make it clear that he had not appointed himself to this position but that he had accepted it from the Lord of hosts, his Father. That is why it is written, "My servant, my chosen one, in whom my soul delights."

And what has he been entrusted with, what does his role consist of? "That he might produce judgment on the nations." When we talk about "judgment," we do not feel comfortable. Most people prefer to avoid judgments, and we think about the judgments of God with some uncertainty and anxiety. But the biblical witnesses speak differently. "Judge me, Lord," entreats the psalmist. For him, God's judgment is something desirable, something that needs to be demanded, for it is a judgment that puts an end to disorder and chaos. The Lord's judgment will put an end to the capriciousness of human judges and decision-makers and bring into the light justice, right, and God's covenant. The Lord's judgment means putting things right, not destroying them. It means normalization, returning to normality, abandoning the abnormal conditions in which we are living in our relations with God, with our neighbor, with nature. A few moments ago we heard these words, taken from another prophecy of Isaiah, about the one who it was promised would carry out God's judgment: "He shall not judge by what his eyes see or decide by what his ears hear; but with righteousness he shall judge the poor and decide with equity for the meek of the earth." All this—including the lamb that lies down with the wolf—is what God's judgment will mean, what it will bring about. "No one shall do evil or harm any longer." This is the task with which God's servant is entrusted: to put right the whole of God's creation, which has been damaged through human sin; to restore it to its normal state; to right injustices; to put an end to war; to destroy pride; to put a stop to the exploitation of the weak and the oppression of the powerless.

It is toward this, toward setting things right in this way, that our God is already working. It is for this that he is calling and arming his servant. Just imagine: He himself is taking on the responsibility of setting right everything that we have damaged through our selfishness, our desire for pleasure, our avarice, through our sin. Broken human relationships, enmity with God and humanity, life that has been devastated and nature that has been laid waste—all this, God has decided, should not remain like this. He is already working on it. He has already chosen and armed his servant. He has given him this task. And his servant "will not fail or be discouraged till he has administered judgment on the earth." On this we can rely, on this we can base our hope, when our gaze wanders sadly over the disfigured face of the earth, over the ruins of human life together. He does not falter; he does not fail.

And how does the Lord's servant carry out his task, what method does he use? A strange one. "He will not cry or lift up his voice, or make it heard in the street; a bent reed he will not break, and a dimly burning wick he will not quench." A strange method. We know other, more effective ones. Lifting up our voice, making it heard in the street, in parliament, on television, making a noise wherever we want to be heard. But that is not the way of the Messiah that the Church of the Old Covenant was waiting for. It is not the way of the Lord Jesus Christ whose coming we are waiting for. It is true that, when Jesus of Nazareth went about Galilee and Judaea, he was sometimes surrounded by a flurry of excitement, but he himself never made any noise or shouted out. Only once was it said of him that he cried out with a loud voice, and that was when he died on the cross. When he went about his work of preaching, healing the sick, and forgiving sins, he did so quietly and inconspicuously. We know that we can achieve many things by making a noise and shouting on the street. But not healing a person in body and soul. Every doctor will tell you that he cannot treat people in the hubbub of the streets, that people need quiet if they are to be cured. And the words of forgiveness cannot be shouted through loudspeakers. Our Lord was gentle and humble of heart. He chose to use this method. To some people, it may seem to be too slow. But try to remember, each one of you, how it was with you. How did this Lord of ours call you and attract you, how did he awaken your trust and faith—was it by shouting or through his quietness and love?

For let us not forget that those bent reeds that he did not break, those dimly burning wicks that he did not quench, were all of us. They are you and me. And I am grateful to him for not treating me more severely, for not breaking the bent reed that I am, for letting me continue to burn dimly. For he came among human beings who were bent and flickering. He came among sinners, so that here his great work of atonement could begin. He began with us, and he did not crush us but straightened us out and rekindled our flame through his love. And he invites us to join him in this and to make use of his method wherever something has to be put right.

This is what our Lord is like, God's servant, yes, God's son. This is the one for whom we are waiting, the one in whom we trust, the one in whom we hope. That is why we look toward him with heads held high, with the joy of Advent. He does not cry or lift up his voice; he does not break the bent reed; he does not quench the dimly burning wick. It is to this Lord that God has entrusted judgment over us and over all nations. He will set right everything that has been damaged. And he will not fail until he has administered judgment on the earth.

31. Through Flood and Fire
Paul W. Nisly

Isa. 43:1–5

But now, this is what the Lord says—
he who created you, O Jacob,
he who formed you, O Israel:
"Fear not, for I have redeemed you;
I have called you by name; you are mine.
When you pass through the waters,
   I will be with you;
and when you pass through the rivers,
   they will not sweep over you.
When you walk through the fire,
   you will not be burned;
   the flames will not set you ablaze.
For I am the Lord, your God,
   the Holy One of Israel, your Savior."

—Isa. 43:1–32

God weeps with us so that one day
we may laugh with him.

—Jürgen Moltmann

On September 18, 1987, a Friday afternoon, our daughter Janelle
was returning home from working at a local hospital. A registered
nurse, she had just completed her first two weeks of "real" work after

---

Paul W. Nisly is associate pastor of Slate Hill Mennonite Church
in south central Pennsylvania. He is also professor of English and
chairman of the language, literature, and fine arts department at
Messiah College in Grantham, Pennsylvania. Nisly holds two masters
degrees and a Ph.D. from the University of Kansas. His articles have
appeared in *Christianity Today.*

a rigorous four years in a baccalaureate degree program. A little over a mile from home, her little car was smashed by an out-of-control tractor-trailer rig and with it were smashed twenty-one years of dreams, aspiration, love.

In the weeks and months since that time, as we have been engulfed in our pain, we have been trying to make some sense of our situation and of God's role in human suffering. My reflections, thus, are both personal and theological. Some thoughts in process are the best I can offer on this ancient/modern dilemma of suffering in a world in which God is supposed to be in charge.

Three simple questions will focus my reflections as they have evolved in these months:

Should believers suffer?
Where is God when we suffer?
Why does God suffer?

Should Believers Suffer?

Should believers suffer? Some Christians—especially in North America—seem to think the answer is no. If we have the needed level of commitment to Jesus Christ, and if we have faith as we ought, then we will not suffer. God is our heavenly Father, the reasoning goes, and if earthly parents want good for their children, surely God wants better for his children. Why would he allow bad things to happen to those who are his dedicated followers?

A few years ago, a visiting speaker in our church said, "If suffering is so wonderful, why don't you all come up here and pray for it?" The fairly obvious implication was that, if we suffer, it is our own fault (lack of commitment, lack of faith) or perhaps even our own misguided choice.

I agree that suffering is awful. It also seems to be inevitable. The prophet says, "When you pass through the waters. . . . When you walk through the flames. . . ." The prophet's words seem to assume suffering as an unavoidable aspect of human experience.

Fire and flood are perhaps the two worst "natural" disasters, and they serve here also as metaphors for all those uncontrollable events that sweep over human life. The flames will come smoking and blazing; the flood will come with tremendous shock waves, carrying everything before it. I think of personal experiences of flood and fire. Several years ago, the Thompson River in Colorado exploded through the valley. Cars, houses, even some large rocks were moved in the torrent. I recall also wheat field fires on the plains of Kansas— where I grew up—great billowing clouds of black smoke visible for miles on the horizon, flames racing high in the dry air, popping, crackling sounds as the fire was driven forward by the south wind. Woe to any truck or combine that was caught in the path of the speeding inferno.

For humans, too, the floods and fire storms come. One of my sisters has for years had severe problems with her back. Surgery seemed to exacerbate the problem rather than relieving it. She could walk or lie down; sitting was impossible. Her husband, my brother-in-law, was a Bible school principal, minister, and evangelist, one who did a considerable amount of traveling in his work. For this they had bought a small recreational vehicle so my sister could also travel, lying on the cot.

Early one morning after a strenuous session at the Bible school, my brother-in-law fell asleep while driving, and the van hurtled down an embankment. My sister's back was broken in the accident, and for a time, life itself hung in the balance. The two were joined in their prayers by their family and many other believers across the Church. Eventually, after weeks of hospitalization and several surgeries, my sister returned home, a paraplegic who needed to relearn much.

Both were people of deep faith; both responded to the situation with grace and courage. Progress was difficult, the recovery slow, but months later my sister was able to accomplish more than one could have anticipated for a woman in her sixties recovering from such grievous injuries. And her loving, devoted husband cared for her better than most nurses could.

Prayers were not fully being answered as we had hoped, but my sister and husband were coping despite their greatly changed circumstances and curtailed activities. But wait—the story isn't finished. My brother-in-law began to experience discomfort: Eventually a doctor's diagnosis pronounced the dreaded word *cancer.* In several months, I preached his memorial sermon. It seemed impossible. He was always the strong one, never ill, always able to help others. He would always care for his wife.

I know of no one with a deeper faith in God, a more committed life of devotion to him—yet my sister suffers the flames and floods of continuing pain and loneliness.

Suffering is awful—and seemingly unavoidable.

Where Is God When We Suffer?

The most incredible, gut-wrenching agony I have ever experienced was the loss of our daughter. Where was God when the tractor-trailer rig rear-ended several cars and then smashed over into the lane of oncoming traffic? Surely, it wouldn't have taken a large miracle for God to have stopped the rig on the median strip—or to have delayed Janelle's return home by a minute.

Where was God?

Basically, there seem to be several answers to this question that sounds so simple—but that allows no easy solution. One response is that it's a matter of simple physics: The physical laws are set into action—and certain results can be expected. A tractor-trailer rig weighing so many tons, traveling at a certain rate of speed: Calculate the answer. God watches; he observes from his position on the balcony of human affairs—he may even be sorry. But there is nothing God can do to stop the physically inevitable. No miracles will bail us out.

The advantage of this view is that God cannot be held responsible for what happens. You can't *blame* God if he doesn't control events. The disadvantage, of course, is that God seems fairly powerless and incapable of helping us.

A second position is almost the obverse of the former: in this view, God regularly performs miracles for his people, if they have faith and call out to him. God is eager to help; if we don't avail ourselves of divine aid, that's our problem, not his.

Various Scriptures are appealed to in support of this view: "Ask and it will be given to you; seek and you will find; knock and the door will be opened to you. For everyone who asks, receives; he who seeks, finds; and to him who knocks, the door will be opened" (Matt. 7:7–8). Or again, "If you believe, you will receive whatever you ask for in prayer" (Matt. 21:22). The instances can be multiplied: "If you remain in me," Jesus said, "and my words remain in you, ask whatever you wish, and it will be given you" (John 15:7).

The advantage of this second view of God should be fairly obvious: He is the great rescuer, the deliverer who takes us through all the Red Seas of our lives. Nothing escapes God's notice; nothing is too large or small for God to do for his children.

The disadvantage, unfortunately, is that it doesn't seem to match our experience. Where was God when my mother prayed for seventeen long years for healing—and yet remained an invalid or semi-invalid for the rest of her life? Where was God when my sister and her husband cried out in their extremity?

A third view emphasizes God's sovereignty. God alone chooses when and how to act. Those holding the third position would see the second view as being too coercive, too demanding: We make of God a divine dispenser of candy bars, favors, and special miracles to be handed out to all takers. No, say those arguing for God's sovereignty, the Lord God alone will choose to act—or not to act—as he pleases.

The advantage of this third view is that God is in control. Nothing ultimately happens outside divine providence. As the children's song says, "He's got the whole world in his hands." Or in the familiar words from Robert Browning's *Pippa Passes:* "God's in his heaven; all's right with the world."

The disadvantage of this view is God's apparent inconsistency. Why does he help sometimes—but at other times remain silent? Why does he reveal himself on occasion—but at other times hide himself? With the prophet, one says, "Truly you are a God who hides himself, O God and Savior of Israel" (Isa. 45:15).

Somehow it would seem simpler if God never intervened; then at least we could know what to expect. The laws of physics, the "laws" of cell growth—with these we would have to cope. Or, on the other hand, if we could always expect him to bail us out of our floundering ship, that would be wonderful. But how can we make sense of this muddle, this divine inconsistency?

And if God really is sovereign, then why does he allow such awful things to occur? Gerald Oosterveen, whose young lad was dying of cancer, writes in *Too Early Frost,* "Occasionally someone would try to comfort or encourage us by reaffirming that God makes no mistakes, that nothing happens without his will, that all of this was part of some wonderful plan he has for our lives. For me, those assurances crumbled each time I stood beside my son's bed as he cried in his sleep or when I saw him walk across the lawn with that slight limp that was just becoming noticeable."

What is the meaning of justice—if God is truly sovereign? Why do people die untimely deaths? The psalmist asked that question: "You have put me in the lowest pit, in the darkest depths. . . . You have taken from me my closest friends. . . . Do those who are dead rise up and praise you?" (Psalm 88).

Why is there no discernible pattern in life—and death? "Surely," the psalmist cries out, "in vain have I kept my heart pure; in vain have I washed my hands in innocence" (Ps. 73:13). How unfair life seems! Janelle never caused her parents a moment's worry about her lifestyle. Never did we stay awake wondering about the company she was keeping. Her morals were impeccable. Yet she was ripped from us.

So how does one answer the questions of God's justice, his fairness, his involvement in the world? I believe in God's ultimate sovereignty—but that is not necessarily comforting. Philip Yancey puts the matter well in *Disappointment with God:* "I have had to conclude that divine sovereignty means at least this: only God can determine what is of value to God."

I come then, finally, somewhat reluctantly, to a fourth position, a position that does not greatly cheer me: God resides in mystery; he will not easily be defined. "I am who I am"—that was his word to Moses. He is self-existent; he doesn't need to depend on anyone else. God is beyond our categories, our definitions, our causal logic. "I am who I am."

But we Westerners have the need to understand, to explain, to rationalize. One explanation for Janelle's accident, an explanation first made to us by a kind bishop in the church, was that Janelle's sudden death affected many people. Perhaps she will now—through her dying—do more for others than had she lived. This reasoning—though well-intentioned—seems specious to me. How quickly the shock wears off for all but those family and friends intimately involved with the situation. On the other hand, had Janelle lived, she would have surely touched at least a hundred people (two hundred people?) each year—in the hospital, in the classroom. Multiply those people by almost fifty years of service, and I find the mathematics irrefutable.

Another explanation—offered in several guises—was that God in his sovereignty was purging us. "Whom the Lord loveth he chasteneth." The argument is hardly new or original: That's what Job's friends thought, too. As Nicholas Wolterstorff puts it in *Lament for a Son,* the friends argued, "God did it, Job; he was the agent of your children's death. He did it because of some wickedness in you; he did it to punish you. Nothing indeed in your public life would seem to merit such retribution; it must then be something in your private inner life." But, says Wolterstorff, "the writer of Job refuses to say that God views the lives and deaths of children as cats-o'-nine-tails with which to lacerate parents."

How, then, shall we explain? I have been forced to say that, even as I can't explain God, neither can I understand the circumstances in which we find ourselves. And while I affirm God's sovereignty, I don't comprehend it. In the midst of our perplexities, we make choices. As C. S. Lewis says, "You bid for God or no God, for a good God or the cosmic sadist, for eternal life or non-entity."

On the Sunday following the accident, the following verse by a Holocaust victim was printed on the church bulletin cover:

> I believe in the sun
>   even when it does not shine;
> I believe in love
>   even when it is not shone;
> I believe in God
>   even when he does not speak.

You make choices—and then you live by those choices. Job, who had lost possessions, health—and, not one child, but all—said, "Though he slay me, yet will I trust him." Despite this ringing affirmation, Job later became increasingly distressed with the injustice of life and the continued questioning of his friends.

Finally, God revealed himself in power and spoke in a mighty storm. God asked Job varied and puzzling questions about the mysteries and powers of nature, questions Job couldn't answer. Job listened and then acknowledged, "I know that you can do all things; no plan of yours can be thwarted." Furthermore, he said, my knowledge of you had been indirect, "but now my eyes have seen you. Therefore I despise myself and repent in dust and ashes" (Job 42:2, 5–6).

The first time that I carefully read the Book of Job was in a world literature class in college. I still recall the sense of outrage I felt at the conclusion of the "debate" with God. What kind of answer is this? It's a non sequitur—it doesn't fit the problem. Job had been asking for justice: He was shown power. Eventually, I have come to accept that we must rest without "answers," that if there is an answer, it is that we cannot fully know God's way.

As God told Moses, "My face you cannot see and live." Pascal says rather enigmatically, "A religion which does not affirm that God is hidden is not true—truly you are a hidden God." I rest, then, in a God who is beyond our knowing, a God whose mystery I cannot fathom, a God whose ways I cannot always justify. But I also believe that God does not abandon us in our pain.

Why Does God Suffer?

Why does God suffer? A curious question, surely, for how could the omnipotent God of the universe, the Creator and Sustainer of all things, the Alpha and the Omega, how could this God *suffer?*

The mystery is that God was in Christ reconciling the world to himself. The mystery is that in the crucified Christ, God shares our pain, our anguished cries of heartache, our unspeakable agony of spirit. He wakes with us in our sleepless hours; he sits with us in our loneliness and wretchedness. "When you pass through the waters, I will be with you. . . . When you walk through the fire, you will not be burned."

The prophet says in words familiar to many, "Surely he hath borne our griefs and carried our sorrows." In the past, I interpreted his word as a metaphoric statement of God's care; now I read it more literally: Our sorrows have become God's. In Jesus' dark night of the soul, he cried, "My soul is exceedingly sorrowful even unto death."

With great power Wolterstorff writes,

> How is faith to endure, O God, when you allow all
> this scraping and tearing on us? You have allowed
> rivers of blood to flow, mountains of suffering to
> pile up, sobs to become humanity's song—all
> without lifting a finger that we could see. You have
> allowed bonds of love beyond number to be
> painfully snapped. If you have not abandoned us,
> explain yourself.
>
> We strain to hear. But instead of hearing an
> answer we catch sight of God himself scraped and
> torn. Through our tears we see the tears of God.

This, then, is the mystery: that the omnipotent God in some unfathomable ways suffers with us. When Daniel's three friends were thrown into the super-heated incinerator, the king expected them to collapse in a moment. No one could survive the fierce heat. But their *ropes* were burned off—not their flesh.

And Nebuchadnezzar, the king, politician, and realist, asks in astonishment, "Didn't we throw three men into the furnace?" "Of course," his advisors respond. "Look," he says, "I see four men walking around in the fire, unbound and unharmed, and the fourth looks like a son of the gods."

I still have no satisfactory answers to the questions of suffering. But I rest in the assurance that the fourth man will walk through the flames with us. Our dark night of the soul has become his.

In Henri Nouwen's marvelous little book *The Wounded Healer,* he writes of the Master, the Wounded Healer:

> The master is coming—not tomorrow,
>   but today,
>   not next year, but this year,
>   not after all our misery is passed,
>   but in the middle of it,
>   not in another place
>   but right here where we are standing.

Through fire and flood, we have the assurance that the Wounded Healer stands with us in the blistering flames and the smashing torrent. He has not abandoned us. Amen.

32. It Is Something to Us
Vernon Murray

Lam. 1:1–22

In 587 B.C., the Babylonian army converged upon Jerusalem and utterly destroyed that city. One eye witness of this dreadful event wrote down his reflections in the form of this funeral song we now call Lamentations. And from this song we can surmise that, in the aftermath of its destruction, many people passed by the smoldering ruins of this once fair city of Yahweh.

Some passed by from a distance, no doubt, to avoid the stench of rotting corpses. Others forced themselves to tolerate the stench in order to plunder the city's wealth.

But whether the approach was near or far, apparently most who passed by ignored the pathos of what they saw and heard; or if they did take note of these cruel atrocities, their response was one of sarcasm and gladness like that recorded later in Lamentations: "All who pass your way clap their hands at you; they scoff and shake their heads at the Daughter of Jerusalem."

But it seems that there are none who take this suffering seriously, none who fathom the depth of Zion's tragic fall. So, ironically, while the pillagers spread out their hands to take the precious things of the city, the treasures of the Temple, and the precious little children, the people of Zion who forged that wealth spread out their hands for a morsel of comfort. But all to no avail: "There is none to comfort, there is none to comfort, there is none to comfort," the poet cries out repeatedly. There is none to comfort! How pathetic!

Vernon Murray is pastor of South Hill Presbyterian Church in South Hill, Virginia. Murray grew up in the Appalachian Mountains of West Virginia and served in the United States Air Force. He holds a master in divinity from Union Theological Seminary in Virginia and a doctor of ministry from McCormick Theological Seminary.

Yes, pathetic indeed, and so the poet becomes the voice of this pathetic city. He cries out on her behalf and asks his desperate question: "Is it nothing to you, all you who pass by?"

Please take note that he does not raise his voice against suffering itself. He knows as well as we do that suffering is a reality of life, that it is inextricably attached to our entrance into this world as well as to our exit, and that all the vicissitudes of life's journey, from beginning to end, travel along on this undercurrent of human suffering. Jesus himself affirms the reality of it as recorded in the Gospel of St. John: "In the world you will have trouble."

And the poet accepts the trouble of his day. He has no delusions about Zion suddenly being restored to her former state. His cry to the passerby is not a cry for them to superhumanly reconstruct the city and raise its dead, so that his suffering may suddenly cease.

No, he accepts the trouble of his day. He enters this mystery of suffering. He may not have comprehended the profundity of it all, but he knows that he must willingly or unwillingly accept it. So he does not protest against suffering itself.

Rather, he raises his objection against the sinful indifference of those who pass by and watch Zion suffer without the slightest effort of lifting their hands to comfort her.

"Is it nothing to you, all you who pass by?" Is it not enough that the city of defense now lies in ruin? Is it not enough that the city of joy now laments? Is it not enough that the city full of people is now empty? Is it not enough that the city of God's pleasure seems now to receive his wrath? Is it not enough that Zion suffers, must she suffer alone? "Is it nothing to you, all you who pass by?"

But to this challenging question, there is not even a semblance of pity for Zion, and so the poet pitifully takes note, "But there is none to comfort." How terribly tragic that Zion suffers alone.

But more tragic still is the passion of our Lord Jesus Christ. Human depravity has never contrived a more brutal form of execution than that of crucifixion. The excruciating pain of punctured hands and feet, aggravated by the full weight of the body upon the wounds, is a horror too intense for words. It was a torture that many had to endure in those days. But for our Savior, the hammer pounds out its bitter torment, and the pain pulsates through his mangled body in a void of comfort.

To be sure, there is no void of human attention. There are many who witness the event of the day. Some pass by; some stand by; some hang by on crosses like that of the Lord. But despite the overabundance of human attention, there is a vacuum of human comfort.

Instead of water, they give him vinegar. Instead of prayers, they issue curses. Instead of praise, they offer derision. Instead of walking by in holy awe, they strut by with head cocked and fists clinched.

And if this ancient Hebrew poet would have been there at the foot of the cross, surely he would have raised his voice once again in passionate protest. "Is it nothing to you, all you who pass by?"

Is it nothing to you lepers, whose hands he cleansed, that now his hands are torn and bleeding? Is it nothing to you whose eyes he washed, whose sight he restored, that now his eyes are matted and blurred by the stream of red that flows from forehead and brow? Is it nothing to you whose thirst he quenched with miraculous wine, that now his only drink is vinegar? Is it nothing to you whose legs he straightened that now his legs are all out of joint? Is it nothing to you whose ears and hearts were blessed with lofty words on Olivet's lofty mount that now he hears only the doubter's curse? Is it nothing to you that he who was a comforter to all, suffers in a void of any comfort whatsoever? "Is it nothing to you, all you who pass by?"

The sights and sounds of Zion's pathos fade into the ancient past; the gruesome images of Golgotha grow dim in the distance of two millenniums. But the tributaries of time dump out two thousand more years of war and destruction, drought and famine, slavery and oppression, sickness and death, heartache and heartbreak.

It all converges into an ocean of human suffering, and yet there is more.

In a dilapidated trailer near an Appalachian town, we see a young boy lying on his bed with stiffened body as he braces himself against the sound of slamming doors, the eruption of profanity, the shuffling and crashing of glass, and the sobbing of brothers and sisters.

In a comfortable American suburb, a disheartened woman sits staring blankly at the wall. Veiled beneath her fashioned hair and her customized cosmetics is a wounded heart, pierced to the quick by the debris of a shattered relationship.

At a grave side, a young father and mother stand helplessly by as the cemetery custodian lowers the child of their youth out of their sight, their dreams vanishing before their eyes in the darkness of the day.

The sights and sounds of human suffering flash a hundred times into our contemporary living rooms in living color. But comfortably separated by TV's glassy screen, we grow hard-hearted and indifferent.

Then the pages of this ancient lament engage our eyes, and there arises from them the echo of the poet's haunting question: "Is it nothing to you, all you who pass by?"

The question penetrates the air of our contemporary world. But ere the last word is spoken, the broad stream of humanity turns its course to seek the pleasantries of life. And as in the days of this ancient poet, so now the question either goes unheard or unanswered. "Is it nothing to you, all you who pass by?"

But there is a remnant who will hear the question and respond. There are a few who will turn from the beaten path and declare from a heart sanctified by God, "Yes, it is something to us, we who pass by. It is something to us that you suffer."

We at South Hill Presbyterian Church would like to think that we are among that remnant who are in tune with the lament of this ancient Hebrew poet and who respond in a positive way.

We have no delusions about our capabilities. We know that we cannot rebuild the walls of your life in one night, no more than the passerby of Zion could rebuild in one night the walls of the ancient Temple.

Moreover, we know that we cannot mend your broken dreams or rekindle your dying hopes at the drop of a hat. And we would not be so foolish as to have you pretend that the gnawing agony in the depths of your innermost being does not exist, for we know that healing can only come when we affirm the reality of the affliction.

But we would answer the ancient poet's question. We would say, "Yes, it is something to us, we who pass by. It is something to us that you suffer." Rather than ignore your suffering or pretend that it does not exist, we would affirm it, affirm its intensity, affirm its devastation. We would acknowledge your dreams and hopes that are broken or buried in a sea of grief. We would remember those dreams and the people who inspired them but who were cut down before their fruition.

We would not be so presumptuous to say that we suffer with you, for we cannot fully know what it is that you suffer. Yet we would say that, while you suffer, you do not suffer alone. We may not be able to suffer with you, but we can be with you while you suffer, and that is where we choose to be, that is what we choose to do.

We would not delude you or ourselves by telling you that Zion's walls were rebuilt overnight or that her inhabitants were restored in one day. But we can tell you that, upon the ash heap of Zion, God did restore Jerusalem and its inhabitants, of which we all are witnesses.

We cannot affirm that Sunday immediately follows Good Friday. But we can tell you that from the darkness of a dreary tomb there did emerge a victorious Christ.

We cannot tell you that the dark night of your soul is of a short duration, but we can tell you that, though weeping remain through a long night, joy will come in the morning of a longer eternity.

While the vast majority of humanity passes you by and ignores the depths of your suffering, while they choose to remain deaf to the desperate cry of the ancient poet, we choose to hear that poet and hear him right well.

To be sure, we do not have all the answers. We certainly do not have a panacea for your broken hearts and your crushed dreams. But we do care. We do remember, and for what it is worth, it is something to us, we who pass by today. It is something to us, this dark night of your soul. It is something to us, and for that reason we gather here today to be with you and to remember with you. Amen.

33. Doing and Being
Byron C. Bangert

Job 3:1–4, 20—4:6; Luke 18:15–17

Have you ever wondered what it is that makes life worth living? What is it about life that keeps us interested, engaged, sufficiently satisfied to go on? Is it what we are able to do? Or is it who we are able to be?

That is probably putting the matter much too simply. Can one really be without doing? Or can one really do without being? Nonetheless, it may be helpful to think about doing and being as if they were two distinguishable approaches to life.

Lately, I have been very busy doing. Sometimes I am able to stop long enough to wish I had more time just to be. At the same time, I know that doing can be a very satisfying experience. There are even some things that I hate to do and yet find satisfaction in the doing. Being able to do things helps give one a sense of accomplishment. I seem to have a need, and I assume others do also, to do things that have identifiable effects. Even things that are not in themselves pleasant to do can be satisfying because one can point to and affirm the results. On the other hand, some things that may seem pleasant to do may yield a certain discontent precisely because they do not result in any tangible evidence of accomplishment. They give us nothing to show for our time and efforts.

To a large extent it seems that the worth of my life is bound up with what I am able to do, and being able to see the results of my efforts assures me of that worth. As a youth, my favorite subject was math. I could readily do the work and see the results in terms of

Byron C. Bangert is pastor of the First Presbyterian Church in Bloomington, Indiana. He received his master of divinity and his doctorate from Vanderbilt Divinity School. Bangert has written for *The Christian Century* and other magazines.

problems solved. In college, however, I found myself unable to see the ultimate usefulness to me of the math itself and consequently ended up doing other things.

It may be more true of men than women, but I think it is true of all of us that our sense of self-worth or self-esteem is linked to what we are able to do. A person who feels inadequate, or of questionable worth, usually associates that feeling with the inability or failure to do certain things. A man may feel inadequate as a husband and father if he is unable to make enough money to provide for his family. A woman may feel inadequate as a wife and mother if she is not a good cook or housekeeper. Changing gender roles may change the occasions for the feelings of inadequacy. Many men now feel inadequate as nurturers, while many women now feel inadequate as breadwinners. In any case, feelings of inadequacy are most likely linked to those expected activities and tasks at which we do not do very well. The person who says, "I can't seem to do anything right," is probably questioning his or her own value and worth. The person who says, "I'm not able to do anything anymore," may be doubting whether life is still worth the living.

Is there anything pernicious in joining the value of our lives to what we are able to do? Perhaps you have read Brian Clark's play *Whose Life Is It Anyway?* or seen the movie starring Richard Dreyfuss. It is a very engaging story about a very appealing young man who wants to be allowed to die. The protagonist, Ken Harrison, has had his spinal cord ruptured in an automobile accident. He is paralyzed from the neck down and can expect to require hospitalization for the rest of his life. He is a gifted young sculptor who can no longer sculpt, fighting a medical establishment that wants to keep him alive. In trying to explain himself, he tells his medical social worker, "I have decided that I do not want to go on living with so much effort for so little result."

The play makes a compelling case for rational suicide. The protagonist engages our sympathies against those in the medical profession who would force him "to go on living with so much effort for so little result." But the play really does not resolve the question of whether Ken Harrison ought to take his life. Even those in the play who work to win him his freedom to do so do not wish to see him take his life. His life is of value to them.

The case of a Ken Harrison is not implausible. One wonders what life would be like without the use of one's arms or legs. Would it be worth living? There are certainly many quadriplegics alive today, all of them requiring some sort of continuous care. If one judges the value of human life in economic terms, most such lives are not worth living. They require great expenditure of medical and personal resources. They place great demands upon others. They are a burden to society. Even with modern electronic technology, most of the Ken Harrisons of the world are not able to make much of an economic contribution to the world. In terms of physical accomplishments, they are not able to do much of anything at all. Mostly, they require so much effort for so little result.

But this only presses upon us the question of whether the value of human life must be tied to what one is able to do. How far are we prepared to go in saying that life is a matter of doing? On the one hand, we tend to think that our lives are worth more the more we can do. The greater our sense of accomplishment, the greater our sense of self-worth. But can we turn this into a general rule? Is the life that is able to do more of greater value? Is the life of a physically normal person of greater value than that of one who is disabled? Is the life of a genius of greater value than that of one who has Down's syndrome? Is the life of a robust person of greater value than that of the sickly individual? It seems to me that there are no pat answers to these questions precisely because the value of human life is not to be comprehended solely by what the individual is able to do.

Ken Harrison decides that his life is not worth living because of what he is no longer able to do and because of the psychological—not physical—pain that is entailed in his helpless state. No one else in the play really wants to see him die, not because they judge his life prospects differently, but because they value his life differently. They value him not for what he can or will be able to do, not even finally because it is in their medical interest to see him live, but because of who he is. They value him for who he is able to be, regardless of what he is able to do. They value him enough to respect his wish to be allowed to die, even if they think that he is wrong.

It is often only in exceptional circumstances that we discover the value and importance of being. Our society would have us think that our real value is to be measured by our doing. From a strictly rationalist, economic point of view, unless our producing exceeds our consuming we are a burden upon others and the world. The law of the marketplace, which governs so many of our daily transactions, is survival of the fittest. There is no room for the unproductive, the

inefficient, the uncompetitive. We speak affirmatively of self-suffi-
ciency, economic independence, and increasing productivity. Planning is goal-directed; organization is achievement-oriented;
management is by objectives. How easily we slip into the track of
thinking that living means nothing more than doing!

But then an illness strikes. Then an accident happens. Then a
loved one dies. Then something happens beyond one's control.
Then comes the question, What can I do? Then one realizes that
doing is not enough. Then one discovers that doing may not help
at all. Then one may begin to understand that being is more important even than doing.

The medical staff members in Brian Clark's play are at first anxious to change Ken Harrison's mind about the future. They are a bit
like the purported friends of Job, Eliphaz the Temanite and the
others, who exhorted Job not to curse his life and not to despair.
They do not hear the depth of his suffering and find it too easy to
believe that this anguish can be dissolved. The medical staff members try to persuade Harrison that he will be able to adjust emotion-
ally to his physical helplessness. They talk about the surprising
advances in technology that will permit him to do things he would
not think possible. They look for the thing to say or do that will turn
him around. It is only as he succeeds in convincing them that their
efforts are doing nothing for him that they are then able to listen to
him, to be present to him as human beings who can share his suffering and not feel that they must do something for him. It is finally
their being, not their doing, that he needs!

There is irony in the play, however. Ken Harrison does not fully
appreciate the value of his own being. He depreciates the significance of his own life for those who care for him. He does not want
to be pitied; he does not want to be patronized; he does not want
to be an object of professional achievement; he does not want to be
the occasion of others' guilt. He is all of these. But he is also the
object of their affection and admiration and love. He means more to
those who care for him than he is able to permit himself to believe.
He does not realize how much they value him for who he is.

I would judge that we mainline Protestants have a worse time
than most when it comes to acknowledging the limits of our doing
and the priority of our being. After all, our basic posture toward life
is rationalist and activist and reformist. If something is wrong, we
analyze it; we work at it; we amend it, fix it, change it. We are by

nature doers. There is much to be said for this posture toward life. There is nothing intrinsically wrong with doing. The person who wants to do something with his or her life is surely more appealing than the person who devotes great energy into trying to be somebody. Doers are people who have at least some sense of responsibility for making a contribution to the lives of others.

The danger lies in supposing that doing is the primary source of one's value and worth. Does one value a friend primarily for what that friend does, or because of who that friend is? Is it not the being of the friend, more than the doing, that makes the friend a friend? We do value others for their contributions to our lives, and we do value our lives for their contributions to others. But these contributions are not just in what we do but in who we are to one another.

The value of one's life to others, and even to oneself, simply cannot be measured by one's doing. When a friend loses a loved one, for example, one may find nothing that one can do, or even say, that will help or make a difference. But being with that friend may matter a great deal. Books on pastoral care and ministry speak of the ministry of presence. Sometimes ministry requires some doing: speaking needed words, helping with some difficult task, performing some rite, reading the Scriptures, offering a prayer. But sometimes ministry simply means being there, present with another. There may be nothing in particular to do but to be. And always the being is prerequisite to the doing. As the gift without the giver is bare, so the doing without the being is bare.

Still, we want to do, not just be. Often we would rather do than be. I find that doing what I think I ought to do is often easier than being who I feel I ought to be. I can more readily effect a change out there in my environment than within me, in who I am. I can *do* better than I can *be!*

But being is prior, more important. Sometimes it takes the experience of being unable to do to discover the value of being. The Gospels record an incident in the life of Jesus that seems to me to say better than anything else I can think of how important it is to be. According to Luke, the people in the crowd were bringing infants to Jesus that he might touch them. Jesus' disciples tried to prevent this, apparently assuming that Jesus would not want to be bothered. What possible interest could Jesus have in such small children? He has more important things to do than mess with babies. But Jesus says, Do not hinder them, for to such belongs the Kingdom of God.

Is there anyone more dependent, more helpless, more unable to do than an infant? An infant can do no work, make no money, earn no keep, produce nothing but messy diapers. All an infant can do is be! Yet we say, How precious! An infant relies wholly upon others for care. An infant is all take and no give. An infant is on the receiving end of life. And Jesus says, "Whoever does not *receive* the Kingdom of God like a child shall not enter it."

What can this mean but that life is not to be attained. It is not an achievement. It is not our doing that makes it whatever it is. To be sure, if we have abilities, if we have talents, if we have energies, we will want to use them and enjoy them and offer them to others. But prior to anything we can do is the life we have received and continue to receive at the hands of others. This is the life that comes to us in being, not doing, in relationships, not in accomplishments. It is valued, as an infant is valued, not for its achievements but because it belongs to the web of existence.

It seems to me that life is most complete, most fulfilling, most worth living when we experience ourselves to be organically related to others, belonging to a network of relationships in which the most important thing is not doing anything so much as being ourselves. What we do does not cease to matter, but who we are somehow matters more. When that happens, life is experienced not as accomplishment but as gift. Life has value, meaning, even purpose because it belongs, because it is accepted, because it is loved. Life is worth living when we know ourselves to be known, accepted, and loved—as we are, for who we are—by others and by God. Amen.

VI. DEVOTIONAL

34. What to Do about God
Welton Gaddy

Gen. 32:22–31

So, you came to worship today to meet God. Really? Do you really want to meet God? If you do, how will you respond? Run, I suspect. Some will run in fear or in excitement or both. Maybe not. Maybe not all of us will respond to God that way. Perhaps some will stay and fight it out—engage God in a struggle. That would not be too uncommon. Precedent for such action exists.

Now before you tell me, let me confess to you that I know this is not particularly a good way to begin a sermon. Even if it is homiletically abominable, however, experientially it is truthful. Please stay with me.

Honestly, is it not much more pleasant to seek God than to find God? Generally speaking, seeking God just means showing up in the right place, assuming an appropriate posture, and mouthing familiar words with no great expectations of real encounter. But, finding God—oh, finding God!—that is something else. You stand trembling or sit shaking. Your insides feel as if you must run as fast as you can, but you can't even move. All the courage in your will wilts. Your voice is reduced to a broken whisper. You are awed, scared, overwhelmed. Seeking God seems so much more pleasant than finding God. Seeking God can go on endlessly—a lifetime with little trouble if you plan it right. Finding God can change your life immediately, trouble you, and make you right. What do you want? Look at the possibilities realistically. What are we to do about God?

Welton Gaddy is a minister living in Macon, Georgia, where he has served as senior minister to Mercer University and as pastor of Highland Hills Baptist Church. He is the author of several books, including *Profile of a Christian Citizen* and *Beginning at the End.*

Actually, the promise of meeting God may well evoke several different responses. Historically, actual personal encounters with God have provoked reactions so similar that they are now almost predictable. Consider some options this morning. One does not preclude the others. As a matter of fact, each option of response may well be a stepping-stone to another level of more meaningful response.

What are we to do about God?

Flee

Flee from God. That is one option—just run away or at least try to run away. Numerous are the people who have made this response to God. Adam and Eve were the first but not the last. They wanted to get away from God just somewhere in the garden, but soon found they had run so fast and so far that they were no longer in the garden. Look at Jonah. What a pathetic prophet running as hard as he could run to get away from the God who had a message of salvation for him and his listeners. Maybe the big fish's belly was good enough for him. Then there was Paul, darting here and there across the Greco-Roman world, seeking to escape God and to execute God's people. A list of those who have run from God would stretch as far as the history of the world from Bible times until now.

Don't be too critical, though. In fact, be very careful about judging those who have fled God. Paul Tillich preached convincingly that a person "who has never tried to flee God has never experienced the God Who is really God." He may be right. Of course, we rub shoulders with, not run from, the gods we create. Who cannot be comfortable with self-styled deities? These gods we shape think like we think, like what we like, vote like we vote. Our pet gods excuse our faults, salve our consciences, and refuse to judge us. Listen carefully to Tillich: "A god whom we can easily bear, a god from whom we do not have to hide, a god whom we do not hate in moments, a god whose destruction we never desire, is not God at all and has no reality."

Who of us wants to be known by God—really, completely known? To be sure, we want God's love—all of us want to be loved by God—but God's love and judgment go together. To be open to receive compassion from God, we must be open to hear instructions from God and to experience transformation by God. An encounter with God can change life completely. Do you see? That is why so many people try to create so much space between themselves and God. Literally, people attempt to flee from possible encounters with God—to noise rather than silence, lest God's voice be heard; to work rather than to worship, lest God's power be felt; to weekend visits at places in the country rather than regular participation in the faith community, lest God's Spirit be sensed.

Ironically, some folks seek to set space between themselves and God by the manipulation of religion. Thus, religion is displayed as a thin veneer of respectability in relation to neighbors but erected as a barrier behind which they attempt to hide from God. We can look very holy and refrain from being godly. Fearing the consequences of a meeting with God, some people run.

You do know this will fail, do you not? Such is the meaning of that dollar-and-a-half word *omnipresent.* God is everywhere. We cannot run fast enough or far enough to escape God. To wherever we run from God, inevitably we will find God. The psalmist tried to prepare us:

> Where could I go to escape from you? Where could
> I get away from your presence? If I went up to
> heaven, you would be there; if I lay down in the
> world of the dead, you would be there. If I flew
> away beyond the east or lived in the farthest place
> in the west, you would be there to help me. (Ps.
> 139:7–10)

We cannot get away from God. God "dogs" us. Understandably, that fact may anger us more and increase the intensity of our resolve to escape. Please know, though, that God pursues us like a persistent mother searching for a lost child, like a compassionate baker seeking out the starving in order to give them bread, like a thoughtful clown looking for a hospital ward in which to make sad people laugh. We cannot get away from God. So what are we to do about God?

Fight

Fight God. That is another option. We can just face into the fact of God's presence and engage God in a struggle on our turf. This option may not be the best one, but it is better than running away. At least this experience moves us beyond any fanciful thoughts of ever escaping God.

Jacob's experience at Jabbok can be instructive to us. This man spent an entire night wrestling with God. Probably, it seemed like a lifetime. Remember, Jacob had been running. The immediate past of his life involved strange places and strange people. Though he had avoided most everybody, in running away from God he ran over a few people like Esau, Isaac, and Laban. Jacob's time of reckoning had come.

Let it be said on Jacob's behalf, he was willing to struggle. Some people do not want any hassle—not even the bother of finding peace with God. Jacob was not like that. He was ready to settle the issue. Jacob and God locked themselves into one more powerful struggle. In fact, at one point God was ready to go, but Jacob would not let the matter rest. He wanted a blessing from God, and he determined to hang on to God until he got it.

Doesn't all of that sound strangely familiar? When we finally do face into the reality of God, we have to settle this matter about who is the Creator and who is the created, who is sovereign and who is subject, who is Savior and who is in need of salvation. The battle grows fierce at points because we want redemption at our price, written into a contract developed by our legal counsel. Yes, we will fight—anyone, including God. We are accustomed to calling a stockbroker, saying, "Sell," and knowing he sold. So we cry to God, "Give me a blessing," and we wait for God to obey.

Who has not fought with God? "Make sense of the mystery," we demand. "Explain this untimely illness!" we implore. "How can you be good and allow so much evil?" we taunt. "Why does there have to be pain?" we beg. "You will tell me how this venture will end, or I will never begin!" we threaten. Sometimes the struggle even gets nastier. We sense we are losing. Deciding we cannot best God, we choose to deny God. That is the way we will get at God. Many atheists came to their creed out of a fight. Thus, we write books about God's disappearance from the world, and we print on the cover of *Time* magazine that God is dead. Now we have got him. He will serve us or we will show Him. Surely, God must laugh at our attempting to get at him by shaking our fist at the heavens. But, no, he doesn't laugh. The struggle is far too serious for that.

Jacob finally got a blessing from God. But it cost him—it cost him a broken hip and a name change. It cost him his identity and his stature. Jacob's struggle ended with God still being God and with a strong-legged Jacob becoming Israel with a limp.

We will never receive a blessing by demand. Don't you know? God's favor comes as a gift. Even then, however, it comes only when we know our need. Jacob now knew he needed God. Maybe, after all, that was the blessing—a recognition that he was not self-sufficient, that he had a limp in his walk, that his spirit needed God's Spirit. Maybe that was the blessing. It is a blessing to realize our need for God.

At sunrise, at the very point when Jacob should have been most tired, Jacob was changed. Where does it happen for us—in a hospital room? at the grave side? in a closet of despair? when screaming questions have left our voices silent and our throats hoarse? when we are unemployed? when we are separated from loved ones? Just when Jacob could have given up, he got up. With God's help, Jacob got up. No longer was he on his own. The one with whom he had struggled was the one with whom he would travel. He was ready to settle into the Promised Land.

No longer was the question one of what to do about God. Now the question was what God was to do about Jacob—about us. That leads to the third response.

Faith

Finally, faith. That is the third option. How nice it would be to start here, but maybe that cannot be. Perhaps the running and the fighting always precede faith. Sooner or later, though, if you stay with God you will come to this.

Please understand the nature of faith. This faith is no mere resignation in fatigue, no pious giving up once we are pinned down. Faith is trust—not blind belief, not creedal confession—trust. Faith is giving ourselves completely to one who cares for us, who gives himself for us. I need not run from God though he is holy and I am sinful. He will judge me, but his judgment will be an act of love. I trust him. Faith is trust.

Faith is confidence. I need not struggle against God. He is all-wise even as he is ever-present. God will not act arbitrarily. I may not understand his ways, but I need not question his ways. God's very presence is my assurance that all is well. Faith is confidence.

Faith is conviction. I will stake my life on God's call, for God's will is the most important factor in life. I am convinced that God's way is *the* way. Oh, sure, struggling and running continue. Now there is a difference, however. If I must run, I will run on God's way. If I must struggle, I will struggle to stay in God's will. That's it. Faith is conviction.

Faith brings us to where we ought to be in responding to God. Be aware, though, it is an awesome place. In faith, we stand open before God, vulnerable to have our wills guided by his will, to have our steps directed by his voice, to have our lives made completely new. We run and struggle, soar and step, think and live by faith.

Look now, look closely at Jacob walking away from this experience. Set against the rising sun on the horizon, you can see clearly his limp—his scar from the struggle, the brokenness that allowed him to be whole. Yes, he is walking with a limp, but suddenly you realize that he has never walked with more certainty. Maybe Jacob lost the struggle, but to lose with God is to win. Jacob now looks like a winner.

So, you came to worship today to meet God. Really? Do you really want to meet God? If you do, how will you respond? Run? Struggle? Faith? Oh, I hope it is faith. I hope you respond to God in faith. That is the way that leads through the dark night of the soul to the brightness of God's love. If you do not believe me, ask that man limping across the horizon, that man bathed in the light of the rising sun. Ask Jacob.

35. What Easter Means to Christians

A. Leonard Griffith

Why do Christians make such a big fuss over Easter? Why is it such an important festival in the Christian year? Most churches are filled today, even those that are normally half empty. Some will hold extra services to accommodate the overflow crowds. And it isn't altogether unlike a college reunion—the alumni returning for their annual visit to their spiritual alma mater. Easter has its own dynamic even for practicing Christians. There is something special about this day. What does it mean for us?

If you want to know what Easter historically means to Christians, read the opening chapters of the Book of Acts, which record the earliest Christian preaching. Those were the sermons preserved in oral tradition before any part of the New Testament was written. They were the first public utterances of the apostles who had known Jesus and witnessed his Resurrection. That's what qualified them to be apostles and that's where their preaching began—not with the life, teaching, ministry, or death of Jesus, but with the fact that God raised him from the dead. Peter proclaimed it on the Day of Pentecost: *"God raised him up, having loosed the pangs of death, because it was not possible for him to be held by it"* (Acts 2:24).

We have to make an important distinction here which I illustrate by recalling a disaster film that you may have seen. It was about an airplane that crashed into the ocean and sank to the ocean bed. It remained intact, though it would soon buckle under the heavy pres-

A. Leonard Griffith was born in Lancashire, England. A member of the Anglican Church of Canada, he has served as a minister of St. Paul's Church in Toronto and the City Temple in London. Dr. Griffith has written twenty-one books, most recently *From Sunday to Sunday: Fifty Years in the Pulpit,* an autobiography.

sure of water. It contained enough oxygen to keep the passengers and crew alive for a while, but that would soon give out. The airplane had no built-in hydraulic mechanism that would cause it to rise to the surface of the water. It was permanently stuck and its occupants doomed unless help came from the outside. That is what happened. Helicopters sighted the sunken craft, rescue ships surrounded the area, divers went down and wrapped cables around the plane, then giant balloons gradually lifted it to the surface and held it there long enough to set the passengers and crew free. The plane didn't *rise;* it was *raised.*

That illustrates the truth of Easter. The Bible plainly states, not that Jesus rose from the dead as daffodils rise from the earth in springtime, but that God raised him as rescue forces raised that sunken plane from the ocean floor. Jesus was dead, as dead as any human corpse interred in a cemetery. Even he had no built-in mechanism, no inherent immortality that would cause him to rise to the surface of the grave. When the disciples saw him alive after he had been pronounced dead, they knew that what they were witnessing was not a miracle of human survival but a mighty act of God. That's what they proclaimed and celebrated. "God raised him up, having loosed the pangs of death, because it was not possible for him to be held by it."

For Christians, God is the principal character in the Easter drama. Other people on this day may celebrate the awakening of the earth and the renewal of life and even the hope of immortality, but *we* celebrate God's mighty act in raising Jesus Christ from the dead. Easter means that our God is forever the God who raised Jesus Christ from the dead. Now let us express that truth in three closely related ways.

I

First, Easter means that *God is always a factor in the human situation.* Too often he is the forgotten factor. Too often we leave him out of our human calculations. In our personal crises, in the Church's struggle, in the problems of the world, we tend to think and behave as though it all depended upon us. When we have done our best and exhausted our strength and used up all our resources, and when every human factor is against us, we sometimes forget that there is still another factor—the love and power of God.

That truth leaps out at us from every part of the Bible. To Moses, the shepherd of Midian, it seemed a hopeless mission to liberate his people from centuries of slavery in Egypt and lead them safely across the Red Sea, through the desert, and back to their own land. Egypt was the oldest and strongest civilization in the world. How could he hope to challenge its power? Every human factor seemed set against it. But Moses had forgotten one factor of which God reminded him by saying, in effect, "All right, Moses. You have done your best. Now you will see what I shall do." And Moses saw. He saw a display of divine power unequalled since the dawn of creation. He saw the human might of Egypt crumble like straw under the mightier hand of God. To be sure, every human factor seemed against God's people in their daring effort to escape from slavery, but they had left one factor out of their calculations—the love and power of God.

The disciples of Jesus left that factor out of their calculations on Good Friday. When they saw his mangled corpse taken down from the cross and sealed in a stone sepulchre, they slunk away like whipped animals to lick their wounds. What fools they had been to believe that their Master was really who he claimed to be and that his way of love could prevail! Every human and physical factor seemed set against it. They had forgotten one factor, however. The Bible says that they rested the next day, being their Sabbath, but what they did not realize was that, even as men rested, the power of God was beginning to work. While deathly defeat gripped the world of earthly sense, another world was astir and in commotion, another mustering of forces was in progress, and the life that lay still in the grave was moving forth in triumph. "But God raised him up, having loosed the pangs of death, because it was not possible for him to be held by it."

The implications of that truth come across from a novel written several years ago by Thomas Savage, entitled *A Bargain with God.* It is the story of an Anglican priest, Father Ferris, who knew and loved all the people in his inner city parish, especially Johnny and Jebby Moss, whom he had married and whose baby he had baptized. One day a fire gutted the building where the Moss family lived, taking the life of their little daughter. Johnny bore the tragedy bravely, but Jebby was numb with grief. She withdrew into herself, refused to speak to anybody, scarcely recognized her husband, and simply sang songs all day to the doll which had belonged to her child. Desperate to see his wife herself again, Johnny went to Father Ferris and poured out his anguish. What could he do? The priest replied, "There's only one thing you can do . . . ask for help." The faint hope in Johnny's eyes vanished. He said dully, "You mean pray?" Father Ferris replied, "Prayers are answered. Not just those for strength and courage, but the others, too." Johnny said, "I never thought much about miracles." The priest answered him gently, "It is hard to believe, but if the greatest miracle happened, of course the little ones can, and we know that the great one happened." Johnny was puzzled. "What do you mean?" he asked. "I mean," said Father Ferris, "that God raised Jesus Christ from the dead."

That's what Easter means to Christians. Because God raised Jesus Christ from the dead, therefore he is always a factor in our human situation, and we must never leave him out of our calculations. We must believe in him and trust him and pray to him and expect from him what may appear to be miracles. Even in the darkest hour we may ever come to know, when we are helpless ourselves and beyond all human help, we can still echo the psalmist who said, "Our help is in the name of the Lord who made heaven and earth."

II

We can express the truth of Easter by saying also that *our God is a God who intervenes.* People of faith have always made that discovery about God. The 124th Psalm, which I just quoted, begins, "If it had not been the Lord who was on our side when men rose up against us . . ." This is one of the psalms that pilgrims sang on the way to Jerusalem, and "the men who rose up against them" were probably bandits and brigands. The psalmist compares them to a primeval monster that swallows up its victims, to raging floodwaters that create chaos, to a trap that snares a helpless animal. There seemed no escape, yet they did escape. It was as though an invisible hand interposed to drive off the monster, push back the floodwaters, and release the deadly trap. Where did this unexpected help come from? The psalmist answers with complete confidence: "Our help is in the name of the Lord who made heaven and earth."

That's what happened at Easter, as Peter proclaimed on the Day of Pentecost when he said to the people, ". . . this Jesus . . . you crucified and killed . . . but God raised him up. . . . " By raising Jesus from the dead, God showed himself to be forever the God who intervenes on the side of the helpless when strong men rise up against them. Men rose up against Jesus, giving grim reality to all those figures of speech coined by the psalmist to describe the peril of the pilgrims. The monster of Roman power swallowed him, the raging floodwaters of religious hypocrisy threw his brief ministry into chaos, a stone sepulchre held his lifeless body in a trap. Then the miracle happened. An invisible hand interposed to drive off the monster, push back the floodwaters, and release the deadly trap. Where did this unexpected help come from? The New Testament writers would echo the psalmist with complete confidence: "Our help is in the name of the Lord who made heaven and earth."

There is a philosophy of history in the Easter truth that our God is a God who intervenes. Thornton Wilder made it the theme of his unusual play *The Skin of Our Teeth,* which tells the story of Mr. and Mrs. Antrobus, a typical American family who represent the human race and span the whole sweep of recorded history. Each act brings the earth's inhabitants to the brink of extinction, first with the approaching Ice Age, then with the Flood, finally with World War Two. Each time the human race appears doomed, but each time an invisible hand intervenes, and the human race, despite its own stupidity, survives by the skin of its teeth. Antrobus himself sums it up in one of his closing speeches: "Oh, I've never forgotten for a long time that living is a struggle. I know that every good and excellent thing in the world stands, moment by moment, on the razor edge of danger and must be fought for. All I ask is the chance to build new worlds, and God has always given us that second chance, and has given us voices to guide us and the memory of our mistakes to warn us. . . . "

That is the story of the Church all down the centuries. Time and again, when men have risen up against it, God has intervened to save it from extinction. We thought that thirty years of communism had destroyed the Church in China. Indeed, a former missionary, who revisited China in 1974, said at the time that only 2 churches in the whole country were open, both in Peking. The Protestant service which he attended drew only seventeen worshipers, three of them Chinese. There was no sermon, only a liturgy. Yet seven years later the same observer told that 120 churches had been repaired and opened for services. He says that powerful sermons on biblical themes were being preached, and thousands of worshipers, half of them under twenty years of age, filled the seats, aisles, and overflow rooms. He said that in one year alone 135,000 Chinese Bibles were published and that a new translation was being prepared by scholars at a recently opened theological seminary. "Without question," he said, "an extraordinary burst of activity on the national, provincial and local levels, is revitalizing the Christian churches of China."

John Calvin said that the story of the Church is a story of many resurrections, and if we can accept the evidence of that truth, we shall regard the Church's future with new hope. Beyond any doubt, the Church has powerful enemies in the secular world culture who rise up to crucify it, and perhaps there is much in the Church's life that ought to be crucified. The Church, as we know it in its present form, could become a corpse; but God can raise a corpse, he can bring the dead to life. Our God has shown himself to be a God who intervenes.

III

We can express the truth of Easter yet another way by saying that the Resurrection of Jesus Christ means that *God will always have the last word.* Of course, nothing seemed further from the truth when Jesus was put to death on Good Friday. Pontius Pilate, who signed the death warrant and said, "What I have written, I have written," thought that he had the last word. The priests who jeered before the cross, "He saved others. He cannot save himself!" thought they had the last word. The Roman soldiers who drove great spikes through his quivering hands and feet and thrust a sword into his side thought they had the last word. The malignant powers of evil and death that hovered like vultures over the dying Son of God thought that they had the last word. Satan, the Prince of Darkness, who had lost many battles against Christ and who now appeared to have won, thought that he had the last word.

But they were all wrong. Behind the cross of Christ, hidden in the shadows, his hand holding the cross, his agony more terrible than the agony of the Crucified, was God, the forgotten factor who intervenes on the side of the helpless when strong men rise up against them. The characters in the passion drama had left God out of their calculations. They didn't know that God wrote the drama and was directing it, dealing once and for all with the evil that crucified his Son and smashing the power of death that held him in its grip. The whole scenario on that Black Friday happened within the sovereign purpose of almighty God, and when it was over, God spoke the last word. That word was *Resurrection.* "God raised him up, having loosed the pangs of death, because it was not possible for him to be held by it."

That is a word we desperately need to hear in our personal and corporate lives. In our personal lives we too readily assume that death will have the last word. We are like those professional mourners in the Gospel story who cried out to the distraught father, when he brought Jesus to heal his sick daughter, "Your daughter is dead; do not trouble the Teacher anymore." For them death was the end, and there could be no arguing with it. But it was not the end for Jesus. He protested against the whole cult of death and our solemn submission in the face of it. He considered that to be a denial of God, who has promised that his purpose for us is not death but life. He underscored that promise in the upper room when he told his disciples that there are other rooms in the Father's house, other worlds beyond this, and that God has all eternity in which to fulfill his purpose for our lives. Not death but God will have the last word, the God of our Lord Jesus Christ who "raised him up, having loosed the pangs of death, because it was not possible for him to be held by it."

The Resurrection of Jesus Christ is God's guarantee that he will have the last word not only in our lives but in our world. That was the theme of an Easter sermon preached two years ago in Northern Ireland by a Roman Catholic priest, John Joseph McCullough. I think it deserves the Nobel peace prize. Reminding his congregation of the joy of the Resurrection, he says,

> It must be almost impossible for so many people
> this morning to find any joy when the Good Friday
> that is Northern Ireland has left its bloodstains, the
> crossmark of suffering, the nailprints of
> bereavement, the calvary of painful memories. . . .
> But maybe the endless Good Friday is our own
> fault. Maybe we have grown accustomed to the
> cross that is so conspicuous in our land. . . . Our
> Easter Day will finally dawn when we begin to
> believe that at last we have been saved from
> ourselves because Jesus died and rose to save us.
> Our Easter Day will finally dawn when together we
> have heaved away the stone of neighborhood
> mistrust, the boulder of the years of pointless
> division. Our Easter Day will finally dawn when we
> discover how pitifully small our differences are

when we hold them up against the endless lines of refugees searching for new life anywhere. Our Easter Day will dawn when we begin to believe that, with the help of God, the slow funeral marches of the past years will give way to the triumphant alleluias. . . . Easter is the celebration of that hope. Because of the risen Christ and our faith in him, we believe that some day things broken will be fixed, friends parted will be gathered, the scars of old wounds will disappear and with them the memories. City ghettoes will no longer scream their denomination at us, the swords will be turned into ploughshares, the hungry will have their fill, the former things will have passed away.[1]

That's why we Christians make such a big fuss over Easter. That's why the churches are filled today. We are celebrating the mighty works of God, especially his mightiest work in raising Jesus Christ from the dead. For us, the Resurrection means that God is always a factor in our human situation, a God who intervenes and who will have the last word in life and the world. Therefore, we praise him, blending our praise with the worship that ascends from a million churches on earth and the hymns of the hosts of heaven. "Jesus Christ is risen today. Hallelujah!"

NOTE

1. John J. McCullough, "Homily for Easter Sunday," in *Best Sermons,* edited by James W. Cox (San Francisco: Harper & Row, 1988), 321ff.

36. Intimacy with God
John Killinger

Song of Sol. 2:8–17

When I saw Jeffrey Archer's play *Beyond Reasonable Doubt* on the London stage, I surprised myself by weeping. Admittedly, the play is a little melodramatic. The main character, a lawyer named David Metcalfe, has been accused of murdering his wife and successfully defends himself in court. Then, in flashbacks, we learn that his wife actually died of an overdose of medication he administered, at her request, to save her from excruciating pain in the final weeks of death by cancer. It is during these flashbacks that we see the extraordinary intimacy and tenderness between the two of them, the absence of which makes David's life without her almost unbearable.

It was the amazing intimacy, I think, that caused me to weep. I could not bear to think of a human being experiencing and then being deprived of it.

Francine Klagsbrun, in her book *Married People,* discusses the nature of intimacy and enumerates several key factors present in it. First, intimacy requires a complete acceptance of the other person just as he or she is, so that each person is unafraid to be open and honest with the other. Second, it implies that each person feels important to the other. Third, it means the creation of an environment in which secrets can be shared with complete confidence. Fourth, it accepts the fact that there will be periods of distancing as well as closeness and that the distancing will not destroy the relation-

John Killinger was until recently senior minister of the First Congregational Church in Los Angeles, California, and is now Distinguished Professor of Religion and Culture at Samford University, Birmingham, Alabama. Dr. Killinger is the author of many books, including *Bread for the Wilderness/Wine for the Journey* and *The Fundamentals of Preaching.*

ship. And finally, intimacy means truly communicating, listening with sensitivity, and assuring the other that he or she is safe in the exchange.

Every human being longs to have intimacy with someone else— to be open and loving and safe together.

But what about with God?

Is it possible to be intimate with God as well, to have this open, sensitive, creative relationship with the eternal One who presides over our destinies?

The Bible suggests that it is.

Oh, we're not to forget that there is always what Kierkegaard called "an infinite qualitative distance" between us and the Almighty. We mustn't assume too much.

But intimacy, communication, a sense of well-being together— yes, that is entirely possible. The Psalms often breathe an air of intimacy. The Song of Solomon, read at a spiritual level, suggests it. The prophet Hosea glories in it. Jesus obviously experienced it—and Paul and John and other New Testament figures.

How can we achieve a sense of intimacy with God?

Let me offer some suggestions.

First, get to know God's story. This is always a first step toward intimacy, isn't it? In any romantic encounter, in the beginning of any friendship, there is the sharing of information, getting to know the other person's history.

"Tell me all about yourself."

Isn't that the lover's plea?

God does have a story. His history is in the Bible and in the books of church history and the books about other people's experiences with him. In fact, God's story is probably better documented than that of any other figure we know. It is woven in and out of all the history books, all the philosophy books, all the books of religious experience ever written.

It amazes and frightens me to think how few people today seem to be interested in discovering as much of God's story as they can. They are busy reading and talking about everything else in the world, from computers to music to sports, but they don't seem to be motivated to learn about God. The *New York Times* best-seller list seldom contains a book about God. It's almost as if we lived in the "brave new world" described by Aldous Huxley, in which the Bible and Shakespeare and all the books about God are locked up in a safe so people can't read them. Only, in our society they don't have to be locked up because most people don't want to read them anyway.

How can we be intimate with a God whose history we don't know? We should all be constantly reading and listening and learning about God; then we will have taken the first step toward intimacy with him.

The second step is to spend time with God. You can't have intimacy with anyone you don't spend time with. You can even lose intimacy, after you've had it, with someone you have stopped spending time with.

I have seen it often with married couples. They come to the counselor, complaining that they don't feel good about each other anymore. Pretty soon, it comes out in the open. "You're hardly ever home any more," she says, "and when you are, you've got your eyes glued to the TV set!" "Oh, yeah?" he says. "Well, you're always on the phone to our daughter or you're running off to some meeting at the church!" In the end, they realize that if they want their marriage to work, if they want intimacy to return, they have to give it time to do so. They literally have to make time for it.

People often remark on the closeness my wife and I enjoy. I will tell you the secret of it. Twenty-two years ago, when I was a young professor busy with teaching, writing, and speaking, I received a sabbatical year. We decided to spend it in Paris. For the first time in my life, I had big chunks of unprogrammed time to use in any way I chose. Our children were both in school for the first time. My wife and I often spent half-days together walking through the beautiful city or sitting on a wall along the river Seine. We had been married fifteen years, but it was as if we had just discovered one another. Ever since then, we have valued the time we have together. We have struggled to create time when our schedules denied it. Being together has produced intimacy.

It is the same with God.

Study the life of any great saint, from Augustine to Mother Teresa. The story never varies. They are people who have time for God, who *make* time for God. Mother Teresa, as busy as she is, working fifteen-hour days, always begins her day with Mass. She begins with God. Then everything she does becomes sacramental.

When you have learned to do this, you miss God if you have to skip a time with him.

Who was it—Paderewski?—who said, "If I don't practice for a month, my audiences notice it. If I don't practice for a week, my friends notice it. If I don't practice for a day, *I* notice it."

That is the way it is with spending time with God. When we miss doing it, if we are accustomed to it, we know it.

Get to know God's story. Spend time with God.

The third step in finding intimacy with God is to seek to please God. That's what we would do next in a human relationship, isn't it? We would try to do something that would give the other person pleasure.

This person buys another flowers. This one brings candy. This one prepares a special meal. This one gets tickets to a play. This one arranges a moonlight trip to Catalina. Courting.

And it doesn't stop when two people get married. It is an essential ingredient of intimacy throughout the relationship.

A few months ago, one of our friends arranged a special birthday celebration for her husband. She took him on a trip that was a series of surprises for him. They drove to a lovely bed-and-breakfast home in the desert. They had a special dinner. After an early breakfast the next morning, she took him on a little drive into the desert and drove up to a colorful hot-air balloon waiting to bear them aloft. They had a wonderful sail out over the coast, stopping en route to pick lemons off a fruit tree.

The husband has not ceased talking about this fantastic trip. You can understand that it has contributed to the intimacy he shares with his wife.

Now, what can you do to please God? There are many things. You can undertake a program of personal change and reform. You can make a pilgrimage to some special place of faith. You can make a significant donation to a church or charity. You can establish a relationship with a needy person and help that person back to solid ground in his or her life. You can offer your services to a church or a charitable agency. There are countless things.

But, as in the case with the woman who arranged the balloon trip for her husband, the best gifts you can give God will be designed in your own imagination. You will think, What can I give the Creator of the world who has shown his love to me in Jesus Christ?

You may even try to think of a new thing each week and make the devising and bestowal of some new gift the pattern of your life.

I promise you, it will carry you along the road to intimacy.

Finally, when you have learned God's story and spent time with God and tried regularly to please God, I recommend that you pause occasionally to reflect on what your life is becoming with God—on how being related to God is changing your existence—and then surrender to the flow of this alteration.

We do this with any new discipline or influence in our lives. When we are undertaking an exercise program, we reassess our progress and adjust the strenuousness of the exercises. When we engage in a course of study, we pause to think about what we have learned and how that impinges upon everything else we know.

When we consider our relationship to God and what it is doing in our lives, we can only give thanks and receive inspiration to intensify the relationship.

I think about a friend in this congregation who has been a Christian for only a few years. It has been exciting, in the last couple of years, to hear him speak self-consciously of what is occurring on his pilgrimage. Some time ago, he was visiting with a former partner in business. She observed that he seemed always to be going to church these days. He said he took the opportunity to tell her about what a difference God has made in his life. She replied that she would like to go to church sometime. Afterward, he reflected on the conversation and realized that he was now witnessing to his faith. He could see his own growth occurring. It was an exciting moment.

I don't mean that we should spend our time feeling our pulses to see how we're doing. But there should be times of introspection when we think about the journey we're making, how far we've come, and what we ought to do to facilitate our future progress.

When I taught courses on prayer in the divinity school, I asked my students to keep journals of their experiences during the semester. Each day, they would write about their prayer lives and other things that impinged upon their spiritual formation. In the years since, I have often had a former student say to me, either in a letter or in person, "I am so glad you had us keep a journal. It began a practice I have never given up, and it still rewards me when I look back and see the distance I have come."

May I summarize for you? First, learn God's story. Second, spend time with God. Third, seek to please God. And fourth, reflect on what your life is becoming with God.

Do these things and you will find yourself growing in intimacy with God.

Maybe you saw the movie *A Field of Dreams.* It is a beautiful, whimsical story about a young farmer who hears a voice in the cornfield say to him, "If you will build it, he will come." Build what, he wants to know. A ball park, he learns. Who will come? Shoeless Joe Jackson, the great star of the Chicago White Sox. So the farmer plows under his corn and builds a ball diamond. And sure enough, one day Shoeless Joe Jackson walks out of the cornfield and begins to play ball. So do seven other White Sox players and then some old New York Giants. It is a lilting, tender story, and it probably sounds crazy if you haven't seen it, but it almost invariably gives people's spirits a lift.

"If you will build it, he will come."

That's the promise we are dealing with, too, isn't it? If we will create the right conditions in our lives, God will come and dwell in them. God doesn't make the intimacy. We do. But God never fails to reveal himself intimately to those who make the overtures, those who take the simple steps of preparing for his presence.

Build your life in these ways, and he will come.

I promise.

37. The Gracious Guest

A SERMON FOR MAUNDY THURSDAY

Albert J. D. Walsh

> For I received from the Lord what I also passed on to you: The Lord Jesus, on the night he was betrayed, took bread, and when he had given thanks, he broke it and said, "This is my body, which is for you; do this in remembrance of me." In the same way, after supper, he took the cup, saying, "This cup is the new covenant in my blood; do this whenever you drink it, in remembrance of me." For whenever you eat this bread and drink this cup, you proclaim the Lord's death until he comes.
>
> (I Cor. 11:23–26)

The Lord Jesus, on the night he was betrayed, reclined at table with his disciples. This was no ordinary meal. Then again, in the presence of Jesus, every meal was extraordinary. It had nothing to do with the menu or the atmosphere. It had everything to do with the way Jesus shared his table with almost anyone. He set no limits. There were no requirements. He simply invited people to share in his friendship and hospitality. I suppose you could say it was because Jesus loved people. Rich and poor, sick and healthy, sinners and saints. Jesus loved people and enjoyed eating with them.

Now, some of the religious leaders had a problem with Jesus' table manners. They wondered why it was that he chose to eat with "tax collectors and sinners." The answer Jesus gave was quite simple. What better way to make them feel accepted than by breaking bread together? Believe me, you need not be a trained theologian to see the wisdom here! Jesus understood that when people recline at table together they are all on the same level. And he used that fact

---

Albert J. D. Walsh serves as pastor of the First United Church of Christ, Schuylkill Haven, Pennsylvania. He is a frequent contributor to *The Ministers Manual* and is author of *Reflections on Death and Grief.*

to bring home to those who felt less than worthy that in his own eyes they were his friends. Of course, if they were Jesus' friends, then they were also friends of God. That's the real meaning of this table fellowship.

You see, there's really no way that we can fully appreciate this meal we are about to share if we haven't first understood what the table fellowship of Jesus was all about. This much I know for sure. Our eucharist this evening is not about some kind of magic; it's not about some ghostlike presence we can neither see nor feel. But it is about Christian fellowship shared in the Spirit of Jesus Christ. To understand this meal we call a "sacrament," we should remember those meals that Jesus shared with "sinners and tax collectors."

Do you remember the story of the little man, Zacchaeus, who climbed high into a tree just for a glimpse of Jesus passing through his village? Zacchaeus never expected Jesus to invite himself to his house for a meal. But if you've read your Gospels, you know that Jesus was full of surprises! So he went to the home of Zacchaeus as a guest. That one act of acceptance was enough to change the life of this little man, forever. A simple act of table fellowship, in the presence of this gracious guest, became a moment of freedom from the bondage to guilt and fear for Zacchaeus.

Again, the people outside the home of Zacchaeus grumbled with displeasure. They said, "This Jesus has gone in to be the guest of a man who is a sinner." They just didn't get it. How else was Jesus to reach the heart of this poor soul, if not by accepting him? The villagers had shunned this sinner, Zacchaeus, for years. All their efforts had not brought this man one inch closer to God. Jesus reached out to Zacchaeus with love and acceptance, and this tax collector did a one-eighty, returning in faith to God! So tell me, which seems like the better way? Being judgmental or being just? I'd say Jesus knew the way to a person's heart!

Then there was the scene with Matthew the tax collector, remember? When Jesus went to Matthew's home for a meal that evening, you can bet your booties he was rubbing elbows with bandits and prostitutes! Not exactly what you'd call the country club set! But they were the people Jesus wanted to reach with the message of forgiveness and acceptance. And isn't it interesting that, with the exception of one Pharisee, Jesus was never invited to recline at table with the religious leaders? Perhaps they did not want Jesus to think himself their equal. If only they had known!

There's a pattern here, isn't there? Jesus ate with sinners and invited himself into their homes and, eventually, their hearts. He may have earned the reputation of being a "drunkard and a glutton," but it doesn't seem to me that he thought himself unworthy of this infamous title. After all, he enjoyed whooping it up with sinners! There was no hidden motive on the part of Jesus. He wasn't there to surprise his host and fellow guests with a "sermon" following the lamb stew! His sole purpose was to be with these folks in order to express the love of God for each one. And I've no doubt they listened and received his words and warmth with thanksgiving.

But I'm equally certain that something of surpassing importance took place following these meals with Jesus. The people who had experienced table fellowship with Jesus could never again break bread together without remembering! That was the spiritual value of his table ministry. Long after he had left their village and their lives, they would remember his presence and his peace. And when they remembered, he was once again with them in the breaking of bread. You see, Jesus taught them a new way to live, laugh, and love together. Table fellowship!

But something else strikes me about the way Jesus shared his table with others. Notice that, whenever Jesus joins folks at table, the line between guest and host begins to fade. In the presence of Jesus Christ, it becomes difficult, if not impossible, to distinguish between the host and the guests. Suddenly there is just this one family breaking and passing the bread, pouring and sharing the cup! Jesus creates a bond of fellowship and care unparalleled in our world. And he does so simply by being the gracious guest among guests. He makes no pretense to a higher place at table. He claims no right to be honored. He simply joins his friends at table. And what he does for them, he wishes them to do for each other.

On that final night, Jesus gathered with his disciples to share one last meal. Yes, this was a solemn occasion. But let's not confuse solemnity with depression! Jesus told his friends that every time they broke bread together, they would remember his presence with them at table. Maybe they would recall his laughter or maybe his loving forgiveness of their stupidities and blunders, not to mention their sins. But as they remembered, he would be there!

Each time they would gather at table, the presence of Jesus would be felt with and within their common friendship. But they were to break bread, as Jesus had done, as an act of acceptance, love, and care. They were to remember his way of eating with those whom society, or the religious Establishment, thought worthless. They would know his presence only when they broke bread, as he had broken bread—with sinners! Now tell me, how could they avoid breaking bread with sinners? They were all sinners!

What's more, they were to share table fellowship without turning the meal into a testimonial dinner for superior saints! At this table, all were equal in the sight of God. They were to break bread in a spirit of unity and peace. Before coming to this table, they were to make right the wrongs committed against a brother or sister. There were to be no grudges, bad feelings, or wounded hearts brought to this table. And if they were brought, then this was the place where they were to be healed! Breaking bread in this spirit made the presence of Christ a reality for all.

So here we are. We are here because we want to remember. We want to remember how Jesus lived and how he died. We want to remember how he cared for sinners and opened his life and love to their pain. We want to remember how Jesus healed the sick and comforted the sorrowful. But most of all, we want to remember his table fellowship. We want to remember how his grace cleared away the guilt from human hearts. We want to remember how his compassion gave support and courage to those who were crushed. And we want to remember how Jesus gave strength to those who felt defeated by life. We want to remember.

And we should. Remember that he is here when we break this bread and share this cup in his name and within his Spirit. Remember that he calls us away from brokenness to bounty, away from sin to salvation, away from loneliness to love, away from isolation to community. With and within the fellowship of this meal, there is neither Protestant nor Catholic, neither factory worker nor executive, neither superior nor inferior. At this table, we are all one to Christ, by Christ, in Christ, and through Christ! For whenever you eat this bread and drink this cup, you proclaim the Lord!

Come to the table of Christ, not because you must, but because you may. Come, not to express an opinion, but to pray for a Spirit. Come, not because you are filled, but because in your emptiness you stand in need of God's mercy and forgiveness. Come to this table with the weight of guilt dragging you down. Come with the questions and cares haunting your heart. Come with the fears and uncertainties plaguing your mind. Come to the table of One who loves you and wants only that you live life more fully. Come to the table of One who knows you better than you know yourself and yet desires that you become his faithful follower. Come to the table of Jesus Christ and remember!

38. Going to Hell for the Right Reason

Tom W. Boyd

Rom. 9:1–5; Matt. 10:26–33

On the fourth reading of *The Adventures of Huckleberry Finn,* I finally began to grasp its religious depth. This novel unveils a primary religious question: For what are we willing to go to hell? And the point is to discover the right reason for being willing to go there.

In a chapter beautifully entitled "You Can't Pray a Lie," Huck finds himself in what he calls "a tight place." He has hidden and protected a runaway slave named Jim on their whirlwind adventures down the Mississippi. Not only is Jim a renegade from legal slavery, he belongs to Miss Watson, a woman who has befriended Huck. Just below Pikesville, their luck runs out, and Jim lies languishing in a cabin prison where he is being held for a reward.

When Huck learns that Jim has been captured, pangs of conscience seize Huck. He realizes that he is under judgment for having hidden a slave and that he is bound for hell as a result. He resolves to write his former benefactress, Miss Watson, and tell her where Jim can be found. He writes the letter, and immediately he feels cleansed, pure, and able now to pray an honest prayer. By doing what he has been taught is the right thing, he has escaped the torments of hell. Huck postpones his prayer as he begins thinking about Jim, the man he is about to send back into slavery:

Tom W. Boyd is Kingfisher Professor of Philosophy of Religion and Ethics at the University of Oklahoma. Ordained to the Presbyterian Church (U.S.A.) in 1963, he has served pastorates in Tennessee, Iowa, and Oklahoma. Boyd has received many teaching awards, and his articles have appeared in scholarly and religious journals.

> . . . I see Jim before me all the time. . . . But
> somehow I couldn't seem to strike no places to
> harden me against him, but only the other kind. I'd
> see him standing my watch on top of his'n, 'stead
> of calling me, so I could go on sleeping; and see
> him how glad he was when I come back out of the
> fog; and when I come to him again in the swamp,
> up there where the feud was; and such-like times;
> and would always call me honey, and pet me, and
> do everything he could think of for me, and how
> good he always was; and at last I struck the time I
> saved him by telling the men we had smallpox and
> he was so grateful, and said I was the best friend
> old Jim ever had in the world, and the *only* one he's
> got now; and then I happened to look around and
> see that paper.

Huck is trapped between the social message that hiding a runaway slave means hell and his desire to protect his friend Jim. Under the burden of this weighty crisis, Huck pauses. Then he says to himself, "All right, then, I'll go to hell," and he tears up the letter to Miss Watson.

Huck is in high company. St. Paul, writing to the Romans, has a similar struggle over the redemption of his own people, Israel. He begins Romans 9 confessing his anguish on their behalf, a suffering so acute that he cries out, "For I could wish that I myself were accursed and cut off from Christ for the sake of my brethren, my kinsmen by race" (9:3). Paul, like Huck, is willing to go to hell . . . for the right reason. What are we to make of such temerity, such foolhardy audacity?

I

When people are struggling with hard decisions and showing stress, one popular response is to ask them, "What is the worst thing that can happen?" We assume that the answer will show that their anxiety is overblown in view of the consequences. When the worst thing that can happen, however, is hell, the situation is grave indeed. Whatever else we may believe about hell, it symbolizes the very worst that can happen and that which we hope, above all else, to avoid.

Jesus is preparing his disciples to go out preaching among "the lost sheep of the house of Israel." He is helping them put fear in perspective, and he is encouraging them not to fear, with one exception. He urges, "And do not fear those who kill the body but cannot kill the soul; rather fear him who can destroy both soul and body in hell" (Matt. 10:28). The suggestion is that the only proper fear for the child of faith is to fear hell.

If hell is the worst that can happen and that which is the most appropriate object of our fear, we do well to understand this symbol. Images of hell pervade Scripture and lie heavy upon our tradition. Some cannot even imagine religion without it. An acquaintance of mine, having found out that some contemporary Christians claim no longer to believe in hell, responded, "If there is no hell, I see no reason for religion or for being good." While this response betrays a motivation to be religious for largely negative reasons—to avoid hell—it also shows how deeply the idea of hell may affect Western religious life.

Stripping away all of the literal images of hell, such as fire and writhing torture, I believe that hell symbolizes separation from God and the consequent anguish. German theologian Pannenburg puts it this way: "To be fully conscious of the nearness of God and yet to be excluded from him is what the ancient dogmas saw as the tortures of hell." Regardless of what we may otherwise affirm or deny about hell, its meaning is isolation, estrangement, "idiocy" in its original sense, "to be totally alone." Hell is the cry of the Ancient Mariner taken to its highest register:

> Alone, alone, all all alone,
> Alone on a wide, wide sea,
> And never a soul took pity on my soul in agony.

II

Why, then, would anyone willingly embrace hell, to say nothing of doing so for a right reason? We confess that there are extremes to which we must, if we are people of faith and devotion, be willing to go. But isn't this will-to-hell going too far?

St. John declares, "Greater love has no one than this, that one lay down life for a friend." Now this is surely far enough! Nothing more can possibly be expected. This laying down of life was what Christ came to do, and if we take up our cross, we may find ourselves approaching, if not facing, such a traumatic test. Even that is unlikely for most of us. But as fearsome as its prospect is, we can imagine this possibility of surrendering life on behalf of another.

Still, St. Paul's "I could wish myself accursed" appears to go beyond the sacrifice of life. It involves a willingness to sacrifice one's soul, one's very being. It goes beyond even the warning of Jesus, "rather, fear him who can destroy both soul and body in hell." Or does it? Have you yet caught the subtle point of Jesus' words? They do not actually foment fear of hell but of the one who has power over hell. Surely the "him" we are to fear is not Satan but God. One might even say that it is just this "fear of the Lord" that might lead one to be willing to go to hell.

A hint to aid our understanding of this matter may be found in that most controversial phrase of the Apostles' Creed: "and he descended into hell." Although there is some biblical warrant for this phrase found in 1 Peter 3 and 4, it was introduced late into the creed and has remained troubling to many. Still, it haunts the history of our faith, suggesting that Jesus may have willingly taken upon himself the fullest agony, not only of dying and of death, but of utter separation. "My God, my God, why have you forsaken me?" He may have willingly gone to hell! But for what good reason?

III

There is a difference between going to hell and being willing to go to hell. When Huck Finn became willing to go to hell, at that very moment, he found heaven! He entered newness of life. He gave up *everything* for Jim. When we allow ourselves to be willing to go to hell for this right reason, deliverance and liberation surprise our lives. And the same is true for St. Paul. He had the right reason: "for the sake of my brethren, my kindred by race."

Huck finds himself willing to go to hell for a black runaway slave who has no status but love. Jim had loved Huck into loving, and Huck now loves Jim so much that going to hell is not asking too much. The reach of Paul's compassion drives him to the same extreme. In this willingness, the second great commandment is pushed beyond its own boundary. One is willing to love one's neighbor to the loss of self. In such love, we discover most graphically what it means to say, "Whoever gains life shall lose it, but whoever loses life for my sake shall gain it."

No one is ever asked, let alone commanded, to go to hell, but there is no grander liberation of spirit than to be set free of that darkest and deepest fear, the fear of hell. To stare into that darkness and say, for the sake of another, "I'll go to hell," is to have penetrated the worst that can happen. With those words we embrace the full paradox of redemption: By letting go of it, we are found in it. We can never, then, be alone.

Conclusion

A friend of mine, John, wrote a short story about Jesus' descent into hell. Fascinated with the question of why Jesus went to hell, John first did some research. One dominant legend from the Middle Ages, he found, is that Jesus went to hell to release Adam and Eve from torment. John found this interpretation inadequate, not radical enough.

In John's story, Jesus shows up at the gate to hell. Satan meets him in a rage, trying to forbid Jesus entering. Jesus cannot be restrained. He tears open the gate and begins his search. As he probes the darkest and most sinister recesses of torment, he releases everyone he finds, but it is clear that he is in quest of some particular one. He hunts ever deeper, ever more strained, into the bowels of ultimate treachery. Finally, far back and away from all other prisons, Jesus finds a cage in horrifying isolation. He approaches it, and as he does so, Satan cries, "No, not that one! That one is my prize!" Oblivious to Satan's objections, Jesus wrenches open the door of the cage and sets the prisoner . . . sets Judas . . . free.

Jesus went to hell for the right reason, for the liberation of the beloved. That is the one right reason—the redeeming reason—for our being willing to descend.

39. Consider the Monkeys
Robert John Versteeg

Matt. 6:26–28

Thomas Jefferson went to see a monkey.

We're able to recover Jefferson's story because we have the memorandum books in which for almost sixty years the chronically cash-poor colonial statesman jotted down his daily expenditures. These ledgers track the day-by-day doings of the great man.

They tell us, for example, that on May 7, 1776, Jefferson, in a phaeton drawn by two horses, "set out for Philadelphia." His first lodgings there proving unsuitable, on May 23 he moved into a new three-story brick house on the southwest corner of Market and Seventh streets, where he was staying when the Continental Congress entrusted him with the creation of one of humanity's most significant documents: "When in the course of human events. . . ."

How do you prepare yourself to write the Declaration of Independence? Some of us who scribble develop elaborate rituals of preparation. We concentrate; we cram our minds with great writings of the past; we retreat to a library; or we sharpen pencils for hours—the same pencil. Of course, Jefferson had been for thirty-three years (he was that young!) preparing himself to write the Declaration. But as he approached those historic days for which he came into the world, from what deep waters was he priming the pump of creativity? On what was Thomas Jefferson nourishing his mind and soul?

His account books reveal that on May 24 Jefferson paid someone named Hillegas twenty-seven shillings for fiddle strings. May 27, Jefferson spent "one and seven" for toys. May 28, he gave two

---

Robert John Versteeg is pastor of Oak Hills United Methodist Church in Cincinnati, Ohio. Formerly director of the conservatory acting program at Virginia Commonwealth University, he has performed and written many dramatic works. Versteeg holds a master of divinity degree from Garrett-Evangelical Theological Seminary.

shillings for a doll. May 31, he "pd 45/ for a silver cover for an ivory book." The ledgers further show that, during the remainder of that momentous session of the Continental Congress, Jefferson also bought fishing tackle, a pair of boots, a hat, and guitar strings.

But evidently by June 1 he was seriously preparing to write, because on that date Jefferson laid out "two and six" for paper. Then again, maybe he gave a fleeting thought to ducking it all and slipping back home to Monticello, because, also on June 1, he parted with "eight and six" for a map. But apparently Thomas Jefferson solved this creative crisis when on that same pregnant day he shelled out—this is the item I love—"one shilling for seeing a monkey."

We've got a revolution on our hands, a cataclysmic international upheaval, erupting hopes and dreams of freedom, and Thomas Jefferson is off looking at a monkey.

"Where is the delegate from Virginia whom we appointed to draft our Declaration of Independence?"

"Tom? He took the day off to go to the zoo."

Of course, there weren't any zoos, and there weren't any "Nature" programs on PBS, so everyday you could not see a monkey. One wonders what influence that monkey might have had on the Declaration. Not that the monkey was independent. I suppose some enterprising fellow, some prototypical P. T. Barnum, had bought it from a traveler, from a sailor maybe, and was making a living going about exhibiting the simian. And one of the happy suckers he hooked was the Honorable Squire Thomas Jefferson, who gladly plunked down "one shilling for seeing a monkey."

Who says that frivolity isn't part of God's creative design? The Puritans, those promulgators of the "Protestant work ethic," said it wasn't. But Jefferson wasn't buying that, and the balance seems to tip in his favor. Although it might have appeared logical to confront Jefferson—"How can you waste valuable time on something so useless as looking at a monkey?"—how logical is it to assume that inspiration—the operation of God's creative Spirit—is bound by our conceptions of "logic"? The wisest people know how to press beyond such limited thinking. Creativity follows its own logic.

Besides, how can Christians who cherish the Christmas story believe that God makes anything that is "frivolous," "unimportant," or "useless"? Rather, God may create things that are fun but not frivolous, unimpressive (to the unimpressed) but not unimportant, beautiful but not useless.

In this creative scheme of things, monkeys have their place. God, in the time of the Flood, did not instruct Noah to draw up the gangway against monkeys. It's a good rule for creative living: Don't prematurely batten the hatches of your ark lest you miss the monkeys.

Do you really need the monkeys on board? I think so, but I'm prejudiced. Man and boy, I've contemplated a lot of monkeys, and I can tell you that there are a barrel of good reasons to meditate on monkeys. Still, anyone who needs a *reason* to look at a monkey may be almost beyond redemption.

The best reason to watch monkeys is for no reason but for sheer delight. Monkeys are part of God's wonderful creation, and our reverence for the Creator may properly include curiosity about and enjoyment of all that God has made for whatever purpose or for no purpose but divine will. God said, "Let there be monkeys." Isn't it holiness to rejoice in the richness of God's creation, to be gladdened by the work of God's hand? Surely such holiness is not "frivolous," "unimportant," or "useless." When we're talking about the Creator Spirit, irrelevance is not necessarily irreverence. You need the monkeys; they're part of God's plan.

With a Continental Congress in session, a Declaration of Independence on the drawing board, and a new world in labor, Thomas Jefferson also had a mind to strings for his fiddle and strings for his guitar, a silver cover for his ivory book, fishing tackle and a hat, a doll and some toys for his children, and "one shilling for seeing a monkey."

Now consider Jesus, who taught his disciples to consider the lilies of the field and the birds of the air (Matt. 6:26–28).

"You've got this whole wide world to save, all the accumulated sin of the world to atone for, and all of fallen creation to redeem. What are you doing off looking at the lilies?" Maybe those weren't the words, but they're essentially the challenge that some of his critics hurled at Jesus, critics who saw in him a man who frittered away his time with wine bibbers and sinners, a man who would rather fiddle-faddle at a wedding feast than endure a rabbinic council.

But maybe part of salvation is looking at lilies, not for any particular purpose or use, but just because God put lilies here for looking at. And to look at the lilies is to salute God and to acknowledge the work of God's hands, and somehow that salutation, that acceptance of God's grace, is part of our salvation.

Of course, there are Puritan-approved and utilitarian purposes to be served by studying God's revelation of God's nature in nature. Jesus also meditated on the way God sent God's gifts of rain and sunshine on both the "just" and the "unjust," and therefrom Jesus concluded that if we wish to behave as children of such a God, we human beings must also do good indiscriminately to all people. And no doubt Jesus hoped that, as a result of looking at lilies, we might let go of some of our anxieties about food and clothing.

We used to joke about the man whose favorite Bible story was of the boy who just "loafs and fishes." I'd be chagrined if anyone took this teaching about lilies and birds as advice to give in to the easy old sin of sloth. Rather, here Jesus is showing us how to disarm the opposite failing: our counterproductive but compulsive hyperactivity caused by anxiousness, or, as we may call it, being uptight.

It's been truly observed that Jesus wasn't crucified because he said, "Consider the lilies, how they grow," but he was crucified because he said, "Consider the leaders, how they steal." We would become ourselves moral conspirators in that stealing if we were to take Jesus's words about lily-looking and bird-watching as an excuse for failing to respond at least as eagerly to his command that we also provide for the poor and feed the hungry. Jesus specifically directs us to feed his lambs. And he tells us that when we clothe the naked and feed the hungry, we clothe and feed him, and when we neglect them, we neglect him, and we enter either the kingdom or outer darkness accordingly.

But it does not necessarily follow that a cavalry charge to the rescue is always the best or the most effective response to hunger or some other need. In an emergency, that may be necessary. But also, in the long run, instead of dashing off on continual cavalry charges, it may be equally necessary and even more effective to pause, to look at a lily, or to be amused by a monkey in order to clear the mind. We may need to enter into a creatively receptive state in which God may lead us to discover a new way: a way to provide for the hungry, say, not only a fish for today but a fishing skill for a lifetime; a way to design better fishing gear; to guarantee cleaner water for coming generations of fish and fishers; and to develop a whole new way of life that neither pollutes, exploits, excludes, nor oppresses.

In any event, actively and sacrificially caring for others is altogether a different matter from being anxious about our own lives. And it's a different matter from going through life uptight. Uptight locks out new visions.

The point is that the same Jesus who loved the world, who cared infinitely for the hungry poor, and who was willing to die for sinners was also the Jesus who was pleased to spend time relaxing with sinners, who was open to receive the gifts of God's creation, and who was glad to enjoy the grace notes of daily existence—the lilies of the field, the birds of the air, the water and the wind, the wedding feast, the children whom he welcomed and took up in his arms for blessing. Jesus, who knew the weight of the world, also knew the secret of allowing himself to be buoyed up by the surrounding delights God has given us richly to enjoy. Such openness and receptivity to grace was an essential part of the Master's creative life-style.

The danger is that people who will not pay "one shilling for seeing a monkey" eventually pay by getting monkeys on their backs. People who won't look at lilies develop tunnel vision. People who won't gaze at the birds of the air grow blind to God's gifts of grace. And people who haven't time or heart to hug little children can't be trusted to hold anything.

Today we're in danger of being swamped by big-time problems ranging from planetary survival, nuclear waste, hunger, poverty, drugs, disease—you know the list—to whatever you consider a big-time problem for you personally: your work, your relationships, your family, your health, your troubles. No one who cares about God's world or cares about you would advise you to ignore those problems. But the Scripture does counsel that, as you struggle to stay afloat in those problems, you should not batten your hatches against monkeys. You should not overlook the possibility that there may be different, even unusual and certainly unpredictable, ways to deal with your problems. Richer, better, more creative approaches open up when you open yourself up to God's all-surrounding gifts and graces, including such apparently "frivolous," "unimportant," and "useless" things as lilies and birds and monkeys.

It's possible that taking time out for opening to grace may produce better results than banging your head against a wall. It's possible that lilies and birds may charm away the boulder that blocks your brain. Incredible or irrelevant as it may seem, it's possible that seeing a monkey may free up Thomas Jefferson to write the Declaration of Independence or you to perform whatever task is given to you.

After all, God did not design this world to be a penitentiary but a paradise, and God created it all for you as well as for every other creature.

Consider the lilies—and don't miss the monkeys.

40. Pretending, Self-Justification, and Grace
Clifford Williams

Psalm 51; Luke 18:9–14; Eph. 2:4–9

I am thinking of announcing that I do not want to be known as a Christian anymore—not that I do not want to be one, but that I do not want to be thought of as one. When people think of Christians, when we Christians think of what it means to be a Christian, we think of high ideals, pure motives, sincere actions, and living in accordance with biblical standards.

When I probe my inner life, I find ulterior motives, insincerity, pharisaical double-mindedness, the savoring of success and esteem, and more—things I am afraid to admit either to you or to myself. If people knew about these, I'm not sure they would like me. So I pretend. I pretend to be a good Christian, and I use this pretension to justify my existence. I convince myself that I really am a good Christian and that God should accept me because of that, thus blinding myself to God's grace.

When we were little, we loved to pretend. We dressed up as Mom or Dad, or we imagined ourselves being someone else. Doing so made us feel important. And it was easy. All we had to do was put on different clothes or a special hat or pick up a baseball bat, and we immediately became our admired person. When I was ten or eleven, one of my heroes was Hank Aaron—the great home run hitter for

---

Clifford Williams is associate professor of philosophy at Trinity College in Deerfield, Illinois. A graduate of Wheaton College in Illinois, he holds a Ph.D. in philosophy from Indiana University. Williams has been published in many magazines and journals and has written *Free Will and Determinism: A Dialogue.*

the Milwaukee Braves. As I lay on the living room floor listening to radio broadcasts, I imagined myself running the bases whenever he hit another home run. And once in a while (when no one was looking), I swung my bat in the backyard just as I imagined he did.

We continue to pretend as adults, though perhaps we do so less consciously. We imagine ourselves being famous or worthy of other people's respect. We act in ways we think others will approve of. It is easy to pretend, and it makes us feel important and good.

When we pretend, we are putting on a show. We are trying to convince others that we are good. Perhaps we are afraid that they will not accept us if they knew what we were really like, if they saw our doubts, fears, hurts, and sins.

We pretend not only to others, but to ourselves as well, for we want to believe that we are worth something. So we act in ways we think are worthy, and we imagine ourselves being looked up to by others. By doing so, we convince ourselves that we really are good and important.

We also pretend to God on occasion, for we sometimes think of him as being like a person we have to impress in order to be accepted.

In a perceptive passage from Sören Kierkegaard's *Attack upon Christendom,* a book that was aimed at reintroducing Christianity into Christiandom, Kierkegaard writes, "Where all are Christians, the situation is this: to call oneself a Christian is the means whereby one secures oneself against all sorts of inconveniences and discomforts . . . and orthodoxy flourishes in the land, no heresy, no schism, orthodoxy everywhere, the orthodoxy which consists in playing the game of Christianity."[1]

Kierkegaard's "attack" was directed against a nineteenth-century state church in which everybody in Denmark was born a Christian, officially proclaimed so at one's baptism as an infant. Kierkegaard's revealing insight in this passage is that, when we are with Christians, we have a tendency to play the game of Christianity. Whenever we are in a church, Bible study, prayer group, or Christian college, we find it hard to avoid imitation Christianity.

Playing the game of Christianity is going through the motions without the inner reality; it is pretending to be a Christian instead of being one for real. More subtly, it is living outside oneself, that is, identifying with the group and its patterns, in much the same way we identified with our childhood heroes.

What is behind this phenomenon of pretending, of playing at Christianity? Two deep-seated motives give rise to pretending: the need for approval and the impulse of self-justification. None of us wants to be too different; we want others' approval, sometimes desperately, so we act in ways that bring that approval—everyday, ordinary ways and spiritual ways as well. Underneath this need for approval is the need for self-esteem, the need for a sense of worth. We sometimes go to great lengths to obtain this sense; when we find ourselves part of a Christian group, we can obtain a sense of worth by acting in ways the group approves. Also underneath the need for approval is the need to overcome separateness and aloneness. Each of us fears that among the millions in the human race, we will be left out. We can overcome aloneness by attracting others to us, which we can do by showing how good we are at being Christians. This need to feel that we are good is behind the impulse of self-justification, which drives us to do things we think will impress others. We feel that our very existence has worth when we do things that we know will make our Christian sisters and brothers think we are spiritual.

What tends to happen, then, when we are part of a Christian group is that we adopt its beliefs and practices, not because of personal conviction, but because of our need for approval and justification. Our acts and words, even our feelings, are not our own. Our faith is someone else's. We become impersonators.

For years my reaction to Ephesians 2:8–9 had been, "Oh, of course, I don't believe in salvation by works. It is by grace we have been saved, and 'not because of works,' as Paul writes there, 'lest anyone should boast.'"

That had been my same reaction to the Ten Commandments. I don't believe in cheating, lying, or killing, and, moreover, I don't do those things. Then about two years ago it occurred to me that one of the reasons God gave us the Ten Commandments was that we have in us the impulse to cheat, lie, and kill. When I dared peek at my impulses, there they were. And I shrunk from that glimpse.

It is the same with Paul's rejection of self-justification. He must have known that our fallen nature strives intensely to justify itself by any means it can other than by grace. Most of what I have done with my life springs from this nearly irresistible passion.

These are the reasons it is so easy to pretend, to play the game of Christianity. These are the reasons pretending and playing at Christianity have a certain satisfaction. They flow from our fundamental needs.

And we have an image to maintain. Churches have an image to maintain, and Christian colleges do as well. We want to show that being a Christian makes a difference and that Christ transforms our lives. True as these are, they push us to cover up our problems, to pretend that everything is okay, and ultimately to justify ourselves because of how we live.

The strength of the impulse to self-justification can be illustrated by the difficulty we have in receiving gifts. We want to give something back in order to even the score or to demonstrate that we are as good as the giver. The same is true of accepting God's grace. We sometimes find ourselves wanting to give something back to God, not so much as a response of gratitude, but as a way of showing that we are worthy of his grace. We want to even the score so that we can demonstrate that we are not so helpless as the gift of grace implies. "To know that God loves us not because we are good but 'just because' is sometimes unbearable."[2] We want to convince God that we are pretty decent people whom he should admire.

But, of course, with God there is no way we can even things up, there is no way we can show that we deserve his gift, and he isn't impressed very much with our schemes and pretensions to convince him that we are decent and admirable.

How do we pretend? When we are bright and cheerful, others think that we are victorious Christians and that nothing is wrong with us—and we know that they think this of us. When we pray before meals or in prayer meetings or carry our Bibles, we are conscious of others observing us. We refrain from confessing our struggles so we will not appear to be weak. At the same time, when we do confess our difficulties, we sense that we are admired for our honesty. (We give up one game to play another.) We keep unacceptable emotions locked up but appropriately display other emotions. We act in ways we know our Christian group will approve of, use the right words to describe our faith, and avoid behavior we know will bring disapproval.

In a way, we need to pretend because we need to feel good and important. Yet we despise pretending because we want to be real and genuine. So we are caught in a dilemma: We can scarcely help pretending, yet we hate it.

There are two kinds of reactions we can have toward pretenders. We can point our finger at them, just as we instinctively point our finger at the Pharisee and at hypocrites. How deliciously delightful is this pointing; how gratifying it is to us. And what acute dismay we experience when we suddenly realize that someone needs to point their finger at us.

Or we can feel toward pretenders as we do toward people who are hurt. When *we* are hurt, we want someone to notice and to give us some understanding. When they do, we open up to them. They have broken through the shell with which we have surrounded ourselves. We find that we don't have to pretend with them or play at being a Christian. We confess a few of our deepest secrets and feel accepted by them in spite of our wounds. Our need to impress them melts away. Perhaps this is how God's grace works.

The truth is that we pretenders are hurt. We sometimes doubt our faith, and that is unsettling because we want the security of knowing the truth. We are lonely, wondering whether anyone likes us. We fight off the gnawing pangs of conscience, as the thought of a past indiscretion springs into our minds. We wrestle with self-rejection and feelings of inadequacy. Some of us are depressed and can scarcely survive each day. Some of us have been betrayed by our parents—hit or criticized or handled sexually or neglected—and are wounded deeply by the memory. Many of us are restless, searching for something more, sometimes with quiet desperation, wanting intensely to tell someone yet even more fearful of doing so.

I would rather you not admire me as a Christian (though part of me secretly wants that). I would rather you think of me as a tax collector, as one who cheats, lies, and skims tax off the top of what I extort so I can live sumptuously. Think of me as being hurt: as having fears and doubts; as wondering sometimes what the point of life is; as being afraid to love; as having various temptations; as trying to impress people to cover self-doubt; as one whose inner life is sometimes disoriented, with ulterior motives and unsavory double-mindedness. And then come up to me, put your arm around me, and say, "I like you the way you are." That might puncture the barriers I have put around myself, and it might incite me to see life through the eyes of the tax collector.

If I could see life through the eyes of the tax collector, some of my impulse to self-justification might lessen in intensity; I might take off some of my masks; I might not strive for success and esteem so much or see these as the source of my self-worth. Maybe I would feel freer to be myself instead of someone else, freer to have my own faith instead of someone else's. Maybe I would feel in my heart, and not just think in my mind, that Christianity isn't just playing a game;

perhaps I would experience God's grace for more than fleeting, scattered moments.

Is there any other way to dissolve pretending than by means of God's grace? Can anything else heal our wounds and salve our hurts? Can anything else satisfy our ceaseless strivings and restless hearts?

NOTES

1. Sören Kierkegaard, *A Kierkegaard Anthology,* edited by Robert Bretall (Princeton: Princeton University Press, 1973), 437.

2. Bruce Ritter, *Sometimes God Has a Kid's Face* (New York: Covenant House, 1988), 26

Index of Scriptural Texts

Genesis **3:6–12, 16,** 160; 32:22–31, 223

Joshua **2:1–24,** 55; **6:20–25,** 55

Job **3:1–4,** 215; **20–4:6,** 215

Psalms **24:1–6,** 184; **51,** 258; **119:105,** 95; **121,** 101; **138,** 140

Song of Solomon **2:8–17,** 237

Isaiah **40:29–31,** 140; **42:1–4,** 197; **43:1–5,** 201; **46:1–4,** 177; **60:1–6,** 39; **61:1–11,** 167

Jeremiah **8:8–13,** 133; **15:10–21,** 189

Lamentations **1:1–22,** 210

Ezekiel **34:11–24,** 41

Matthew **1:18–25,** 18, 83; **2:1–12,** 39; **5:9–12,** 184; **6:26–28,** 253; **10:26–33,** 248; **20:1–16,** 124;

25:31–46, 41; **28:1–10,** 64, 89; **28:16–20,** 24

Mark **1:1–8,** 10

Luke **4:1–13,** 147; **18:9–14,** 258; **18:15–17,** 215; **19:1–10,** 77; **19:41–44,** 133

John **1:1–18,** 3; **3:1–8,** 29; **8:31–59,** 167; **9:1–12, 29–41,** 111; **9:1–41,** 69; **16:31–33,** 189

Romans **9:1–5,** 248

1 Corinthians **11:23–26,** 243

Galatians **6:1–10,** 154

Ephesians **2:4–9,** 258; **3:2–3, 5–6,** 39

Hebrews **11:30–31,** 55; **12:1–2,** 89, 118

James **2:21–26,** 55

Revelation **7:2–4, 9–12,** 184

Index of Sermon Titles

A Kind of Loving, for Me, 140
An Hour's Work and a Day's Pay, 124
Caught in the Act, 154
Consider the Monkeys, 253
Dirty Work, 77
Doing and Being, 215
God and the "L-Word", 167
God Remembers, 107
Going to Hell for the Right Reason, 248
Have You Ever Heard John Preach?, 10
He Is Going before You, 89
He's Back, 64
How to Become a Christian, 29
Infant Arms: Epiphany, 39
Intimacy with God, 237
Is Sex Ever Safe?, 160
It Is Something to Us, 210
Jesus, the Liberator, 111
Joseph, 83
Joseph's Story, 18
Mary, Mother of God, 48
Not All Saints, But Surely Some Saints, 184

Pretending, Self-Justification, and Grace, 258
Remember Rahab, 55
Spread, O Spread, Thou Mighty Word, 24
The Bible: Its Diversity and Its Unity, 95
The Big One and the Not-So-Big One, 101
The Distorted and the Natural, 147
The Gracious Guest, 243
The Saints: Dogged Blunderers toward Heaven, 118
The Servant of the Lord, 197
The Things That Make for Peace, 133
The Tragicomedy of the Gospel, 69
The Word Comes among Us, 3
Through Flood and Fire, 201
What Easter Means to Christians, 229
What to Do about God, 223
When All Is Said and Done, 41
When Life Crashes In, 189
Your Religion: Method or Motive—Which?, 177

Index of Contributors

Achtemeier, Elizabeth, 133
Ayers, James, 154
Bangert, Byron C., 215
Beasley-Murray, George, 3
Boyd, Tom W., 248
Burghardt, Walter J., 140
Craddock, Fred, 10
Filipi, Pavel, 197
Fuhrman, C. Michael, 69
Gaddy, Welton, 223
Griffith, A. Leonard, 229
Groves, Richard, 160
Horne, Chevis F., 89
Kelso, John E., 18
Killinger, John, 237
Leininger, David E., 29
Leonard, Bill J., 111
Macleod, Donald, 177
Metzger, Bruce M., 95
Murray, Vernon, 210

Nisly, Paul W., 201
Parrent, Allan M., 147
Pringle, Neta, 83
Roberts, Howard W., 167
Ruff, Jeffrey L., 77
Sands, Leo, 39
Sasser, L. Allan, 124
Simcox, Carroll E., 118
Sisk, Ronald D., 101
Stendahl, Krister, 107
Towner, W. Sibley, 184
Trotter, Mark, 41
Tuck, William Powell, 189
Versteeg, Robert John, 253
Vitrano, Steven P., 48
Walsh, Albert J. D., 243
Waring, J. Donald, 24
Wilkinson, David R., 55
Williams, Clifford, 258
Willimon, William H., 64